HOUGHTON MIFFLIN
KEYBOARDING
and Applications

Judith A. Chiri / *Smoky Hill High School, Aurora, Colorado*

Jacquelyn P. Kutsko / *Smoky Hill High School, Aurora, Colorado*

Patricia E. Seraydarian / *Oakland Community College, Farmington Hills, Michigan*

Ted D. Stoddard / *Brigham Young University, Provo, Utah*

Houghton Mifflin Company / Boston

Atlanta   Dallas   Geneva, Illinois   Lawrenceville, New Jersey   Palo Alto   Toronto

Authors

Judith A. Chiri is Business Education Department Chairperson at Smoky Hill High School in Aurora, Colorado. She has taught typewriting, electronic keyboarding, and other business courses at the middle school through college levels. In addition to writing for business journals and conducting workshops for teachers and secretaries, Ms. Chiri is involved in FBLA, Colorado Educators For/About Business, and other professional organizations; and works with her district Vocational Advisory Committee.

Jacquelyn P. Kutsko teaches keyboarding and word processing on electric and electronic keyboards at Smoky Hill High School in Aurora, Colorado. An FBLA adviser, she has also taught business English, office procedures, and most other courses in the business education curriculum at the secondary and postsecondary levels. In addition, Ms. Kutsko is self-employed as a business office consultant. She has written numerous articles and conducted teacher workshops throughout the United States.

Patricia E. Seraydarian is Department Chairperson of Office Information Systems at Oakland Community College in Farmington Hills, Michigan. A recognized expert in information processing, Dr. Seraydarian lectures on the topic around the country and has served as consultant to the Michigan Department of Education. She is also an on-site professor for General Motors Corporation. Dr. Seraydarian is the author of a variety of materials for secretarial training as well as for the professional secretary.

Ted D. Stoddard, Professor of Information Management at Brigham Young University in Provo, Utah, has lectured and written extensively in the areas of keyboarding, typewriting, shorthand, and microcomputing. He is a specialist in business/computer education, business communication, and computer information systems. Dr. Stoddard has served in numerous leadership positions in professional organizations, including that of president of the Western Business Education Association.

Printed in the U.S.A.

ISBN: 0-395-40568-8

BCDEFGHI-JH-898\76

Credits

Cover

Concept by Linda Wade
Photography by Martucci Studio

Illustrations

Dorothea Sierra: 1, 84

Lisa Sparks: viii, ix, xii (bottom right), xiv (top right), xv (top right), 3 (top right), 4, 7, 20, 22, 38, 48, 62, A-1, A-2, A-3, A-4, A-5, A-6.

David Archambault: x, xii (bottom left), xiv (bottom right), 3 (bottom left), 5, 6, 8, 9, 13, 17, 25, 30.

Roger Ink: 3

Steve Alexander: 25

Handwriting by Marsha Goldberg

All other art by Graphics, etcetera, Inc.

Contents

Part 1   Developing Keyboarding Skills   1

Unit 1   Alphabetic Keys   Lessons 1–16   2

Alphabetic keys / Keyboarding techniques / Default settings / Margin settings / Line spacing / Word wrap/Margin signal / Printing (basic function) / Space bar / Shift keys / Cursor/carrier return / Identify misstrokes / Paragraph tabs

Unit 2   Number and Symbol Keys   Lessons 17–32   46

Top-row number and symbol keys / Math/programming symbol keys / Keyboard composition / Spacing with symbols and punctuation / Cursor movement / Command underscoring / Correction techniques / Insert/delete / MEASURING MASTERY

Part 2   Building Formatting Skills   84

Unit 3   Personal/Business Letters   Lessons 33–45   85

Block format letters / Envelopes/OCR format / Proofreader's marks / Word division rules / Naming documents / Storing documents / Retrieving documents / Printing documents / Deleting documents / MEASURING MASTERY

Unit 4   Horizontal and Vertical Centering   Lessons 46–56   118

Horizontal centering of words and lines / Vertical centering / Horizontally and vertically centered tables / Automatic centering / Decimal tab / Page layout / Formatting new margins / MEASURING MASTERY

Unit 5   Unbound Reports   Lessons 57–70   143

Unbound report format / Advanced cursor movement / Advanced page layout / Subscript / Superscript / Endnotes / Bibliography / Title page / Quotations within a report / MEASURING MASTERY

Unit 6   Progress Review   Lessons 71–75   174

MINISIMULATION / MEASURING MASTERY

Appendixes (follow page 89)

Preface

The rapid growth of technology has resulted in changes in every facet of our lives—business, personal, and professional. One significant change is that keyboarding skills are in greater demand for an increased number of people whose careers or personal interests bring them in contact with this electronic technology.

The skills required for keyboarding in the electronic age are not identical to the skills taught in the traditional typewriting course, nor is the methodology for developing these skills identical. To develop an appropriate level of keyboarding skills in our students, we need to appreciate *how* and *where* their keyboarding skills will be applied and to adjust our curriculum accordingly. Two needs emerge from this analysis. First, more than ever, we need to use sound techniques for developing "touch" keyboarding skills. Second, we need to shift the classroom emphasis from one of production to one of inputting and accessing information. Specifically, our students must be able to input both text and data efficiently and to access the capabilities of the microcomputer. The keyboarding course that addresses these needs can open the door to the technological future for many of our students.

Objectives

Houghton Mifflin Keyboarding and Applications is a comprehensive program carefully designed to train persons to input data efficiently and accurately through the use of a keyboard. This broadly stated goal encompasses a hierarchy of objectives:

- To develop a "touch" keyboarding skill for inputting both alphabetic and numeric data
- To develop the ability to format typical documents
- To develop a knowledge of information processing terms associated with the skill of keyboarding
- To develop proofreading and basic language arts skills
- To develop the ability to compose at the keyboard
- To develop desirable interpersonal skills needed in a world of electronic communications: flexibility/adaptability, decision making, time management, and positive attitudes
- To develop the ability to use equipment and to access its capabilities efficiently

Components

A complete package of instructional materials has been developed to meet these objectives. The package includes: a student textbook with ample material for up to one semester; a Teacher's Manual containing a complete testing program; and a Student Activities workbook correlated to the textbook.

Features

Houghton Mifflin Keyboarding and Applications promotes student mastery of keyboarding and the development of formatting skills through a variety of special features.

Skill-Building Program Intensive technique development through technique timings, speed-building drills, and accuracy practices is the basis of the skill-building program, enabling students to develop speed and accuracy.

Simplified Instructions The directions for completing each job, as well as explanations of formats and procedures, are presented in simple, easy-to-read language. Students can learn independently while they are developing their ability to read and follow directions.

Realistic Work Assignments Students key from rough-draft, handwritten, unarranged, and incomplete copy, as well as their own compositions, to gain experience in working with different kinds of source documents.

Communication Skills Keyboard Composition activities give students opportunities to input original work at the keyboard, while Language Arts and Apply the Rule activities review basic capitalization, punctuation, and related language skills.

Decision-Making Skills Activities are structured to give students increasing responsibility for the details of their work. The sequence is *show, tell, remind,* and *remember.* Initially, students key from completely formatted copy in the Project Previews. The next few applications are accompanied by complete instructions. In later applications, these detailed instructions are replaced by reminders in the form of "cues" and "checkpoints." Finally, students are expected to remember the format—or look it up in convenient Need to Knows.

Computer Literacy Lesson content and the topics and vocabulary presented in timed paragraphs and other drill materials enhance students' understanding of computers, their capabilities, and some of their uses.

Simulation To provide realistic practice in handling input, a minisimulation is included in Lessons 71–73. This minisimulation exposes students to a number of ways in which electronic keyboards are being used to process information more efficiently.

Testing Program The Measuring Mastery lessons in the student textbook can be used for informal or formal evaluation of student progress. Alternate tests provided in the Teacher's Manual on blackline masters contain objective questions and application problems to check student comprehension of basic keyboarding concepts.

Acknowledgments

This textbook represents a group effort, with many people contributing their ideas and assistance. Among those who deserve special mention are our students and colleagues, who reviewed and used drafts of our materials in their classes; the teachers and students who participated in the learner verification study; and the hundreds of teachers who have shared their insights, problems, solutions, and enthusiasm for teaching in today's electronic environment. To all of them go our sincere thanks and appreciation for their valuable suggestions and encouragement.

J. Chiri, J. Kutsko, P. Seraydarian, T. Stoddard

Index

Monitor is an electronic screen that displays data. The monitor may also be called a CRT (Cathode Ray Tube) or a VDT (Video Display Terminal).

Prompt is a line displayed on the monitor to request specific input from the user.

Right Shift Key is used to capitalize letters keyed with the left hand.

Space Bar spaces the cursor forward one space at a time.

Tab Key moves the cursor directly to a tab stop.

Ten-Key Enter/Return is used to enter numeric data from the ten-key numeric pad.

Ten-Key Numeric Keyboard (Pad) is a set of keys that resembles a calculator and is used to enter numeric data.

Disk Drive is the component of a microcomputer system that reads and writes data on a disk.

Enter/Return Key is used to enter information into a microcomputer or to return the cursor to the beginning of a new line.

Function Keys are those keys other than the alpha/numeric keys that allow the user to perform special functions such as automatic centering.

Keyboard is a device similar to a typewriter keyboard containing alphabetic, numeric, and special function keys.

Left Shift Key is used to capitalize letters keyed with the right hand.

Menu is a list of functions available in a software program.

Backspace Key moves the cursor to the left (backward) one space at a time. On some equipment, it may delete characters.

Caps Lock Key is used to key all capital letters.

Control Key is usually used with other keys to perform specific functions such as automatic centering.

Cursor is a lighted indicator on the display screen that shows a user's exact position within a document.

Cursor Movement Keys allow the cursor to be moved up, down, left, or right within text.

Disk (Diskette/Floppy Disk) is the most common storage medium used with microcomputers. Disks are usually made of thin plastic, magnetically coated. Disks are protected by a jacket with openings to allow the disk drive to read or write information.

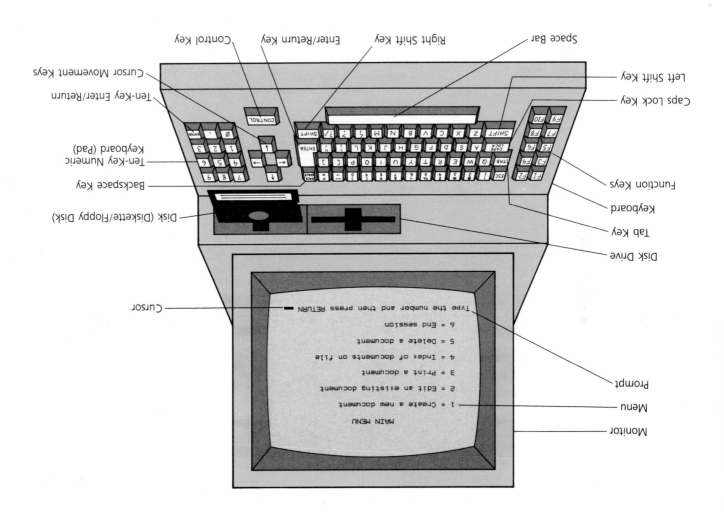

Microcomputer

Control Key • Enter/Return Key • Right Shift Key • Space Bar • Cursor Movement Keys • Ten-Key Enter/Return • Ten-Key Numeric Keyboard (Pad) • Backspace Key • Disk (Diskette/Floppy Disk) • Left Shift Key • Caps Lock Key • Function Keys • Keyboard • Tab Key • Disk Drive • Cursor • Prompt • Menu • Monitor

MAIN MENU

1 = Create a new document
2 = Edit an existing document
3 = Print a document
4 = Index of documents on file
5 = Delete a document
6 = End session

Type the number and then press RETURN

Electronic Typewriter

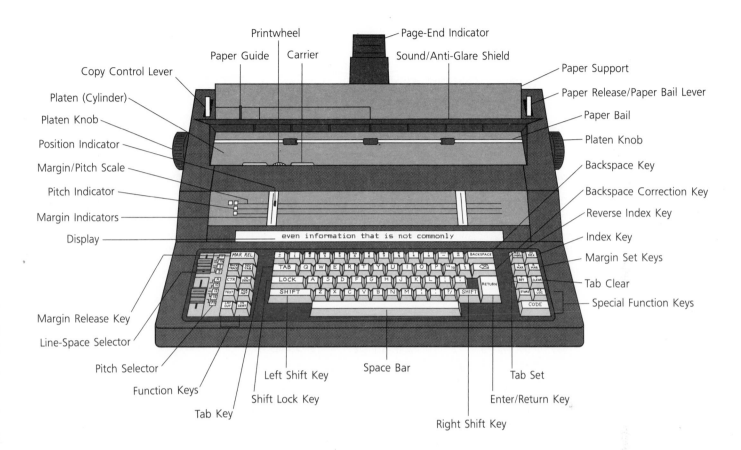

Backspace Correction Key backspaces and removes an incorrect character.

Backspace Key moves the carrier to the left (backward) one space at a time.

Carrier is the movable unit containing the printwheel and ribbon carrier.

Copy Control Lever moves the platen forward or backward to adjust for paper thickness.

Display shows keyed text for checking accuracy.

Enter/Return Key enters information into memory and/or returns the carrier to the left margin while moving the paper up to a new line.

Function Keys are those keys other than the alpha/numeric keys that allow the user to perform special functions such as automatic centering.

Index Key moves the paper up without returning the carrier to the beginning of a line.

Left Shift Key is used to capitalize letters keyed with the right hand.

Line-Space Selector controls the space between lines of text.

Margin Indicators are adjustable tabs on the margin scale that can be positioned to show where current margins are set.

Margin/Pitch Scale indicates horizontal spaces, the position of the carrier, and the pitches available. It may also show the position of the margin sets.

Margin Release Key allows the carrier to move beyond the margin stops.

Margin Set Keys set the margins to control the beginning and ending of lines.

Page-End Indicator shows the lines/inches left on a standard 8½ x 11-inch sheet of paper.

Paper Bail holds the paper against the platen.

Paper Guide guides the paper into the machine so it is consistently in the same position.

Paper Release/Paper Bail Lever frees the paper for removing or straightening.

Paper Support supports the paper for reviewing.

Pitch Indicator shows the pitch that has been selected.

Pitch Selector allows the user to choose a pitch from those available on the machine.

Platen (Cylinder) is the large roller around which the paper turns.

Platen Knobs are used to turn the platen by hand.

Position Indicator shows the position of the carrier on a line.

Printwheel is a circular disk containing all the keyboard characters.

Reverse Index Key moves the paper down without returning the carrier to the beginning of a line.

Right Shift Key is used to capitalize letters keyed with the left hand.

Shift Lock Key is used to key all capital letters.

Sound/Anti-Glare Shield reduces noise and adjusts for glare.

Space Bar spaces the carrier forward one space at a time.

Special Function Keys are those keys that do not produce a letter, number, or special symbol.

Tab Clear clears, or removes, tab stops.

Tab Key moves the carrier directly to a tab stop.

Tab Set sets, or puts in, tab stops.

Element Typewriter

Paper Release Lever frees the paper for straightening or removing.

Pitch Identification indicates 10- or 12-pitch type.

Platen (Cylinder) is the large roller around which the paper turns.

Platen Knobs are used to turn the platen by hand.

Position Indicator indicates position of the type element on a line.

Right Shift Key is used to capitalize letters keyed with the left hand.

Shift Lock is used to key all capital letters.

Space Bar spaces the carrier forward one space at a time.

Tab Clear/Set clears and sets tab stops.

Tab Key moves the carrier directly to tab stops.

Type Element is the ball-shaped device containing all the keyboard characters.

Variable Line Spacer returns the carrier to the original text line.

Left Shift Key is used to capitalize letters keyed with the right hand.

Line Finder allows for keying above or below a line and then returning to the same line.

Line-Space Lever controls the space between lines of text.

Margin Release Key allows the carrier to move beyond the margin stops.

Margin Sets control the beginning and ending of lines.

Margin/Pitch Scale indicates horizontal spaces, shows position of printing point, and shows position of margin sets.

Multiple Copy Control adjusts for insertion of multiple pages (such as carbon packs).

On/Off Control turns the electric power on and off.

Paper Bail holds the paper against the platen.

Paper Centering Scale centers the paper on the platen.

Paper Guide guides the paper into the machine.

Aligning Scale helps locate the text line when reinserting paper.

Backspace Key moves the carrier to the left (backward) one space at a time.

Card Holder holds cards and envelopes against the platen.

Carrier is the movable unit containing the platen.

Carrier Return Key returns the carrier to the left margin and moves the paper up to a new line.

Correcting Key backspaces to the error and moves the lift-off tape into position to make a correction.

Dual-Pitch Lever (special models only) resets spacing for 10 pitch or 12 pitch.

Express Backspace Key moves the carrier rapidly to the left without spacing the paper up.

Half-Backspace Lever moves the carrier to the left a half space at a time.

Index Key moves the paper up without returning the carrier to the begin-ning of a line.

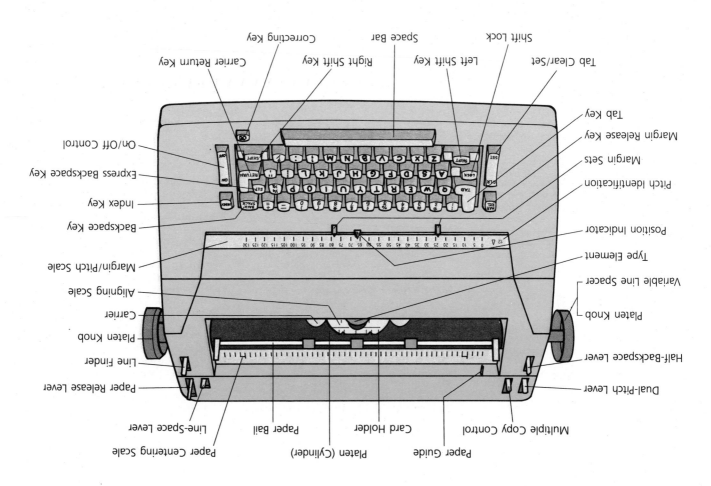

On/Off Control — Express Backspace Key — Index Key — Backspace Key — Margin/Pitch Scale — Aligning Scale — Carrier — Platen Knob — Line Finder — Paper Release Lever — Line-Space Lever — Paper Centering Scale — Paper Bail — Platen (Cylinder) — Card Holder — Paper Guide — Multiple Copy Control — Dual-Pitch Lever — Half-Backspace Lever — Platen Knob — Variable Line Spacer — Type Element — Position Indicator — Pitch Identification — Margin Sets — Margin Release Key — Tab Key — Tab Clear/Set — Shift Lock — Left Shift Key — Space Bar — Right Shift Key — Correcting Key — Carrier Return Key

Learn About Software

Disks

A **disk** is a magnetic device that is similar to, but slightly smaller than a 45-rpm record. Disks are sealed in a protective jacket. Through holes in the jacket, the disk drive "reads" information from or "writes" information to the disk. Never insert or remove a disk while the red "in use" light of the disk drive is on.

Disks must be handled with care to avoid damaging information stored on them. To avoid damage, follow these guidelines:

Hold the disk by the corner. Do not touch the exposed recording surface of the disk.

Do not bend or fold the disk.

Do not expose the disk to extreme heat or cold. Never store the disk in direct sunlight.

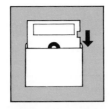

Store disks in their protective envelopes in an upright position away from liquids, dust, smoke, and ashes.

Do not store disks near x-ray devices and magnetic fields such as telephones, dictation equipment, magnets, monitors, and other electronic equipment.

If it is necessary to write on a disk label, use only a felt tip pen. Do not use ballpoints, pencils, or paper clips.

Menus

The **menu** lists the functions a software program can perform. When the microcomputer is operating and a program disk has been inserted properly, a menu will appear on the display screen. A **prompt** will also appear. The prompt tells you what to do to choose a menu option.

Learn About Pitch (Type) and Paper Size

Pitch (Type) Size

Size of type, or **pitch,** is the number of horizontal spaces/characters to an inch. Most printwheels or elements are either 10 pitch (10 characters to a horizontal inch) or 12 pitch (12 characters to a horizontal inch). Some equipment also has 15 pitch (15 characters to a horizontal inch). More advanced software programs and printers may allow you to print in still other sizes. Notice the difference in the three major pitch sizes shown in the next column.

This is a sample of 10-pitch type.

This is a sample of 12-pitch type.

This is a sample of 15-pitch type.

Determine the Pitch of Your Equipment

M Microcomputers

Hard copy is text printed on paper. To obtain a hard copy of text prepared on a microcomputer, you must connect the microcomputer to a printer. The two most common kinds of printers are letter-quality printers and dot-matrix printers.

Letter-Quality Printers

Letter-quality printers produce typewriter-quality text. Most letter-quality printers are equipped with either a 10-pitch or a 12-pitch printwheel. However, other pitch sizes may be available. The pitch may be set through the software, usually by an option on the print menu. The pitch is also marked on the face of the printwheel. Determine the pitch of your printer and choose the appropriate pitch selection from the menu. Set your margins to correspond to the pitch of the printwheel.

Dot-Matrix Printers

Dot-matrix printers form letters with a series of closely spaced dots. The pitch and style of the letters depend on the software and the kind of printer in use. Many software packages offer a variety of pitch sizes. However, some dot-matrix printers are very close in size to 10- or 12-pitch typewriter type. When using a dot-matrix printer, choose the 10-pitch selection from the menu, and use appropriate margin settings.

T Typewriters

Dual-pitch typewriters can print in either 10 pitch or 12 pitch. When using a dual-pitch typewriter, always check to see if the printwheel or element is 10 or 12 pitch. Set the pitch selector to correspond to the pitch marked on the printwheel or element. Be sure yours is set correctly.

Dual-pitch typewriters also have 10- and 12-pitch margin scales. Be sure to use the proper scale to set the margins for the pitch you are using.

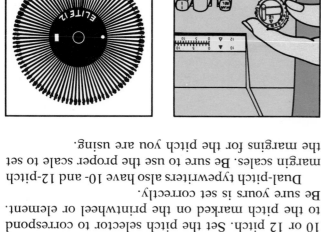

If you are not using a dual-pitch typewriter, align the left edge of the paper with zero on the margin/pitch scale. If the right edge of the paper ends at 85, you have a 10-pitch typewriter (8½ inches × 10 spaces = 85). If the right edge ends at 102, you have a 12-pitch typewriter (8½ inches × 12 spaces = 102).

Paper Size

Standard size paper is 8½ inches wide by 11 inches long (21.59 × 27.94 cm). With 10 pitch, there are 85 horizontal spaces across the page (8½ inches × 10 spaces = 85). With 12 pitch, there are 102 spaces across the page (8½ inches × 12 spaces = 102). With 15 pitch, there are 127 spaces across the page.

The center point of the paper for 10 pitch is half the number of spaces in the line, or 42½. Drop the half, and use 42 as the center point. For 12 pitch, the center point is 51. For 15 pitch, the center point is 63.

Standard vertical line spacing is 6 line spaces to 1 vertical inch. Therefore, a sheet of paper 11 inches long (27.94 cm) has 66 lines (11 inches × 6 lines = 66).

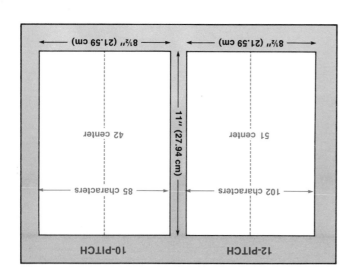

If your margin scale does not start at zero, key a line of characters and measure off 1 inch. Count the number of characters in the 1-inch space to determine whether you have a 10- or a 12-pitch typewriter.

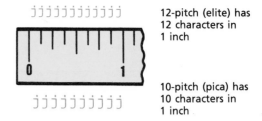

12-pitch (elite) has 12 characters in 1 inch

10-pitch (pica) has 10 characters in 1 inch

Adjust Your Paper

M Microcomputers

Two kinds of paper may be used in computer printers: Continuous feed and individual sheets of standard-size paper. With continuous-feed paper, the perforation should align with zero, or to the right of the first print position. If your paper cannot be adjusted, adjust your left margin to allow for the extra paper to the left of the perforation.

If your printer uses individual sheets, set the paper guide or align the paper with zero on the paper scale, or with the first print position.

T Typewriters

The paper guide helps you to insert paper into the typewriter so that it is consistently in the same position. The paper guide also helps to keep the paper straight. Adjust the paper guide before you insert a sheet of paper into the typewriter. Slide the paper guide to the left or right so it aligns with zero on the paper guide scale, paper bail scale, or margin/pitch scale.

Figure Your Margins

Once you have determined the pitch of your equipment and adjusted the paper, you need to determine where to set the margins. Margins allow you to control the amount of space on either side of the printed line. For most documents, left and right margins are equal in width. For example, reports usually have 1-inch side margins.

To determine margin settings, multiply the number of characters per inch (usually 10 or 12) by the number of inches you want in the side margin. The result is the left margin setting. For example, the left margin setting for a 1-inch margin using a 12-pitch machine is 12 (12 characters × 1 inch = 12). On a 10-pitch machine, the left margin setting is 10 (10 characters × 1 inch = 10).

To get the right margin setting (when margins are equal), subtract the left margin setting from the total spaces across the page. On a 12-pitch machine, the right margin setting for a 1-inch margin is 90 (102 − 12 = 90). On a 10-pitch machine, the right margin is 75 (85 − 10 = 75).

Note: Some software uses line length rather than side margin settings. To determine the line length of a document when margins are given, subtract the left margin from the right margin. For example, if your side margins are 12 and 90, subtract 12 (the left margin) from 90 (the right margin) to get a line length of 78 characters.

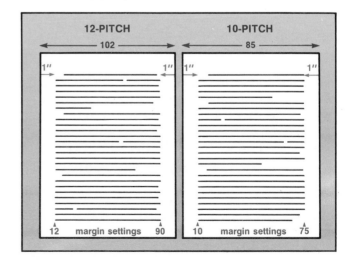

Set Your Margins

The following procedures are for most standard kinds of margin sets. If the procedure for setting margins on your computer or typewriter is not given here, refer to the equipment's operating manual or ask your teacher for help.

M Microcomputers

Most software has default (preset) margins. These margins are automatically set when you load the software into the computer. Changing the default margins is usually done in one of the following ways.

Special Command

1. At the left edge of the screen, enter the special command used by your software to change default settings.
2. A prompt appears on the screen and asks you for the desired margin set number.
3. Respond to the prompt by keying in the desired margin settings.

Ruler Line

1. Move the cursor along the ruler line displayed on the screen. A margin symbol will move as you space left or right.
2. When the symbol is at the desired setting, operate the enter/return.

Print Menu

Some software programs require you to set margins when you are ready to print a document.

1. Access the print menu. The print menu lists options for changing margins.
2. Select the option you want to change.
3. Enter the new margin settings.

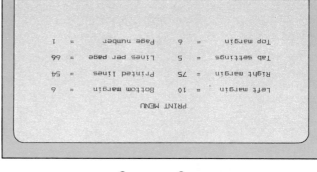

```
                    PRINT MENU

Left margin    = 10    Bottom margin   = 6
Right margin   = 75    Printed lines   = 54
Tab settings   = 5     Lines per page  = 66
Top margin     = 6     Page number     = 1
```

E Electronic Typewriters

1. Locate the left and right margin-set keys on your keyboard.
2. Move the printwheel or element to the desired setting for the left margin. (You may need to use the margin release to move past a previously set margin).
3. Press the appropriate margin-set key.
4. Follow the procedure outlined above to set the right margin.

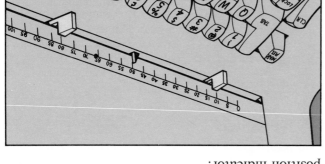

T Element Typewriters

1. Push in the left margin-set lever.
2. Slide it to the left or right to the desired setting on the margin/pitch scale.
3. Release the lever.
4. Repeat this procedure to set the right margin.

Note: You may have to move the carrier to the right before you can slide the margin set past the position indicator.

Set Your Tab Stops

The tab key is used to move the cursor/carrier directly to a specific position on a line.

M Microcomputers

Use the method required by your program to set new tab stops. The two most common methods of setting tab stops are as follows:

Special Command

1. Give the tab set command for your program.
2. When the prompt asks for a column number, key in the column number for the first tab setting.
2. Repeat this procedure to set the remaining tab stops.

Ruler Line

1. Access the ruler line.
2. Move the cursor to the first desired tab position.
3. Press the appropriate key for setting tabs (usually the tab key or the letter T).
4. Repeat this procedure to set the remaining tab stops.

T Typewriters

Before you set tab stops, clear any previously set tab stops.

To clear all tabs at once, check your typewriter to see if it has a total tab clear key. If it does, press the total tab clear key to clear all tab stops.

If you have an element typewriter, move the carrier to the far right. Hold down the tab clear while you return the carrier.

To clear tab stops one at a time, move the carrier to the left margin. Tab to the first stop and press the tab clear. Continue this procedure until all tab stops are cleared.

To set a tab stop, move your carrier to the desired position and press down the tab set.

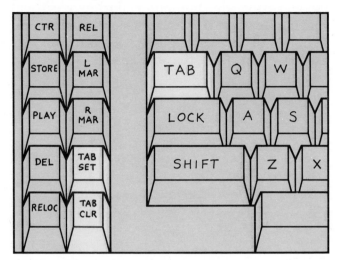

Electronic Typewriter

Type Element

Set Your Line Spacing

When you select single spacing (SS), text appears on every line. When you select double spacing (DS), one blank line is left between printed lines. When you select triple spacing (TS), two blank lines are left between printed lines, and so on, as shown in the following illustration.

1	single	double	triple	quadruple
2	single	blank	blank	blank
3	single	double	blank	blank
4	single	blank	triple	blank
5	single	double		quadruple

M Microcomputers

Most software programs use a default line-space value of 1 for single spacing. Line spacing may be set on the ruler line, or may be an option of the print menu. To change the default setting, you may need to use a command or enter the desired setting.

T Typewriters

On some typewriters, the line-space selector/lever can be set on 1 for single spacing, or 2 for double spacing. Some machines also have settings for triple spacing and for half-line spacing (1½ or 2½). The settings may be indicated by a light on the line-space selector, or by notches or numbers beside the line-space lever.

in a safe, dry, clean area. Arrange the connector and power cables so they cannot be tripped over. This will help prevent personal injury as well as damage to the connectors.

When you are using the computer, always keep food and liquids away from the area. Avoid using the computer during electrical storms. In fact, it is wise to unplug the computer until the storm passes. Keep the display screen clean. Dust the screen with a very soft cloth.

To avoid damaging diskettes, handle them only by the protective jacket. Do not touch the exposed areas. Never insert or remove a diskette when the disk drive is operating. Store diskettes in a vertical position in a dry, dust-free holder.

Your computer is likely to give you many years of good service if you follow these simple suggestions for proper care of your system.

JOB 2 Announcement

File name: L75J2   DS; center vertically and horizontally.

Mideast Technical Institute
Open House
honoring
Presidential Scholars
4:00 p.m.
Sunday, March 15, 19--
Adams Hall

JOB 3 Table

File name: L75J3   DS   Center vertically and horizontally. Leave 10 spaces between columns.

Software Memory Requirements

Basic Programming	128K
Spell Check	128K
Color Chart	256K
Rapid File	256K
Report Writer	256K
Easy-step Accounting	512K

JOB 4 Personal Business Letter

File name: L75J4   Key on a plain sheet of paper. Supply an appropriate salutation.

Mr. Robert Houser / Camp Wapiti / P.O. Box 1180 / Jackson, WY 83025 / A friend and I are making plans for summer vacation. We have read about Camp Wapiti and are interested in participating in a computer workshop there. ¶ We plan to vacation the week of July 20–27. We would like one double room. Do you have accommodations available during that time? Also, please send us additional information describing other activities that are to take place during that week. ¶ As soon as we receive a confirmation from you, we will send our deposit of $100 each. / Sincerely / Lauren McCoskey / 145 Pike Street / Maysville, KY 41455

JOB 5 Business Letter/Envelope

File name: L75J5   Key the letter with an envelope. Use letterhead stationery or plain paper. Supply an appropriate salutation.

Ms. Diana K. Waters / Sales Specialist / Graphic Aids, Inc. / 8005 Arcadia Avenue / Milford, CT 06460 / Have you had an opportunity to see a demonstration of the new E-Z color printer? ¶ The E-Z offers you many advantages. It does spreadsheets, word processing, and graphics. It prints in six brilliant colors. The E-Z also produces letter-quality print, and can be attached to most leading personal computers. ¶ The new E-Z color printer is the latest in our complete line of superior printers. All our models are on display in our showroom. Let our trained sales staff help you select the printer that best meets your needs. / Sincerely / Mark G. Merriweather / Sales Manager

Part **1** // Developing Keyboarding Skills

LESSONS *74–75* *Measuring Mastery*

74–75A

Warmup

Key each line twice. DS after each pair.

Confusing words: your and you're

Goal: To strengthen keyboarding skills 5′

1 Use <u>your</u> to show possession and <u>you're</u> when writing <u>you are</u>.
2 When you're through, your results will be sent to your home.
3 You're sure to win if you plan your work and work your plan.

| 1 | 2 | 3 | 4 | 5 | 6 | 7 | 8 | 9 | 10 | 11 | 12 |

74–75B

Goal Writing

Default or DS

Take two 3-minute goal writings.

If you finish before time is called, start again.

Record your speed and accuracy.

Goal: To measure timed-writing progress 10′

	1′	3′
Supervisors must like and enjoy working with people.	11	4
They must be able to communicate on an individual basis as	23	8
well as on a group level. They must be able to organize the	35	12
work flow and evaluate its effectiveness. They must be	46	15
willing and able to take responsibility for the unpleasant	58	19
tasks as well--disciplining any careless worker, settling	69	23
disputes among workers, and helping to solve problems.	80	27
When these jobs open up, the company will most often	91	30
look first to the ranks of its own workers for a person to	103	34
fill the job.	105	35

1′ | 1 | 2 | 3 | 4 | 5 | 6 | 7 | 8 | 9 | 10 | 11 | 12 | AWL
3′ | 1 | 2 | 3 | 4 | 5.7

74–75C

Production Measurement

Goal: To measure production skills 85′

JOB 1 Report

File name: L75J1   Key this report with a title page in unbound format.

CARING FOR YOUR COMPUTER

Choosing a computer for your personal use is a decision that requires careful study and planning. Once you have made the purchase, there are some guidelines you should follow to increase the life of your system.

To begin, be sure to read the manual before setting up your computer. Carefully follow all instructions for installing and operating the computer. Be sure to install the computer

(Continued next page)

Unit 1 / Alphabetic Keys

"Every home will have a computer." How many times have you heard or read this statement recently? The computer is being used more every day—at home, at school, on the job. Soon, everyone will need to know how to use computers. One of the first steps in learning to use computers is to develop good keyboarding skills.

The arrangement of the keyboard is basically the same for all kinds of equipment: computers, electronic typewriters, and electric typewriters. There are a few keys that are unique to each kind of equipment, but these can be learned easily.

In your keyboarding class, you will learn to key the alphabet, number, and symbol keys by touch. That is, you will learn to key without looking at your fingers as you strike the keys. Also, you will learn to use the equipment in your classroom—microcomputers, electronic typewriters, or electric typewriters. You will learn to use menus; to store, retrieve, and print; and to format documents.

In this unit, Lessons 1–16, you will learn to:

1. Key all alphabetic keys by touch.
2. Locate selected machine parts and use them correctly.
3. Use proper techniques in striking the keys and using various machine parts.
4. Figure your speed on timed writings.
5. Identify errors.

Micro Dictionary

command	an instruction given to the computer usually by means of the keyboard
default settings	settings that are preset in software or in equipment's memory
file name	a name given to a document when it is stored
format	the arrangement of text on a screen or on paper
menu	a list of functions that a computer performs in relation to the software program that is being used
monitor	the display screen of a microcomputer that allows the user to view all data entered through the software or the keyboard
option	one of the functions that can be selected from a software menu
print	the process of converting screen copy to hard (paper) copy
program disk	a disk upon which the word processing program is stored
prompt	a message that appears on the display screen and asks the user to respond
scrolling	the process of moving screen text up, down, to the left, or to the right
software	a set of programmed instructions that tells the computer what to do
store	the placement of documents on a floppy disk or in memory so they may be recalled at a later time
student disk	a disk that stores the data keyed by a student
word wrap	the automatic movement of a word from one line to the next when the word goes beyond the right margin setting

Correspondence Secretary

JOB 6 Letter/Enclosure

File name: L71J6 Letterhead/Envelope Send to: Ms. Julia Brandt / Training Specialist / CompuData Communications Consultants / 945 West Houston / San Antonio, TX 78285. Supply an appropriate salutation and use your name as Correspondence Secretary.

The enclosed notice confirms the dates, times, and places for the training sessions you will be conducting on electronic mail at Smythe's Office Products. ¶ We look forward to having you here at our company headquarters. You'll be training all 85 of our employees. We have divided them into four groups. Each of the four groups has a three-hour session scheduled. ¶ The management at Smythe's is eager to have all employees use the electronic mail system. We believe it is a way to improve our productivity by simplifying office communications, and we are pleased to work with you to achieve our goal. / Sincerely / Correspondence Secretary / Enclosure

Enclosure

File name: L71J6E Arrange the following copy into four double-spaced columns. Center the table vertically and horizontally. Leave 4 spaces between columns.

Electronic Mail Training Seminar

Monday	8:00-11:00	Last names A-F	Room A12
Monday	1:00-4:00	Last names G-M	Room B11
Tuesday	8:00-11:00	Last names N-S	Room A12
Tuesday	1:00-4:00	Last names T-Z	Room B11

JOB 7 Centered Announcement

File name: L71J7 Center the following announcement vertically and each line horizontally. DS.

ELECTRONIC MAIL is HERE!

Training seminars

for all smythe's employees

will be held

the first Monday of next month

OR

the first Tuesday of Next Month

Watch your mail—

DETAILS TO BE ANNOUNCED SOON!

Executive

JOB 8 Electronic Message

File name: L71J8 Compose and key an electronic message to Sally Hartnett in the Shipping Department. Key her name, department, and the file name on separate lines. DS, then compose the message.

Congratulate Sally on a job well done. Tell her that through the use of the new electronic mail system, the amount of time between receiving an order and shipping that order has been lowered by almost 30 percent. ¶ Explain to her that her efficiency and time management ratings are high, and that she and her coworkers are to be commended for putting forth the necessary effort to learn the new system and for working as a team to accomplish this goal. Tell her to keep up the good work!

Financial Officer

JOB 9 Form

Retrieve file L71J4 (the form you prepared in JOB 4). Set a tab stop 30 columns/spaces from the left margin. Fill in the form with the information given below. Begin to key new information at the tab. Be sure to align decimal points in dollar amounts. Use the current date for DATE SUBMITTED. Figure the total expenses, and key in the amount on the form.

(Your Name) / 4260 East Maplewood Avenue / San Antonio, TX 78212 / Social Security #532-87-2677 / Boston Data Technical Seminar / Boston, MA / July 9 and 10 / Expenses: Airfare, $389.00; Hotel, 180.00; Meals, 210.98; Ground transportation, 45.50; Entertainment, 46.50; Miscellaneous, 25.75.

Checkpoint: Be sure to verify the total expenses before keying that amount.

1A

Read and Do   Goal: To learn to arrange your work area   5′

Follow these steps to arrange your work area:

1. Clear your desk of everything you don't need.
2. Move the equipment so the front edge of the keyboard is even with the front edge of your desk or table.
3. Place your textbook to the right of your keyboard at a comfortable reading angle.
4. Place other necessary supplies (such as paper or pencil) on the other side of your desk or table.

Checkpoint: Is your work area arranged neatly, like the one in the illustration?

1B

Read and Do   Goal: To learn proper position at the keyboard   5′

Refer to the illustrations as you read and follow the instructions.

Curve your fingers

Correct position at the keyboard

Sitting in correct position at the keyboard is important as you learn and build keyboarding skills.

1. Sit up straight with your back touching the chair.
2. Sit directly in front of the keyboard.
3. Put both feet flat on the floor with one foot slightly in front of the other. This foot position provides support so that you do not become tired.
4. Place your fingers on the keys.
5. Hold your forearms so they slant with the keyboard.
6. Keep your wrists low, but do not rest them on the keyboard.
7. Curve your fingers.
8. Position your chair so that your elbows are down by your sides. If you sit too close to or far from the keyboard, you cannot keep your hands in correct position.

Mandell, Steven L., and Mandell, Colleen J. *Computer Fundamentals with BASIC Programming.* St. Paul: West Publishing Company, 1985.

Spencer, Donald D. *An Introduction to Computers.* Columbus: Charles E. Merrill Publishing Co., 1983.

JOB 3   Table

File name: L71J3   From the following list, prepare a 3-column table showing the top sales person from each territory, that person's territory, and the amount of sales. Title the table TOP SALES REPRESENTATIVES. DS the table and leave 6 spaces between columns.

Central: Greg Louthis, $765,560; Jo Michelletto, $851,700; Sandy Lotito, $850,210
Northeast: Lew Tong, $794,590; Mark Sandrini, $457,570; Tony Giradina, $800,000
Northwest: Margaret Gomez, $885,000; Chris Zuppio, $774,650.
Southeast: Ray Fouillard, $487,800; Dianne Buggenhagen, $530,360
Southwest: Keith McElreath, $670,980; Lois Levin, $565,740

JOB 4   Form

File name: L71J4   Key the following form using 1-inch side margins. Key the title on line 13. DS the form. Indent the SS items 5 spaces. Store the document or save your hard copy for use in JOB 9.

```
                    EXPENSE REPORT
                                   TS
      NAME

      STREET ADDRESS

      CITY, STATE, ZIP

      SOCIAL SECURITY NUMBER

      CONFERENCE NAME

      LOCATION (CITY/STATE)

      DATES ATTENDED

      EXPENSES

         5  AIRFARE
            GROUND TRANSPORTATION
            HOTEL
            MEALS
            MISCELLANEOUS
            ENTERTAINMENT

      TOTAL EXPENSES

      DATE SUBMITTED
```

JOB 5   Program

File name: L71J5

Use default or 1-inch side margins.

Key the following program. Be sure to follow the spacing shown. Remember to release the caps/shift lock when keying numbers.

```
10000  PRINT@966, "PRESS ENTER TO CONTINUE OR S TO STOP.";

10010  A$=INKEY$ : IF A$=" THEN GOTO 10010

10020  IF A$="S" THEN ST%=1 : RETURN

10030  IF A$<>CHR$(13) THEN GOTO 10010

10040  ST%=0 : RETURN

11000  TD%=A1%(A%) : GOSUB 17000

11010  TY%=A4%(A%)

11020  IF TY%<>1 THEN GOTO 11040

11030  GET 2, A3%(A%) : AM#=CVD(ZF$) : DC$=ZH$ : GOTO 11100

11040  GET 1, A3%(A%) : AM#=CVD(Z7$)

11050  IF TY%<>2 THEN GOTO 11070

11060  DC$="D" : EX$="PURCHASES JOURNAL" : GOTO 11100

11070  IF TY%<>4 THEN GOTO 11090

11080  DC$="C" : EX$="CASH RECEIPTS JOURNAL" : GOTO 11100

11090  DC$="D" : EX$="CASH PAYMENTS JOURNAL"

11100  RETURN
```

Read and Do

Goal: To learn how to load a disk or insert paper 5′   1-1

The symbols **M** **E**, and **T** are used in this textbook to identify directions and activities for specific keyboarding equipment.

The symbol **M**, shown in the first activity, indicates that these directions are to be used with microcomputers.

Note: You will need word processing software for your microcomputer.

If you are using a typewriter, ignore the directions marked **M**. Instead, complete the activity marked with the symbol **T**.

The symbol **E** is used in later lessons to mark directions and activities designed for the electronic typewriter.

M *Microcomputer*

1. Open the door to the disk drive.
2. Insert the program disk into Drive 1 and close the door.
3. Insert the student disk into Drive 2 and close the door. (If you have a single disk drive, follow the screen prompts to determine when to remove the program disk and load the student disk.)
4. Turn on the monitor.
5. Turn on the microcomputer.
6. Follow the prompts on the screen.
7. If required to give a file name, use: **Lesson1**.

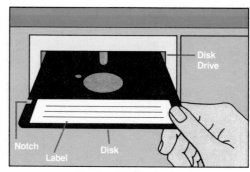

Insert the disk in the disk drive with the label facing up and the notched side facing left.

T *Typewriter*

1. Turn on the typewriter.
2. Set the paper guide so that the left edge of the paper lines up with zero on the margin/pitch scale.

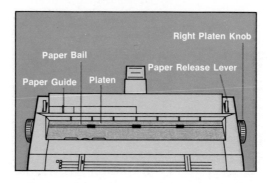

3. Place the paper behind the platen, with the longer edge against the paper guide.

4. Pull the paper-load lever/bail toward you (or up on some machines).

5. Feed the paper into the machine using the paper-feed key or by turning the platen knob.
6. Check to see if your paper is straight

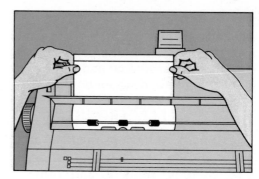

by turning the paper up a few inches and lining up the side edges. If the paper is not straight, pull the paper release lever forward and straighten the paper. Return the paper release lever to its proper position.
7. Place the paper-load lever/bail back into position. Adjust the paper bail rollers so they divide your paper into approximately equal sections.
8. Roll your paper down to the appropriate top margin. Unless you are told otherwise, you should always leave about 1 inch at the top of your paper.
9. Return the carrier to the left margin.

Administrative Assistant

JOB 1 Outline

File name: L71J1   Key the outline as shown. Use 1-inch side margins and follow the spacing indicated. Center and key the title in all caps on line 13.

```
LM          line 13 ↓ ELECTRONIC MAIL
 |                                    TS
 | 1sp |
→I.   The uses of electronic mail
   |                              DS
   5→ A.   Establishing communication
   |   4→ 1.   Business associates
   |       2.   Suppliers
   |       3.   Customers
   | B.   Gaining access to information
   |                                    DS
II.   The advantages of electronic mail
   |                                    DS
   | A.   Less expensive
   | B.   Higher employee productivity
   |      1.   Eliminates telephone tag
   |      2.   Easy to access
```

JOB 2 Report

File name: L71J2   Key this report in unbound format. Also prepare a title page and a bibliography. Use the company name and address instead of the author's name and school on the title page.

ELECTRONIC MAIL

Put aside your pens, pencils, and paper! Say "good-by" to handwritten, rough drafts of letters, memos, reports, and other documents. Electronic mail will save you from the needless drudgery and time wasted on written communications and telephone calls.

With electronic mail, rough-draft communications are keyed directly into the computer. Corrections are easy to make, and editing functions, such as moving or changing paragraphs, are simple to effect. Once edited and corrected, any document can be transmitted instantly to the electronic "mailbox" of the recipient. The recipient can "call up" the message to appear on the screen. The message can then be printed, filed, forwarded, deleted, or responded to by the receiver.

With electronic mail, any employee is only seconds away from valuable information. The keyboard provides access to inventory, data bases, client references, mailing lists, backlog updates, price increases, and other necessary information that will help employees to perform more efficiently. Participating suppliers can instantly respond with delivery dates, back-order quantities, and other helpful information. Customers can place orders directly into the computer.

When compared with other mail-delivery services, electronic mail is less expensive, yet significantly faster. Most long-distance electronic mail can be transmitted for the cost of a one-minute long-distance phone call. Less time-sensitive mail can be sent after 11 p.m. at lower rates.

Electronic mail can result in high levels of productivity for all employees. It can eliminate or reduce significantly, the calling back and forth on the telephone trying to reach someone ("telephone tag"). It can also reduce the time spent waiting for a message to be delivered and a response to be returned. Electronic mail is flexible, operating 24 hours a day, 7 days a week for incoming and outgoing information. Easy access is assured to all users. The contents of the electronic mailbox are accessible from any telephone line. A personal access code ensures privacy.

Although electronic mail is not likely to replace hand-carried mail totally, it will continue to grow in popularity. Because of its efficiency, electronic mail can help decrease employee workloads and increase employee productivity. Increased productivity means more time for customers—the lifeblood of our organization.

BIBLIOGRAPHY

Kurshan, Barbara L.; November, Alan C.; and Stove, Jane D. *Computer Literacy Through Applications*. Boston: Houghton Mifflin Company, 1986.

Kutsko, Jackie. "Electronic Messages—Instant Communication is Here." *Business Exchange*, March 1985, pp. 24–27.

(Continued next page)

New-Key Orientation

Study the keyboard chart to the right. Note which finger strikes each home key.

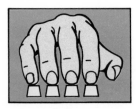

Correct alignment

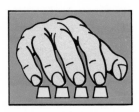

Incorrect alignment

Goal: To learn the home-key position 5′

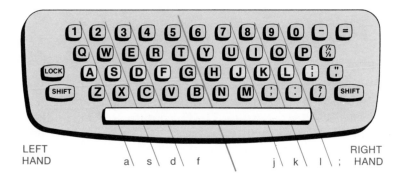

1. Place your left index finger on **F** and your right index finger on **J**. This positions your hands on the home keys: left hand on **A S D F**; right hand on **J K L ;**. Keep your fingers curved and aligned on the keys.
2. Using the correct fingers, lightly touch each key as you say the letters to yourself: asdfjkl;
3. Remove your hands from the keyboard.
4. Replace your fingers on the home keys. Check for correct finger and wrist position: fingers curved and wrists low, but not resting on the keyboard.
5. Strike each home key with the correct finger while saying each letter to yourself. Use a quick, sharp stroke: asdfjkl;
6. Strike each home key again as you say each letter: asdfjkl;

1E

Read and Do

Goal: To learn the proper technique for the enter/return key 7′ *1-2*

When you reach the end of a line, you must return the cursor/carrier to the beginning of a new line. To do this, use the enter/return (E/R) key.

1. Locate the enter/return key.
2. Place your fingers in home-key position.
3. Key the letters: asdfjkl;
4. Keep your other fingers on the home keys while you extend the **sem** finger to the enter/return key.
5. Tap the enter/return key lightly.
6. Return your **sem** finger to its home-key position immediately after striking the enter/return key.

Using the **sem** (semicolon) finger, tap the enter/return key lightly and release it quickly.

7. On the new line, key: asdfjkl;. Then operate the enter/return key to begin a new line.

1F

Read and Do

Goal: To learn to operate the space bar 5′

The space bar is used to space between words and after marks of punctuation (such as the semicolon).

1. Locate the space bar below the letter keys.

2. Place your fingers in home-key position and key: asdf
3. Hold your right thumb over the space bar and keep your fingers in home-key position. Strike the space

(Continued next page)

Unit 6 // Progress Review

This unit contains lessons designed to help you review the formats and procedures presented in Units 1–5 and evaluate how well you have learned them. Lessons 71–73 contain a Minisimulation. In the Minisimulation, you will complete a variety of keyboarding assignments related to a single company, Smythe's Office Products. Each assignment reviews and reinforces important keyboarding concepts and formats.

When you have completed the Minisimulation, you should be ready for Lessons 74–75, Measuring Mastery. These lessons can be used to evaluate your keyboarding skills and knowledge of:

1. Block-format letters.
2. OCR-format envelopes.
3. Horizontal and vertical centering.
4. Unbound reports.
5. Proofreading and error-correction techniques.

Lessons 71–73 Minisimulation

Smythe's Office Products

You are working for Smythe's Office Products, located at 357 Parkview Drive, San Antonio, Texas 78211. Smythe's also has stores in Dallas, Fort Worth, and Houston. Smythe's Office Products specializes in retail sales and service of office supplies and equipment.

Smythe's offices are fully automated. All personnel have access to microcomputers to prepare documents. With the addition of electronic mail, employees at all levels are using the microcomputer keyboard to communicate with other employees in Smythe's branch stores located in other cities. The efficient use of the keyboards keeps information flowing smoothly to all parts of the company.

While working at Smythe's, you will assume the role of the following people as you key their documents and electronic messages.

Administrative Assistant outline, report, table, program, form
Correspondence Secretary letter, centered announcement, table
Executive electronic message
Financial Officer form

Key each job in the order given, and complete one job before you go on to the next. Proofread your work and correct all errors. Use the current date on all documents.

Use the stationery supplies in your workbook or plain paper for these jobs. As you complete a job, file it in a folder (in the order completed). Then turn the folder in to your teacher when all jobs are completed.

bar with your right thumb using a quick, down-and-in motion. (Keep your left thumb tucked out of the way.)

4. Key: jkl; then *quickly* strike the space bar.

5. Do not pause before or after striking the space bar.

6. Key: asdf. Then space quickly and key: jkl;

7. Operate your enter/return to begin a new line.

1G

Technique Timing

Take two 1-minute timings.

Tap the space bar the number of times shown in the boxes. Pause briefly between boxes.

Use your enter/return when you see E/R.

Goal: To improve keyboarding techniques 4′

Tap the space bar with your right thumb, using a quick, down-and-in motion. Keep your left thumb tucked out of the way.

1 sp	2 sp	3 sp	2 sp	1 sp	3 sp	E/R	1 sp	4 sp
2 sp	3 sp	5 sp	2 sp	E/R	3 sp	1 sp	1 sp	4 sp
2 sp	E/R	1 sp	2 sp	2 sp	E/R	3 sp	4 sp	1 sp
3 sp	1 sp	E/R	1 sp	2 sp	3 sp	4 sp	2 sp	E/R

1H

Technique Timing

Take a 1-minute timing on each line.

Think and say each letter to yourself as you strike it.

Space once between letter groups.

Goal: To improve keyboarding techniques 6′

Enter/return quickly when you come to the end of a line. Do not space before using the enter/return key.

F and J 1 ff jj ff jj ff jj fj fj fj fj fj fjf fjf

D and K 2 dd kk dd kk dd kk dk dk dk dk dk dkd dkd

S and L 3 ss ll ss ll ss ll sl sl sl sl sl sls sls

A and ; 4 aa ;; aa ;; aa ;; a; a; a; a; a; a;a a;a

1I

Keyboard Practice

Key each line twice.

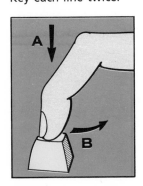

Goal: To practice proper keystroking techniques 5′   *1-3*

Strike the keys with a quick, sharp stroke (A). As you strike the key, snap the finger toward the palm of your hand (B).

1 as ask as ask all lass all lass as ask a E/R   Repeat each line.

2 ad ad lad lad ad lad all a lad all a lad E/R

3 all all fall fall all all fall fall fall E/R

4 a lass; a lass; a lass asks; a lass asks E/R

5 ask a lad; a lass asks; a lad; ask a lad E/R

M Note: As you continue to key lines of text, the text may begin to scroll (disappear) off the screen.

70B

Goal Writing

Goal: To measure timed-writing progress 10′

Default or DS

Take two 3-minute goal writings.

If you finish before time is called, start again.

Record your speed and accuracy.

	1′	3′
Salespeople very often write letters to tell their cus-	11	4
tomers all about new products or services. Because personal	24	8
letters are often the most effective, the salesperson may	35	12
send the same letter to many different people.	44	15
A word processor has memory capability, and, as a re-	55	18
sult, the body of a letter describing a product can be input	68	23
one time and then stored. By using the merge function, a	79	26
keyboard operator can recall the letter at any time and	90	30
input a list of names and addresses to whom the letter is to	103	34
be sent. The printer can automatically print the letter as	115	38
many times as it is needed, filling in a new name and ad-	126	42
dress each time.	129	43

1′ | 1 | 2 | 3 | 4 | 5 | 6 | 7 | 8 | 9 | 10 | 11 | 12 | AWL
3′ | 1 | 2 | 3 | 4 | 5.7

70C

Production Measurement

Goal: To measure formatting skills 35′

File name: L70C   Key this report in unbound format. The title is All About Modems. Prepare a title page. Use your name as the author.

Sooner or later every computer user has the desire to connect to something "out there."[1] If you have a microcomputer, you probably won't be an exception. You may want to access a new service, communicate with other people, or telecommute to work. The device that allows you to do all these things is the modem.

What is a modem? The dictionary defines modem as "a device that converts data from one form into another, as from one usable in data processing to one usable in telephone transmission."[2] Another writer describes the modem as follows:

The word modem is a contraction of "modulator/demodulator," which is exactly what the modem does. The modem converts computer data into the form that phone lines can carry. In effect, computers and telephones speak two different languages. The modem acts as the translator.[3]

The prospective modem buyer needs to be familiar with transmission speeds. The usual speed for the home user is 300 bits per second; a speed of 300 bps equates to about 30 characters per second. That speed is slower than many daisy-wheel printers run.[4]

Once your modem is connected, you are ready to enter the exciting world of information your computer can bring to you.

NOTES

1. William Barden, Jr., "The Hayes Micromodem II," *Popular Computing*, February 1983, pp. 66–72.

2. *The American Heritage Dictionary*, Second College Edition (1982), s.v. "Modem."

3. David B. Powell, "Buyer's Guide to Modems," *Popular Computing*, July 1984, pp. 111–120.

4. David A. Gabel, "Modems," *Personal Computing*, January 1985, pp. 109–119.

Read and Do

Refer to the illustrations as you read and follow the instructions for your equipment.

Goal: To end the lesson 3'

M *Microcomputer*

Ending procedures vary. Follow the specific instructions for your equipment or these general steps:

Always store disks in their protective envelopes to prevent damage to stored documents.

T *Typewriter*

Use the paper-feed key or paper-release lever to remove the paper from your typewriter.

1. Read and respond to any prompts that appear on the screen.
2. If necessary, store your document using the store key or command for your software.
3. Be sure the red light of the disk drive is off before you open the door of the disk drive.
4. Carefully remove the disk from the disk drive.
5. Place the disk into its protective envelope.
6. Turn off the power to the monitor and to the microcomputer.
7. Store the disk following your instructor's guidelines.
8. Clean up your work area.

1. To remove the paper from the typewriter, follow these steps:
   a. Pull the paper-load lever/bail toward you. (On some machines this will cause the paper to eject. If so, go to Step 2.)
   b. Operate the paper-feed key or paper-release lever.
   c. Take the paper out of the machine and return the paper-load lever/ bail or the paper-release lever to its original position.
2. Turn off the typewriter.
3. Cover the machine if told to do so.
4. Clean up your work area.

Lesson 2

M Default Settings
T SS SM 2" (12-pitch), 24–78; 1½" (10 pitch), 15–70

Read and Do (Review)

Do each activity to the right as you read it.

Goal: To get ready to key 3'

Clear your desk of books or other materials you won't need during your keyboarding class. Arrange your work area as described in 1A. Prepare your equipment by completing the steps on the next page.

(Continued next page)

Choose an answer from the box on page 171 to complete each sentence.

6. The bottom margin of an unbound report is ____ lines.
7. Each entry on the endnotes page is single spaced with a ____ space between entries.
8. The first line of a(n) ____ entry is indented five spaces.
9. The first line of a(n) ____ entry begins at the left margin; other lines are indented five spaces.
10. Bibliography entries are placed in ____ order.

69E

Application: Reports

File name: L69E

Goal: To key the title page for an unbound report   6′

Prepare a title page for your report, Preparing a Research Paper. Use your name and school on the title page.

> **Checkpoint:**   Did you key the current date a DS below your school's name?

69F

Read and Do
Read and follow the instructions to the right as you put your report together.

Goal: To proofread and assemble the pages of a report   16′

Proofread and assemble the pages of the report you prepared in Lessons 64–69. The file name under which the report is stored is L64E.

1. Proofread. Read your entire report word-for-word, both for accuracy and for understanding.
2. Correct all errors.
3. Print the report (microcomputers).
4. Assemble the pages. Place the title page first, followed by the pages of the report (in numerical order), the endnotes, and the bibliography.
5. Fasten the pages together. Follow your teacher's instructions for stapling the pages together.

Lesson 70 / Measuring Mastery

70A

Warmup

Goal: To strengthen keyboarding skills   5′

Key each line twice. DS after each pair of lines.

```
Speed          1  Yes, the manager plans to cover the reasons with them today.
Accuracy       2  Please also ask Sam about last year's sales data situations.
Number/Symbol  3  The "Tri-Wool" carpet sells for $1,586.99 less 15% discount.
Data Entry     4  Left and right brackets ([]) were used to designate subsets.
                  |  1  |  2  |  3  |  4  |  5  |  6  |  7  |  8  |  9  |  10  |  11  |  12  |
```

Complete the steps that apply to your equipment.

M *Microcomputer*

1. Insert the disks in proper sequence as described in 1C.
2. Turn on the monitor.
3. Turn on the microcomputer.

T *Typewriter*

1. Turn on the typewriter.
2. Adjust the paper guide so that the left edge of your paper aligns with zero.
3. Insert a sheet of typing paper and straighten it if necessary.

> **Checkpoint:** Is your keyboard even with the front edge of your desk or table?

2B

Need to Know

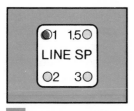

E Line-space key

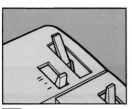

T Line-space lever

Goal: To learn about line spacing   5′

M *Microcomputer*

On most microcomputers, the line spacing is determined by a default setting that is preset in the software. Usually, the default setting is single spacing (SS). When you SS, text appears on every line. When you see the instruction to double space (DS) in the following lessons, operate the enter/return key two times.

E **T** *Typewriter*

The line-space key/lever controls the number of lines your paper spaces up when you operate the return. Set your line spacing for single spacing (SS) as shown in the color band at the beginning of this lesson. When you SS, text appears on every line. When you see the instruction to double space (DS) in the following lessons, operate the return key two times.

▶ 2C

Read and Do

12-pitch (elite) has 12 characters to 1 inch

ｊｊｊｊｊｊｊｊｊｊｊｊ

ｊｊｊｊｊｊｊｊｊｊ

10-pitch (pica) has 10 characters to 1 inch

Goal: To learn about setting margins   6′   *2-1*

All microcomputers and typewriters have margin settings that allow you to control the length of a line of text and to position that line of text horizontally on the page.

Most printers and many typewriters can print in either 10-pitch or 12-pitch. Determine the pitch of your equipment.

Next you need to decide how wide to make the side margins. The correct side margins for each lesson and the actual margin settings are shown in the color band at the beginning of the lesson.

M *Microcomputer*

All software programs have default margins. Use default margins unless otherwise directed.

Changing margins is often a print function and will be taught in a later lesson.

(Continued next page)

Speed Practice

Take a 12- or 10-second timing on each line. If you complete a line in the time allowed, go on to the next one.

Goal: To build keyboarding speed 5'

GWAM
12" | 10"

1 The department will open next week.   35 | 42
2 I will send the goods to the other town.   40 | 48
3 I would like to thank you for the fine gifts.   45 | 54
4 He paid us to visit the firms when he got to town.   50 | 60
5 Officers are nominated in January and elected in March.   55 | 66

| 1 | 2 | 3 | 4 | 5 | 6 | 7 | 8 | 9 | 10 | 11 |

69C

Need to Know

Refer to the illustration as you read about the format for a title page.

Goal: To learn how to prepare a title page 6'

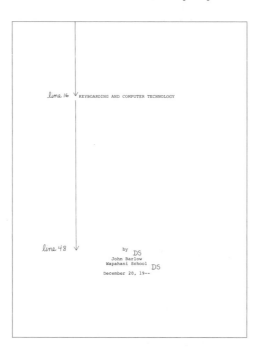

line 16 KEYBOARDING AND COMPUTER TECHNOLOGY

line 48 by DS
John Barlow
Wapahani School DS
December 20, 19--

The title page for a report contains the title of the report, the author's name, and the date. For a school report, the title page may also include the name of the school, the course, and other information the teacher requests. This information is keyed on a separate page and is placed at the beginning of the report.

1. Enter/return to line 16. If you are using a microcomputer, include the default top margin in your count.
2. Center and key the report title in all caps.
3. Space down 32 additional lines to line 48 and center the word *by*.
4. DS and center your name.
5. SS and center the school's name.
6. DS and center the current date.

69D

Self-Check

Choose the word or phrase that correctly completes each statement.

Key the number and the completed statement.

Check your answers in Appendix C.

Goal: To review formats for an unbound report, endnotes, and bibliography 12'

Answers:	alphabetical	1"	double
	bibliography	13	triple
	7	endnote	6

1. The title of a report, endnotes, or bibliography is placed on line ____.
2. A ____ space is used after the title or heading.
3. The body of a report is ____ spaced.
4. On the second page of a report, the body begins on line ____.
5. An unbound report uses ____ side margins.

(Continued next page)

Set your margins as indicated in the copy at the right.

T *Typewriter*

Align the left edge of your paper at zero on the margin scale. Then set your margins at the proper settings for your machine.

12-pitch (SM 2″)		10-pitch (SM 1½″)	
left margin	24	left margin	15
right margin	78	right margin	70

2D

Read and Do (Review)

Left hand on Ⓐ Ⓢ Ⓓ Ⓕ
Right hand on Ⓙ Ⓚ Ⓛ Ⓢ

Goal: To review home-key position 3′

1. Place your fingers in home-key position.
2. Keep your wrists side-by-side and even with the slant of the keyboard.
3. Keep your wrists low, but not resting on the keyboard.
4. Curve your fingers.
5. Hold your right thumb over the space bar. Keep your left thumb tucked out of the way.
6. Tap the space bar several times with a quick, down-and-in motion: *space, space, space.*

2E

Technique Timing

Sit in home-key position. Then take two 1-minute timings on each line. Work on improving the technique shown.

Space once between letter groups.

Goal: To improve keyboarding techniques 9′

Strike each key with a quick, sharp stroke. Release the key quickly.

1 ff jj dd kk ss ll aa ;; fj dk sl a; ;lkj E/R
2 aa ;; ss ll dd kk ff jj a; sl dk fj fdsa E/R

Keep your wrists low, but do not rest them on your keyboard.

3 asd fjk l; aa ;; a; ss ll sl dd kk dk fj E/R
4 sad lads; as dad asks; sad lass asks dad E/R

2F

Technique Timing

Review the correct techniques for the enter/return.

Goal: To improve keyboarding techniques 4′

Place your fingers in home-key position. Keeping your other fingers on the home keys, reach the **sem** finger to the enter/return key. Tap the key lightly and release it quickly. Remember: Do not space before striking the enter/return key at the end of a line.

(Continued next page)

68F

Project Preview

File name: L68F
Full sheet
SM: 1"
Tab: ¶

Key as much of the bibliography as you can in 5 minutes. If you finish before time is called, start again.

Goal: To key a bibliography 7'

line 13 ↓ BIBLIOGRAPHY TS

Estrin, Herman. "How to Write for Scientific and Technical
    ⁵→ Journals." The Journal of Business Communication 18
        (Summer 1981): 55–58. DS
Hauser, Travis L., and Gray, Lee Learner. Writing the Research
    ⁵→ and Term Paper. New York: Dell Publishing Company, Inc.,
        1977. DS
Holmes, Ralph M. The Reference Guide: A Handbook for Office
    ⁵→ Personnel. Boston: Houghton Mifflin Company, 1980. DS

68G

Application: Reports

Goal: To prepare a bibliography for an unbound report 10'

File name: L68G   Full sheet   Prepare a bibliography for the report in 64E. Use the same margins you used on page 1 of the report.

BIBLIOGRAPHY

Estrin, Herman. "How to Write for Scientific and Technical Journals." *The Journal of Business Communication* 18 (Summer 1981): 55–58.

Hauser, Travis L., and Gray, Lee Learner. *Writing the Research and Term Paper.* New York: Dell Publishing Company, Inc., 1977.

Holmes, Ralph M. *The Reference Guide: A Handbook for Office Personnel.* Boston: Houghton Mifflin Company, 1980.

Kahn, Gilbert, and Mulkerne, Donald J. D. *The Term Paper: Step by Step.* Garden City: Doubleday & Company, Inc., 1964.

Modern Language Association. *MLA Handbook for Writers of Research Papers, Theses, and Dissertations.* New York: Modern Language Association, 1984.

Turabian, Kate L. *A Manual for Writers of Term Papers, Theses, and Dissertations.* 4th ed. Chicago: The University of Chicago Press, 1973.

Checkpoint: Did you underscore only those marks of punctuation that are part of the titles?

Lesson 69

M Default Settings
T SS   SM 1½" (12); 1" (10)   Tab ¶

69A

Warmup

Key each line twice.
DS after each pair.

"al" combinations

Goal: To strengthen keyboarding skills 5'

1 album balcony algebra calypso dental alien electoral calvary
2 balderdash Albania Alberta female Alcott galore Alfonso bale
3 Alice alphabetized principal female names for the Alsatians.

| 1 | 2 | 3 | 4 | 5 | 6 | 7 | 8 | 9 | 10 | 11 | 12 |

Take two 1-minute timings.

Enter/return when you see E/R, not at the end of a line.

```
a as ad ads all fall
as sad; ask lads ads

a lad lads lass fall
as a lad; a sad dad;

a fall; a lad falls;
all lads; ask a lass
```

Do not space before operating the enter/return. Quickly return the **sem** finger to home-key position after operating the enter/return.

```
a as ad ads all fall   E/R   as sad; ask lads ads   E/R E/R
a lad lads lass fall   E/R   as a lad; a sad dad;   E/R E/R
a fall; a lad falls;   E/R   all lads; ask a lass   E/R E/R
```

Checkpoint: Do your lines look similar to those shown in the left margin?

2G

Need to Know

Goal: To learn about double spacing 3′   2-2

If you followed the directions correctly in Activity 2F, you should have a blank line between some of your keyed lines. You left the blank line by operating your enter/return key twice.

M *Microcomputer*

Most software programs have a default setting for line spacing. The default line setting is usually for single spacing (SS). You may double space when the default setting is in effect by operating the enter/return key two times. Double spacing may also be done by selecting the appropriate option on the print **menu** or by giving a command. However, these techniques for double spacing will be taught in a later lesson.

T *Typewriter*

When your machine is set for single spacing (SS), you can leave a blank line by operating your return two times.

Your typewriter should be set for single spacing for the early lessons in this textbook as shown in the color band at the beginning of each lesson. Be sure to set the appropriate line spacing at the beginning of each class. For more information, refer to the *About Your Equipment* section of this book.

2H

Keyboard Practice

Key each line twice.

Double space (DS) after each pair of lines by operating your enter/return two times.

Goal: To practice proper keystroking techniques 8′

Cue: Keep your eyes on the textbook copy as you key.

```
1 aj ak al a; sj sk sl s; dj dk dl d; a;sl      Repeat each line.
2 fj fk fl f; ja js jd jf ka ks kd kf a;sl
3 la ls ld lf ;a ;s ;d ;f a; sl dk fj a;sl
4 as as ask ask asks asks ad ad ads ads as
5 sad sad dad dad fad fad lad lad all fall
6 all fall dad dads ask asks lad lads lass
```

Checkpoint: Did you remember to enter/return two times for a double space between groups?

---

4. His teacher at faulkner junior high school was ms. rutherford.
5. The soccer team at lexall university played in the pearl bowl.
6. She saw a shakespearean play in dallas at the westone theatre.
7. Did ms. wilkes work for the knox company in saginaw, michigan?
8. Ask mr. leu to compare marxist doctrine with russian policies.

68D

Keyboard Composition

Default or DS

Key as much as you can in 8 minutes.

Do not correct errors.

Goal: To compose at the keyboard   10′

Choose one of these topics to discuss in one or two paragraphs. You may want to use some of the words and phrases listed for each topic as you key your paragraphs.

1. Topic: MY PLANS FOR THE FUTURE

Some suggested words and phrases for you to use are:

when I finish school	apply for a job
job responsibilities	buy a ____
travel	improve my ____
save money	learn more about ____

2. Topic: A PERSON I ADMIRE

Some suggested words and phrases for you to use are:

accomplishments	helps other people by ____
personality	famous
outlook on life	can ____ better than most people
look up to	works hard to ____

68E

Need to Know

Refer to the illustration as you read about the format for a bibliography page.

Goal: To learn to key a bibliography   5′

68-1

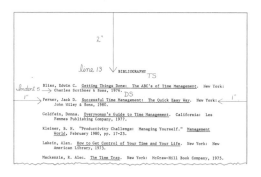

The bibliography is an alphabetic listing of all the sources referred to or used by the writer in preparing a report. It includes books, magazines, government publications, and newspaper articles. The bibliography is keyed on a separate page and placed at the end of the report.

1. Center and key in all caps the heading BIBLIOGRAPHY on line 13.
2. TS after the heading.
3. Use the same side margins as you used in the report.
4. Key the sources in alphabetical order by author or, if the author is not known, by title.
5. Key each source in this order: author's name, title of the source, and publication data.
6. Start the first line of each source at the left margin. Indent the second and all other lines five spaces from the left margin.
7. SS the lines of each source. DS between sources.

Technique Timing

Take a 2-minute timing on each pair of lines. Work on improving the technique shown.

If you finish before time is called, start again.

DS after each timing.

Goal: To improve keyboarding techniques 7′

Quickly return to home-key position after operating the enter/return.

1 a;sldkfj a;sldkfj a;sldkfj a;sldkfj lad;

2 a fall; a flask; all fall; all dads; ask

Sit up straight with your feet flat on the floor.

3 all fall fads; a fall flask; as all lads

4 all ads; a fall ad; a sad lass; as a dad

Strike the space bar with a quick down-and-in motion.

5 aa ;; ss ll dd kk ff jj a;sldkfj jak jak

6 fall lass dad fad dads lads ask asks sad

2J

Read and Do (Review)

Goal: To end the lesson 2′

M *Microcomputer*

1. Read and respond to any prompts.
2. If necessary, store your document.
3. Carefully remove the disk from the disk drive.
4. Place the disk into its protective envelope.
5. Turn off the power to the monitor and to the microcomputer.

T *Typewriter*

1. Remove the paper from the typewriter.
2. Turn off the machine.
3. Cover the machine if directed to do so.
4. Clean up your work area.

Lesson **3**

| **M** Default Settings |
| **T** SS   SM 2″ (12-pitch), 24–78; 1½″ (10-pitch), 15–70 |

3A

Read and Do (Review)

Goal: To get ready to key 3′

Clear your desk of everything you don't need, and arrange your work area as described in 1A.

M *Microcomputer*

1. Insert the disks in proper sequence as described in 1C.
2. Turn on the monitor.
3. Turn on the microcomputer.

T *Typewriter*

1. Turn on the typewriter.
2. Adjust the paper guide.
3. Insert a sheet of paper into the typewriter and straighten it if necessary.
4. Set the line spacing for single spacing (SS).
5. Set the margins as directed in the color band at the beginning of the lesson. Refer to 2C.

Cue: Decide which punctuation marks are to be underscored before you begin the document.

NOTES

1. Ralph M. Holmes, *The Reference Guide: A Handbook for Office Personnel* (Boston: Houghton Mifflin Company, 1980), p. 158.
2. Holmes, p. 158.
3. Kate L. Turabian, *A Manual for Writers of Term Papers, Theses, and Dissertations*, 4th ed. (Chicago: The University of Chicago Press, 1973), p. 64.
4. Holmes, p. 160.
5. Holmes, p. 160.
6. Modern Language Association, *MLA Handbook for Writers of Research Papers, Theses, and Dissertations* (New York: Modern Language Association, 1984), p. 181.
7. Turabian, p. 58.

Lesson 68

M Default Settings
T SS   SM 1½" (12); 1" (10)   Tab ¶

68A

Warmup

Key each line twice. DS after each pair.

Confusing words: precede and proceed

Goal: To strengthen keyboarding skills 5′

1 According to procedure, I cannot precede Mark in the parade.
2 The preceding comment is okay. You may proceed to print it.
3 The holiday precedes the meetings, so I can proceed at once.

| 1 | 2 | 3 | 4 | 5 | 6 | 7 | 8 | 9 | 10 | 11 | 12 |

68B

Accuracy Practice

DS after each group of lines.

Goal: To build keyboarding accuracy 5′

Take a 3-minute accuracy timing on the lines in 68A. If you make an error, start again. Stay on a line until you have keyed it without error.

Checkpoint: How many error-free lines did you key?

68C

Language Arts

Read the rule in the box at the right.

Then key the numbered sentences, supplying correct capitalization where needed.

Check your work with the key in Appendix B.

Goal: To review rules for capitalization 8′

Capitalize proper nouns and proper adjectives. A proper noun names a specific person, place, or thing. A proper adjective comes from a proper noun and describes the noun it precedes.

Example:

It was Johanna's practice to read English poetry in New York City.

1. Can sue study greek in athens while she and fay are in greece?
2. My friend, dean, is in the u.s. navy in san diego, california.
3. Will raylen be attending franklin roosevelt college this year?

(Continued next page)

Warmup

Key each line twice.

DS after each pair of lines.

1 a;sldkfj a;sldkfj a;sldkfj a;sldkfj a;sl

2 fjfj dkdk slsl a;a; a;sldkfj a;sldkfj a;

3 all lad ask fad lass ad dad all fall ads

4 as a lad; ask a dad; all fall; a sad lad

Checkpoint: Are you seated with your back against the chair and feet flat on the floor?

Technique Timing

Take two 1-minute timings on each line. Work on improving the technique shown.

DS after each timing.

Space between words without pausing. Use a quick down-and-in motion.

1 all lads ask dad; a sad lass; ask a lass

Quickly return to home-key position after operating the enter/return.

2 a fall; a flask; all fall; all dads; ask

Keep your eyes on the textbook copy.

3 sad dad fad lad fall all as a asks salad

New-Key Orientation

1. Locate the new key on the keyboard chart.
2. Next, locate the key on your keyboard.
3. Before keying the practice lines, read the instructions for each new key.
4. Practice the first line, returning to home-key position after making the reach to the new key.
5. Practice the second line for 2 minutes or until you can key it without looking at your hands.

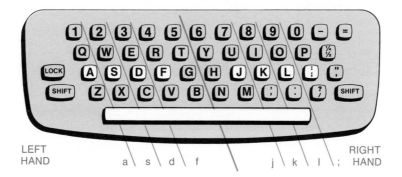

LEFT HAND   a s d f   j k l ;   RIGHT HAND

 Practice the reach to Ⓔ with the **d** finger. The **f** finger may lift slightly, but keep your other fingers in home-key position.

1 de de de de de de de de de de de de de

2 see lee fee led fed lead dead feed sea

H Practice the reach to Ⓗ with the **j** finger. Keep your other fingers in home-key position.

3 jh jh jh jh jh jh jh jh jh jh jh jh jh

4 hal had has he she heal head hall lash

(Continued next page)

Supply quotations as needed.

Check your work with the key in Appendix B.

1. Pioneers of the Old West was the title of the first chapter.
2. He wrote an article entitled A Computer for You last August.
3. They made Rhythmic Raindrops a song remembered by everybody.
4. James read Longfellow's The Village Blacksmith to the class.
5. Sign of the Times was the first movie filmed by Mitch Alder.
6. Bonatello's Circle of Gold was the best speech he ever gave.

67D

Need to Know

Refer to the illustration as you read about the use of notes to identify the sources of information in a report.

Goal: To learn to key endnotes 5′   67-1

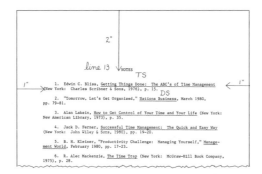

Notes keyed at the foot of a page on which material is cited are called *footnotes*. Notes keyed on a separate page and placed at the end of a report are called *endnotes*. To key endnotes:

1. Center and key in all caps the heading NOTES on line 13. TS after the heading.

2. Use the same side margins as in the report.
3. Key the notes in numerical order.
4. Indent the first line of each note five spaces.
5. Key the note number, a period, two spaces, and the reference. Key each reference in this order: author's name, title of source, publication information, and page number. (For later references to the same source, use the author's last name, a comma, and the page number.)
6. SS the lines of each note. Start the second and all other lines at the left margin. DS between notes.

Note: A page with a title or a centered heading is not numbered.

67E

Project Preview

Full sheet
SM: 1″

Tab: ¶

Key as much of the endnotes as you can in 4 minutes. If you finish before time is called, start again.

Goal: To learn the format for endnotes 6′

line 13 ↓ NOTES
                    TS

⁵→ 1.   Karen R. Krupar, Communication·Games (New York: The Free Press, 1973), p. 158.
                    DS

⁵→ 2.   Krupar, p. 158.
                    DS

⁵→ 3.   John T. Molloy, Dress·for·Success (New York: Warner Books, Incorporated, 1975), p. 56.

67F

Application: Reports

Goal: To prepare the endnotes page for an unbound report 16′

File name: L67F   Full sheet / Key the endnotes for the report in 64E. Underscore the titles shown in italics.

(Continued next page)

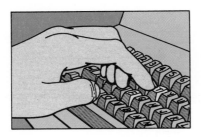

Practice the reach to Ⓣ with the **f** finger. Keep your other fingers in home-key position. Do not let your wrist move up as you strike Ⓣ.

Ⓣ

5 ft ft ft ft ft ft ft ft ft ft ft ft ft

6 tea set fat sat jet let tell feet test

3E

Technique Timing

Take a 1-minute timing on each line. Work on improving the technique shown.

DS after each timing.

Goal: To improve keyboarding techniques 12′

Return to home-key position after making reaches to the new keys.

1 feel keel leaf jell seal seek leased fed

2 hash heal shell sheds sashes ashes heads

3 jet least let fat east feat teak sat eat

Keep your eyes on your textbook copy as you key.

Repeat lines 1–3.

Keep your wrists low, but do not rest them on your keyboard.

4 the last jet; he has a fast jet; she has

5 the lake had; take all; at last; a death

6 the last deal; the sale has; she takes a

3F

Keyboard Practice

Key each line twice.

DS after each pair of lines.

Goal: To practice proper keystroking techniques 8′

1 at least tell; all the sales; a sad jest

2 she has a lease; sell the jet; see these

3 take the tea sets; shed these hats; take

4 the test; feed these fat lads; ask these

3G

Read and Do (Review)

Do each activity to the right as you read it.

Goal: To end the lesson 2′

M *Microcomputer*

1. Read and respond to any prompts.
2. If necessary, store your document.
3. Carefully remove the disk from the disk drive.
4. Place the disk into its protective envelope.
5. Turn off the power to the monitor and to the microcomputer.

(Continued next page)

M Default Settings

T SS   SM 1½" (12); 1" (10)   Tab ¶

67A

Warmup

Goal: To strengthen keyboarding skills 5'

Key each line twice. DS after each pair of lines.

Speed   1 Notify us of the days their firm intends to finish the jobs.
Accuracy   2 However, three more general credit references are necessary.
Number/Symbol   3 The correct items are $24.67 or 15.67% and $12.65 or 78.34%.
Data Entry   4 Try the new formula to solve the problem: E = (A + B) + C*D

| 1 | 2 | 3 | 4 | 5 | 6 | 7 | 8 | 9 | 10 | 11 | 12 |

67B

Goal Writing

Goal: To measure timed-writing progress 10'

Default or DS

Take two 3-minute goal writings.

If you finish before time is called, start again.

Record your speed and accuracy.

	1'	3'
Good listening is as important as good speaking. It is	11	4
a skill you can develop. Whenever you listen, you have a	23	8
purpose. You may listen for specific information. When you	35	12
listen to a commercial, you will judge the new product to	47	16
decide whether or not you want to buy it. This is called	58	19
critical listening. You may practice conversational listen-	71	24
ing when you talk with some of your friends. You may even	82	27
combine all three ways of listening. Each type of listening	95	32
will require you to be an active listener. You need to pay	107	36
attention and think about what you are hearing if you are to	119	40
become a good listener.	123	41

1'| 1 | 2 | 3 | 4 | 5 | 6 | 7 | 8 | 9 | 10 | 11 | 12 | AWL
3'| 1 | 2 | 3 | 4 | 5.7

67C

Language Arts

Goal: To review use of quotation marks 8'

Read the rule in the box at the right.

Then key each numbered sentence, supplying quotation marks where needed.

> Place quotation marks around the titles of articles, speeches, book chapters, songs, poems, and movies.
>
> **Examples:**
>
> Ann Lyle wrote "Word Processing for Today" for the next issue.
> Lincoln's "Gettysburg Address" has become a model for brevity.

(Continued next page)

Do each activity to the right as you read it.

T *Typewriter*

1. Remove the paper from the typewriter.
2. Turn off the machine.
3. Cover the machine if directed to do so.
4. Clean up your work area.

Lesson 4

M Default Settings
T SS   SM 2″ (12-pitch), 24–78; 1½″ (10-pitch), 15–70

4A

Read and Do (Review)

Follow the steps at the right to get your equipment ready.

Goal: To get ready to key 3′

Clear your desk of everything you don't need, and arrange your work area.

M *Microcomputer*

1. Insert the disks in proper sequence.
2. Turn on the monitor.
3. Turn on the microcomputer.

T *Typewriter*

1. Turn on the typewriter.
2. Adjust the paper guide.
3. Insert a sheet of typing paper and straighten it if necessary.
4. Set the line spacing for single spacing (SS).
5. Set the margins as directed in the color band at the beginning of the lesson.

4B

Warmup

Key each line twice.

DS after each pair of lines.

Goal: To strengthen keyboarding skills 5′

```
1 a;sldkfj a;sldkfj a;sldkfj a;sldkfj a;sl
2 jade fake leak deal self jest seek least
3 these death seals feels leads teeth feet
4 task salad dash steel lakes eat kale fee
```

4C

Technique Timing

Take two 2-minute timings on each group of lines. Work on improving the technique shown.

DS after each timing.

Goal: To improve keyboarding techniques 10′

Keep your fingers curved and your wrists low.

```
1 the last jet; a fast jet; seek the deal;
2 at least ask a dad; the fast jet had the
3 these lads feel that the sale has a lead
```

Checkpoint: Were you able to maintain good techniques while you keyed the lines?

(Continued next page)

Comparison Copy

Default or DS

Take two 2-minute timings on each paragraph.

Try to increase your speed on the second timing.

Try to keep your speed on the handwritten and rough-draft copy as high as your straight-copy speed.

Goal: To build speed on a variety of copy   14'

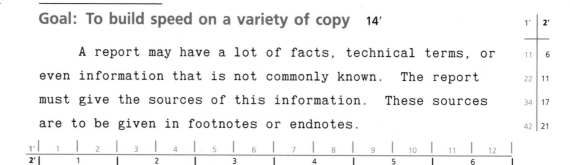

	1'	2'
A report may have a lot of facts, technical terms, or	11	6
even information that is not commonly known. The report	22	11
must give the sources of this information. These sources	34	17
are to be given in footnotes or endnotes.	42	21

```
1' | 1 | 2 | 3 | 4 | 5 | 6 | 7 | 8 | 9 | 10 | 11 | 12 |
2' |   1   |   2   |   3   |   4   |   5   |   6   |
```

	1'	2'
To help find and locate information that was taken from	11	6
other sources, a raised Arabic number must be keyed at the	23	12
end of the statement. To do this, key the numbers a half-	35	18
line space above the print line. Number the references	46	23
consecutively throughout the rest of the report.	56	28

	1'	2'
¶At the conclusion of the research report, there is a sepa-	8	4
rate page listing these references. Each reference is	20	10
numbered to correspond with numbered statements within	32	16
the body of report. these are references, called notes	44	22
or footnotes identify the source of the material used.	59	30

Language Arts

Read the rules in the box at the right.

Then key each numbered sentence, underscoring titles of published works where needed.

Check your work with the key in Appendix B.

Goal: To review use of the underscore   8'

Underscore titles of books, magazines, newspapers, or plays. Underscore all words, spaces, and punctuation marks that are part of the title itself. When keying from printed material, underscore titles shown in italics.

Example:

Houses, A Homebuyer's Guide was reviewed in the Tulsa Clarion.

1. Linda is reading my copy of the book Stories of the Wild West.
2. She wrote six automotive columns for Lake Charles Weekly News.
3. His book Byways was reviewed in this issue of Literary Digest.
4. They will use this textbook: Our Business and Economic World.
5. The magazines I like best are Sports World, Flying, and Forum.

Application: Reports

Goal: To key an unbound report   18'

Continue the report in 64E, File L64E. Try to complete page 3.

Checkpoint: Did you proofread and correct errors?

Take two 2-minute timings on the group of lines.

Keep your wrists and hands almost motionless as you strike each key.

4 head lasses; sell the shell; take a jet;

5 sell that dead leaf; she fed these seals

6 take the last sash; feel these felt hats

4D

New-Key Orientation

1. Locate the new key on the keyboard chart.
2. Next, locate the key on your keyboard.
3. Before keying the practice lines, read the instructions for each new key.
4. Practice the first line, returning to home-key position after making the reach to the new key.
5. Practice the second line for 2 minutes or until you can key it without looking at your hands.

Goal: To learn the location of Ⓘ Ⓖ and Ⓝ 12'

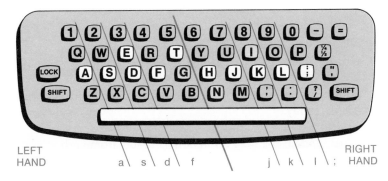

Ⓘ Practice the reach to Ⓘ with your **k** finger. The **j** finger may lift slightly, but keep your other fingers in home-key position.

1 ki ki ki ki ki ki ki ki ki ki ki ki ki

2 it kit sit fit hit lit his lid hid kid

Ⓖ Practice the reach to Ⓖ with your **f** finger. Keep your other fingers in home-key position.

3 fg fg fg fg fg fg fg fg fg fg fg fg fg

4 fgf jag hag leg keg lag sage aged glad

Ⓝ Practice the reach down to Ⓝ with your **j** finger. Keep your other fingers in home-key position.

5 jn jn jn jn jn jn jn jn jn jn jn jn jn

6 nat net ned den hen fan sand land hand

4E

Technique Timing

Take a 1-minute timing on each line. Work on improving the technique shown.

DS after each timing.

Goal: To improve keyboarding techniques 11'

Return to home-key position after making reaches to the new keys.

1 it kid list fist kiss hills field filled

2 egg leg sag gag gas gagged lagged gaggle

3 fan tan than thank send sand land handle

Keep your eyes on your textbook copy as you key.

Repeat lines 1–3.

(Continued next page)

Self-Check

Key the statement number and your answer: True or False.

Check your answers in Appendix C.

Goal: To review the format for quotations 8'

1. A long quotation to be set off within text contains four or more printed lines.
2. Long quotations are indented 10 spaces from each margin.
3. Long quotations are enclosed in quotation marks.
4. Long quotations are followed by a superior figure.
5. A double space is used before and after a long quotation.
6. Quotation marks indicate that a person's exact words are being used.

65E

Application: Reports

Goal: To key an unbound report 18'

Continue the report in 64E, File name L64E. Try to complete page 2 of the report today.

Cue: Indent the long quotations 5 spaces from each margin.

Lesson 66

M Default Settings
T SS   SM 1½" (12); 1" (10)   Tab ¶

66A

Warmup

Key each line twice. DS after each pair.

Goal: To strengthen keyboarding skills 5'

```
1 Your learning is more effective when progress goals are set.
2 Some goals will be long-term, and others will be short-term.
3 Short-range goals help you map your progress and feel great.
```
| 1 | 2 | 3 | 4 | 5 | 6 | 7 | 8 | 9 | 10 | 11 | 12 |

66B

Speed Practice

Take a 12- or a 10-second timing on each line. If you complete a line in the time allowed, go on to the next one.

Goal: To build keyboarding speed 5'

GWAM

	12"	10"
1 I will terminate our contract soon.	35	42
2 It was nearly eight when I reached home.	40	48
3 Steve thinks that all the units will be sold.	45	54
4 We think you will like the site for the new plant.	50	60
5 Carolyn has been a close friend of mine for five years.	55	66

| 1 | 2 | 3 | 4 | 5 | 6 | 7 | 8 | 9 | 10 | 11 |

Take a 1-minute timing on each line.

Space between words without pausing. Use a quick, down-and-in motion.

4 `tin sing kind hint shine kindle gain tag`

5 `dank dangle glisten fling knitting inlet`

6 `sitting tingle giggle listen link single`

4F

Keyboard Practice

Key each line twice.

DS after each pair of lines.

Goal: To practice proper keystroking techniques 7′

1 `let the king land the ninth jet in haste`

2 `he said that the king felt fine at night`

3 `she lied as she said she had faith in it`

4 `he asked that she feed the fast fat seal`

4G

Read and Do (Review)

Follow these procedures at the end of each keyboarding class.

Goal: To end the lesson 2′

 Microcomputer

1. Read and respond to any prompts.
2. If necessary, store your document.
3. Carefully remove the disk from the disk drive.
4. Place the disk into its protective envelope.
5. Turn off the power to the monitor and to the microcomputer.

T *Typewriter*

1. Remove the typing paper from the typewriter.
2. Turn off the machine.
3. Cover the machine if directed to do so.
4. Clean up your work area.

Lesson 5

M Default Settings
T SS   SM 2″ (12-pitch), 24–78; 1½″ (10-pitch), 15–70

5A

Warmup

Key each line twice.

DS after each pair of lines.

Goal: To strengthen keyboarding skills 5′

1 `a;sldkfja;sldkfja;sldkfja;sldkfja;sldkfj`

2 `the then these this that thin than think`

3 `night sight lights fights height delight`

4 `hang gang sang fang dangle jangle tangle`

> **Checkpoint:** Did you remember to arrange your work area as described in Lesson 4A?

---

enclose the title of a chapter in a book in quotation marks, but underline the book title itself. Enclose the title of a magazine in quotation marks, but underline the magazine name itself.

Consistency is important when preparing reports. Reference manuals provide rules that ensure that a consistent style is followed. Some style manuals present very traditional ways to key reports, while others feature more current, easy-to-use formats. Despite differences in details, all style manuals show "correct" ways to key reports. Whatever style is used, it is the writer's responsibility to follow it consistently throughout the report.

Lesson 65

M Default Settings
T SS   SM 1½" (12); 1" (10)   Tab ¶

65A

Warmup

Key each line twice. DS after each pair.

Confusing words: your and you're

Goal: To strengthen keyboarding skills 5'

1 Use your to show possession and you're when writing you are.
2 When you're through, your results will be sent to your home.
3 You're sure to win if you plan your work and work your plan.

| 1 | 2 | 3 | 4 | 5 | 6 | 7 | 8 | 9 | 10 | 11 | 12 |

65B

Language Arts

Read the rule in the box at the right.

Then key each numbered sentence, supplying semicolons where needed.

Check your work with the key in Appendix B.

Goal: To review use of the semicolon 9'

Use a semicolon to separate items in a series when there are commas within the items.

Example:

Past winners include Hall, 1978; Sandic, 1980; and Lowenstein, 1982.

1. Send copies to Roth, Dallas Solti, Toronto and Wise, Akron.
2. We ordered these: A35, 10 sets A61, 3 sets and K37, 2 sets.
3. Invite Casey, Operations Alves, Personnel and Ricks, Sales.
4. On Monday, we sold 130 on Thursday, 175 and on Friday, 220.
5. She travels to Boise, Idaho Peru, Indiana and Dallas, Texas.
6. Trophy winners were Dick, 1984 Jeanne, 1983 and Tommy, 1982.

65C

Keyboard Composition

Default or DS

Key as much as you can in 8 minutes.

Do not correct errors.

Goal: To compose at the keyboard 10'

Choose two of these questions to answer. Answer each question in one or two paragraphs.

1. What are some of the things you like about yourself?
2. Why is it a good idea to learn how to keyboard?
3. What would you do if you lost your wallet?

Technique Timing

Take two 2-minute timings on each pair of lines. Work on improving the technique shown.

Key each line once. If you finish before time is called, start again.

DS after each timing.

Goal: To improve keyboarding techniques   10′

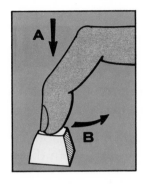

Strike each key with a quick, sharp stroke. Snap the finger toward the palm after each stroke as shown in the illustration.

1 he thinks that; she feels the; list that
2 kindle; assign; knitting; knight; kitten

Tap the space bar using a quick, down-and-in motion. Do not space at the end of a line.

3 sing king ding fling sling single jingle
4 at the jail; see a light; fish all night

5C

Keyboard Practice

Key each line twice.

DS after each pair of lines.

Goal: To practice proper keystroking techniques   14′

Cue: Keep your eyes on the textbook copy.

1 the light; the jail; the fish; the shine
2 has a fine kite; sing a little; the sign
3 a tall tale; a keen knight; a fine sight
4 she thinks that she has signed the lists
5 he felt he needed the things at the sale
6 he thinks the kindness is a keen delight

Cue: Keep your wrists and hands almost motionless as you strike each key.

7 he gnashed his teeth at the killing gale
8 the lads asked the king at the east gate
9 the sale at the kingfish is in his hands
10 he sang in jest at the sight in the jail
11 she asks in jest; she needs his kindness
12 he is a fine dad; she said he had a kite

Application: **Goal: To key an unbound report**   22′
Report

File name: L64E   Key page 1 of the report. Do not key the author's name on page 1. You will prepare a title page in Lesson 69.

PREPARING A RESEARCH PAPER

Term papers or other formal reports should be keyed in an accepted report format. A variety of style manuals for keying reports can be found in libraries and book stores all across the country. Even though these reference manuals may differ slightly in format specifications, the most widely used reference manuals do apply some common rules. This paper will outline the basic guidelines to follow when keying reports.

If the report has a title page, it should include at least the report title, the author's name, and the date. Other items of information on the title page are optional. The report title is centered horizontally in all capital letters. All other information related to the title (a subtitle, author's name, or date) is keyed in initial capital letters. The title of the report also appears on the first page of the body of the report. Here, too, it is centered in all capital letters. The title is followed directly by a triple space to the body of the report.

Because most reports involve research, some factual or quoted material is usually included. "The conventions of documentation are a means to an end: to lend authority and credibility to your work and to enable the reader to locate sources with ease."[1] Any factual information that is not commonly known or any direct or indirect quotation of words from a particular source must be specially identified. A direct quotation may be handled in one of two ways. Quotations of three or fewer typewritten lines are double spaced and enclosed in quotation marks. Quotations of four or more lines, however, are single spaced and do not have quotation marks at the beginning or at the end of the quotation.[2] These longer direct quotations are separated from the rest of the report copy by a double space and are keyed with adjusted margins.

If quotations of four or more typed lines appear, single space them and indent five spaces from both the left and the right margins. Quotations of less than four typed lines may be double spaced and run into the text.[3]

Information about the source of the fact or quotation used in the report is included in footnotes or endnotes. Footnotes present this information at the bottom, or "foot," of the page on which the fact or quotation appears. Endnotes present the same information, but they appear at the end of the report, on a separate page.

Footnotes may also be keyed together in a list on a separate page at the end of the report. If this practice is followed, center the word "notes," typed in all capital letters, 2 inches from the top of the page. Then triple space and type the notes in numerical order, single spaced, with a double space between notes.[4]

Information in footnotes and endnotes is keyed in a standard format. A book reference, for example, includes the author's name (in normal order), the title of the book (underlined), publication information, and page references.[5] A single "p." is used if only one page is cited in one note, whereas "pp." is used if two or more pages are cited. Frequently one source will be cited in several notes. The first time the reference is used, the complete information listed above is given. The second and later references to that same source appear in shortened form. A shortened note for a book usually includes the author's name, a comma, and relevant page numbers (with a p. or pp.).[6] Reference manuals provide rules for documenting many kinds of sources, not only for notes, but for bibliographies as well.

In footnotes, endnotes, or bibliography listings, remember to "underline the titles of whole published works and to put the titles of parts of these works in quotation marks."[7] For example,

Technique Timing

Take two 2-minute timings.

Return when you see E/R, not at the end of a line.

If you finish before time is called, start again.

DS after each timing.

Goal: To improve keyboarding techniques 5'

Do not look up as you enter/return. Begin keying the next line without pausing.

dish fishing telling E/R delight assign shine E/R kiss
jangle knitting E/R killing shilling jig E/R fail flesh
tennis it E/R think link sink kink E/R thing sing king
sign E/R height kitten needle

> **Checkpoint:** How often did you look at your hands when you entered/returned? *Not at all; Once or twice; Several times; Usually.*

Keyboard Practice

Key each line twice.

DS after each pair of lines.

Goal: To practice proper keystroking techniques 10'

1 fail said jail laid hail tail nail aided
2 sealing dealing keeling kneeling healing
3 nil neat night nines needle nigh needing
4 get gain gale gill gift glen geese glean
5 if it is in idle its ideal ignite island
6 lead the list; tells a tale; hit the net
7 lends a dish; lift the lid; take a taste
8 set these dates; get in line; take sides
9 get the geese as a gift; glean that glen
10 nine neat needles night needing nil nets

Self-Check

Read each statement to the right and decide whether it is true or false.

On a sheet of paper, handwrite the statement number and your answer: True or False.

Check your answers in Appendix C.

Goal: To review good keyboarding techniques 6'

1. You should look at your fingers, not at your textbook, when working at the keyboard.
2. When sitting at the keyboard, sit up straight with your back touching the chair.
3. You should not space before entering/returning at the end of a line.
4. For best results, press the space bar firmly and release it slowly.
5. Both feet should be placed flat on the floor, one slightly ahead of the other.
6. Rest the palms of your hands on the keyboard when you key.
7. You should always look up when you operate the enter/return to be sure you are at the beginning of a new line.
8. By operating the enter/return two times, you leave one blank line between keyed lines.

Goal Writing

Goal: To measure timed-writing progress 10'

	1'	3'

Default or DS

Take two 3-minute goal writings.

If you finish before time is called, start again.

Record your speed and accuracy.

Employee benefits, also called fringe benefits, are an | 11 | 4
important part of your job. Just as salaries may vary from | 23 | 8
company to company, so too do benefits. The most common | 35 | 12
benefit is vacation time. Many companies offer two weeks | 46 | 15
of vacation after one year, three weeks after five years, | 58 | 19
and four weeks after ten years. Group medical and dental | 69 | 23
insurance may be offered at a reduced rate. The company may | 82 | 27
also pay a certain part of the insurance. To encourage you | 94 | 31
to continue your education, the company may pay part or all | 106 | 35
of your tuition for an evening course you may take to im— | 117 | 39
prove your skills. | 121 | 40

1' | 1 | 2 | 3 | 4 | 5 | 6 | 7 | 8 | 9 | 10 | 11 | 12 | AWL
3' | | 1 | | 2 | | 3 | | 4 | | 5.7

64C

Language Arts

Goal: To review the use of quotation marks 8'

Read the rule in the box at the right.

Then key each numbered sentence, supplying quotation marks where needed.

Check your work with the key in Appendix B.

> Use quotation marks to set off a direct quotation (a person's exact words).
>
> **Examples:**
>
> Maria said, "You must handle the diskette carefully to avoid damage."
> "Do you suppose," Mr. Wilkinson asked, "that you can finish today?"

1. Ms. Donner said, Be very judicious in the use of the copier.
2. Jenny asked, How many copies of the report will you require?
3. Do you suppose, Mr. Canady asked, that you could help him?
4. Ms. Leu told Timothy that he would have to reprint the letter.
5. Incidentally, Janet said, the copier needs to be repaired.
6. The order from Boston must be processed today, said Mr. Lee.

64D

Need to Know

Goal: To learn how to key quotations 5'

64-1

A quotation of three or fewer lines is keyed within the normal paragraph copy and is enclosed in quotation marks. A quotation of four or more lines is keyed following these instructions:

1. Indent the left and right margins five spaces.
2. SS the quotation.
3. Key a superior figure at the end of the quotation.
4. Do not enclose the quotation in quotation marks.
5. Leave a DS before and after the long quotation.

6A

Warmup

Key each line twice.

DS after each pair of lines.

Goal: To strengthen keyboarding skills 5′

1 fin din sin gin kin sit lit kit hit fit;

2 jell jets jade jest jilt hand half halt;

3 skiff slash slate sleek slide sneak snag

4 slight height flight delighted sightless

6B

Technique Timing

Take two 2-minute timings.

If you finish before time is called, start again.

DS after each timing.

Goal: To improve keyboarding techniques 5′

Sit in correct position: back against the chair and feet flat on the floor, one slightly in front of the other.

1 find kind nine line fine tine fins tins;

2 is the; in the; if the; let the; see the

3 the thing is; find a site; take a flight

4 the night; a sight; the light; the fight

6C

New-Key Orientation

1. Locate the new key on the keyboard chart.
2. Next, locate the key on your keyboard.
3. Before keying the practice lines, read the instructions for each new key.
4. Practice the first line, returning to home-key position after making the reach to the new key.
5. Practice the second line for 2 minutes or until you can key it without looking at your hands.

Goal: To learn the location of O R and left SHIFT 12′

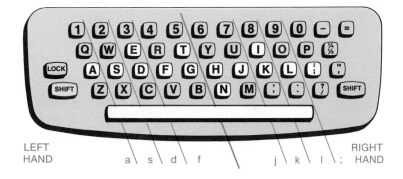

LEFT HAND   a s d f   j k l ;   RIGHT HAND

 Practice the reach to O with the l finger. The k finger may lift slightly, but keep your other fingers in home-key position.

1 lo lo lo lo lo lo lo lo lo lo lo lo lo

2 lot log old hole gone done tooth jolts

(Continued next page)

Self-Check

Choose the word or number that answers each question. Key the number and your answer in complete sentences.

Check your answers in Appendix C.

Goal: To review the format for continuing pages 8′

Answers:	double	single	4	7
	triple	13	2	6

1. On what line is the page number placed on continuing pages of a report?
2. On what line of page 2 does the body of the report begin?
3. The page number is keyed how many spaces before the right margin?
4. Is single or double spacing used for the body of the continuing pages?
5. The bottom margin on a continuing page has how many blank lines?

63F

Application: Superscripts

Goal: To key copy containing superior figures 5′

Default or DS / Key the exercises that follow. Use correct spacing after the superior figures.

Exercise 1: Space once after a superior figure that follows a comma or a semicolon. Ignore quotation marks when determining spacing.

1 jets,^{1} for this 3 jets;^{1} for this
2 jets,"^{1} for this 4 jets;"^{1} for this

Exercise 2: Space twice after a superior figure that follows a period or a colon. Ignore quotation marks when determining spacing.

1 jets.^{1} For this 3 jets:^{1} for this
2 jets."^{1} For this 4 jets:"^{1} for this

63G

Application: Reports

DS

Goal: To key page 2 of an unbound report 15′

Retrieve L62G or insert your paper in the typewriter. Then continue the report in 62G.

Lesson **64**

M Default Settings

T SS   SM 1½″ (12); 1″ (10)   Tab ¶

64A

Warmup

Goal: To strengthen keyboarding skills 5′

Key each line twice. DS after each pair of lines.

Speed | 1 The club shares the dish with its neighbor most of the time.
Accuracy | 2 We wanted to welcome a few new workers at Western Warehouse.
Number/Symbol | 3 Two changes (2109 N. 1450 E. and 1129 W. 650 N.) were noted.
Data Entry | 4 410 PRINT "ANTICIPATED ADDED AREA IS";3.14159*R*R;" SQ. FT."

| 1 | 2 | 3 | 4 | 5 | 6 | 7 | 8 | 9 | 10 | 11 | 12 |

Follow steps 1–5 on page 19 to learn the reaches to the new keys.

 Practice the reach to Ⓡ with the **f** finger. Keep your other fingers in home-key position.

3 fr fr fr fr fr fr fr fr fr fr fr fr fr

4 fir far tar jars dart dirt first third

Use a one-two count to operate the left shift key. **One**—depress the left shift key with the **a** finger. **Two**—strike the desired key with the correct finger of the right hand. Quickly release the shift key and return the **a** finger to its home-key position.

 Practice the reach to the left shift key with the **a** finger. Keep your other fingers in home-key position.

5 La La La La La La La La La La La La La

6 He His Ned Nan Jan Nate Jake Jets Kate

6D

Technique Timing

Take a 1-minute timing on each line. Work on improving the technique shown.

DS after each timing.

Goal: To improve keyboarding techniques 11′

Return to home-key position after making reaches to the new keys.

1 fool fold told sold song thong good hood

2 red rag ran far free rail hard lark rake

3 He is; Hal sat; Nan gets; Is it; Jake is

Keep your eyes on the textbook copy.

Repeat lines 1–3.

Quickly release the shift key and return the **a** finger to home-key position.

4 Join this one; Hank is the one; Here are

5 Let her tell those stories to Janet soon

6 His Her Lee Ida Karl Jake John Ned Lorna

6E

Keyboard Practice

Key each line twice.

DS after each pair of lines.

Goal: To practice proper keyboarding techniques 8′

Cue: Avoid pauses when using the left shift key.

1 Jo said Jan has seen the old red rooster

2 Ora had a great session on the third hit

3 He had Lee and Karl and Jake for his jet

4 Ida rode a Jetstar for the entire season

5 I said that Joanna and Neal are the ones

(Continued next page)

Lesson 6

63B

Speed Practice

Take a 12- or 10-second timing on each line. If you complete a line in the time allowed, go on to the next one.

Goal: To build keyboarding speed 5′

		GWAM 12″	10″
1	I streamlined my working procedure.	35	42
2	I've been pacing myself to avoid stress.	40	48
3	I'll try to be flexible with daily schedules.	45	54
4	If we realize our limits, we can plan around them.	50	60
5	Try to see all of life's situations in positive lights.	55	66

| 1 | 2 | 3 | 4 | 5 | 6 | 7 | 8 | 9 | 10 | 11 |

63C

Keyboard Composition

Default or DS

Key as much as you can in 5 minutes.

Do not correct errors.

Goal: To compose at the keyboard 7′

Choose one sentence to complete, and use it as the beginning of a short paragraph.

1 If I could play any musical instrument, it would be . . .

2 My earliest memory of school is . . .

3 My favorite book is . . .

Checkpoint: Did you keep the cursor/carrier moving as you composed your paragraph?

> 63D

Need to Know

Goal: To learn to key superscripts 5′

Superscripts are numbers, letters, or symbols that print one-half line above the text line. Superscripts are used in mathematical equations. One form of superscript is the **superior figure** that is used by authors to identify sources of factual information.

Automatic Superscripts

To use superscripts on a microcomputer, you must have software and a printer with this capability. Some electronic typewriters also are equipped with automatic superscripts or half-line up options. Determine the command or the keys to use for superscripts on your equipment. Superscripts are usually preceded and followed by a series of keyed commands or by depressing a special function key. For example, one program uses CODE + 1/2 ↑ before and CODE + 1/2 ↓ after the superscript number.

The procedure for keying superscripts usually includes the following steps:

1. Give the command or press the special function key to begin the function.
2. Key the superscript.
3. Give the command or press the special function key to end the function.

Superscripts may not appear one-half line up on your microcomputer screen. However, superscripts will print in the raised position.

Manual Superscripts

1. Locate the line finder. Pull the lever forward.
2. Manually turn the platen knob toward you a half-line space.
3. Key the superscript.
4. Push the line finder back to its original position.
5. Return the platen to its original line space.

Key each line twice.

6 Learn the right things and get the sales

7 Jail is the right thing for John and Lee

6F

Technique Timing

Take two 2-minute timings on each group of lines. Work on improving the technique shown.

Key each line once. If you finish before time is called, start again.

DS after each timing.

Goal: To improve keyboarding techniques 9'

Do not pause between words. Try to keep the cursor/carrier moving.

1 note nose none done lone tone gone groan

2 tore sore fore soar dare road roan thorn

3 fright freight grief relate render grate

Keep the wrists low, but not resting on the keyboard.

4 the ladies; the girls; this is; there is

5 their goods; their food; their one thing

6 Here are the letters; I sold those goods

Lesson 7

M Default Settings

T SS SM 2" (12-pitch), 24–78; 1½" (10-pitch), 15–70

7A

Warmup

Key each line twice.

DS after each pair of lines.

Goal: To strengthen keyboarding skills 5'

1 night tight light fight sight right then

2 tone gone none lone done this that north

3 for her; for those; for this; for their;

4 that is not; there is not; there are no;

7B

Technique Timing

Take a 1-minute timing on each line.

DS after each timing.

Goal: To improve keyboarding techniques 5'

Keep your **s**, **d**, and **f** fingers in home-key position as you hold, then quickly release, the shift key.

1 He is here; I need that one; Lee has it;

2 I think I need an O; an H; an L; and a K

3 He asked Jane to send the letter to Karl

4 Here are the things that she sent to Jed

> **Checkpoint:** Did you remember to use the **a** finger on the shift key?

Application: Reports

Goal: To key page 1 of a two-page report 17′

File name: L62G   Full sheet   DS

Key page 1 of the two-page report. Use your name as the author.

> **Cue:** Key two hyphens to make a dash. Do not space before or after the dash.

Three Ages to Now

Although recorded history goes back thousands of years, the history of man can be divided into three different ages. The first age lasted the longest, spanning thousands of years. The second age began less than two centuries ago, and the third age is just beginning. These ages—the Age of Tools, the Age of Power, and the Age of Computers—are quite different.

The Age of Tools began when the first human picked up a rock, a shell, or a stick of wood and used it as a tool or weapon. During the Age of Tools, the tools changed in material, from stone to bronze to iron. However, the tools had a common bond: all were powered by human or animal energy.

The Industrial Revolution was a revolution in the type of power used to run machinery. Coal, steam, and oil replaced animal energy. Productivity increased at a rapid rate. A single pound of coal now produced more energy than a full eight hours of human energy. Prior to 1750, about 90 percent of the population worked as farmers. Today in America, although less than 5 percent of the population farms, America exports food to the rest of the world!

In 1947, a major step was taken that ushered in the Age of the Computer. A 30-ton digital computer (ENIAC) was constructed. By the 1960s, the computer age had arrived, with computers costing millions of dollars being used by business and government. In 1971, Intel Corporation invented the silicon chip. A wafer-thin piece of silicon, the integrated circuit chip replaced thousands of transistors to provide a portable and inexpensive computer. In fact, a single silicon chip stored up to ten times as much information at 1/30,000 the cost as the first ENIAC computer.

Today the computer is changing our lives. There are silicon chips that can be implanted in the scalp to restore some sight to certain blind people. Other chips allow robots in factories to perform many tasks that people once performed. With the help of computers, astronauts can travel beyond this planet to other parts of the universe. As improvements are made in computer technology in the future, our lives will continue to change. In a few years, perhaps computers will make it possible for all of us to fly to the moon!

> **Checkpoint:** Did you proofread and correct all errors?

Lesson 63

M Default Settings
T SS   SM 1½″ (12); 1″ (10)   Tab ¶

Warmup

Goal: To strengthen keyboarding skills 5′

Key each line twice.
DS after each pair.

"tw" combinations

```
1 twin twine tweed tweezers tweet twelve twice twilight twitch
2 Twyla untwisted the heavy twine until she had twenty pieces.
3 The twin birds tweeted twelve times every night at twilight.
```

| 1 | 2 | 3 | 4 | 5 | 6 | 7 | 8 | 9 | 10 | 11 | 12 |

New-Key Orientation

1. Locate the new key on the keyboard chart.
2. Next, locate the key on your key-board.
3. Before keying the practice lines, read the instructions for each new key.
4. Practice the first line, returning to home-key position after making the reach to the new key.
5. Practice the second line for 2 minutes or until you can key it without looking at your hands.

Goal: To learn the location of Ⓤ Ⓦ and ⊙ 12′

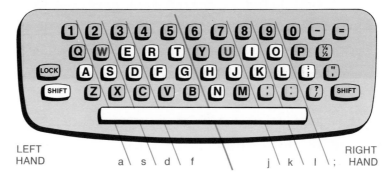

LEFT
HAND   a s d f   j k l ;   RIGHT
                                                                 HAND

Ⓤ Practice the reach to Ⓤ with the **j** finger. Keep your other fingers in home-key position. Do not lift your wrist as you strike Ⓤ.

1 ju ju ju ju ju ju ju ju ju ju ju ju ju

2 jut jug gun run dug hug rugs just ruin

Ⓦ Practice the reach to Ⓦ with the **s** finger. The **d** finger might lift slightly, but keep your other fingers in home-key position.

3 sw sw sw sw sw sw sw sw sw sw sw sw sw sw

4 sow saw sew wit wig win was with shown

Practice the reach to ⊙ with the **l** finger. The **sem** finger might lift slightly, but keep your other fingers in home-key position.

⊙ 5 l. l. l. l. l. l. l. l. l. l. l. l.

6 L. ft. in. Ill. Ind. Oreg. La. No. Jr.

Technique Timing

Take a 1-minute timing on each line. Work on improving the technique shown.

DS after each timing.

Goal: To improve keyboarding techniques 11′

Return to home-key position after making the reach to the new keys.

1 unfit usual until unit under unjust dust

2 who whose what where when how while will

3 L. J. is a ft. taller than Jr. and Nana.

Keep your eyes on the textbook copy.

Repeat lines 1–3.

(Continued next page)

62D

Rough Draft

Goal: To key rough-draft copy 5′

Default or DS

Read the copy before you begin keying. Then key the paragraph making the changes indicated.

Correct errors.

What ~~kinds of~~ skills will |have / you| by the time you
graduate from ~~H~~igh ~~S~~chool? Does a demand exist for people
with your skills? What kind of ~~a wage~~ *income* can you ex~~ec~~pt to
earn with yo~~ur~~ skills? ¶All too often, students in high
school ~~have~~ *do* not given *lc* Enough thought to the futre even
though it is probably *one of* the most important ~~things~~ *considerations* they will
need to think about *in* their li~~n~~es. Have you taken advantage
of *the* courses that are offered at your school that will give
you a skil *l* that ~~an~~ earn you an income?

62E

Need to Know

Goal: To learn to key subscripts 5′

Subscripts are characters that appear one-half line below the text line. Subscripts are used in chemical notations, such as H_2O, and in certain mathematical applications.

Automatic Subscripts

To use subscripts on a microcomputer, you must have software and a printer with this capability. Some electronic typewriters also are equipped with automatic subscripts or half-line down options. Determine the command or the keys to use for subscripts on your equipment. They are usually preceded and followed by a series of keyed commands or by depressing special function keys. For example, one program uses the CODE + 1/2 ↓ keys before and CODE + 1/2 ↑ after the subscript.

The procedure for keying subscripts usually includes the following steps:

1. Give the command or press the special function keys to begin the function.
2. Key the subscript.
3. Give the command or press the special function keys to end the function.

The subscripts may not appear one-half line down on your microcomputer screen. However, subscripts will print in the lowered position.

Manual Subscripts

1. Locate the line finder. Pull the lever forward.
2. Manually turn the platen knob away from you a half-line space.
3. Key the subscript.
4. Push the line finder back to its original position.
5. Return the platen to its original line space.

62F

Application: Subscripts

Goal: To key copy containing subscripts 5′

Default or DS

Key each of the sentences. Key subscripts where indicated.

1. I thought everyone knew that H_2O stands for water.
2. Did you know the formula for carbon dioxide: CO_2?
3. The doctor prescribed higher doses of vitamin B_{12}.
4. Figure 1.3 shows the greater monetary value at X_4.
5. The molecular formula was determined to be $C_4H_8O_2$.

Keep the wrist from turning outward as you strike ⊙ with the I finger.

4 K. U. Hunt was our unusual Latin Leader.

5 K. U. K. Kar Kare will let J. L. use it.

6 N. U. Hill and H. U. Heath were willing.

7E

Apply the Rule

Read the rule and the examples.

Then key the sen-tences in the *Application* section. As you key them, use the correct spacing after the periods.

Goal: To learn the spacing after the period 6′

Rule

1. Space once after a period used with an initial or an abbreviation.
2. Space twice after a period used at the end of a sentence.

Examples

Kathie left at noon. K. L. left at one.

Ned went to Ohio U. J. L. was at O. S. U.

Application

1 Let us work with N. H. Oaks at the sale.

2 I was with Kate. Nan wants H. J. to go.

3 I sang. Jorge jogged. Helena did also.

4 J. U. Last is here. Let Lorrie see her.

7F

Keyboard Practice

Key each line three times.

DS after each group of lines.

Goal: To practice proper keystroking techniques 5′

> **Cue:** When shifting for capitals, use a one-two count.

1 Let her go. I will. Ned Jones will go.

2 I had a ft. of wire and an in. of twine.

3 Lou is here now. Jed will see her soon.

4 O. J. wrote Jo often when she was there.

7G

Technique Timing

Take two 2-minute timings.

Key each line once. If time allows, start again.

DS after each timing.

Goal: To improve keyboarding techniques 6′

Quickly return to home-key position after striking enter/return and begin keying without pausing.

1 H; How; J; Jet; K; Keg; L; Let; I; India

2 Ned Harris left. Ora Howe will go soon.

3 Oregon Iowa Utah Kansas Illinois Indiana

4 Linda K. Hanson will go to Utah in June.

T *Typewriters*

Insert your paper in the typewriter. If you are completing page 1, align the paper to begin on the next line. If you are starting page 2, space down to number the page. Then continue the report in 60H.

Cue: Use the format for an unbound report.

Lesson **62**

M Default Settings
T SS   SM 1½" (12); 1" (10)   Tab ¶

62A

Warmup

Key each line twice.
DS after each pair.

Confusing words:
loose and lose

Goal: To strengthen keyboarding skills 5'

1 Whenever an item is loose, it's free, unfastened, or untied.
2 When your team gets defeated, you lose--not loose--the game.
3 Tie down every one of the loose ends in case you lose today.

| 1 | 2 | 3 | 4 | 5 | 6 | 7 | 8 | 9 | 10 | 11 | 12 |

62B

Accuracy Practice

DS after each group of lines.

Goal: To build keyboarding accuracy 5'

Take a 3-minute accuracy timing on the lines in 62A. If you make an error, start again. Stay on a line until you have keyed it without error.

Checkpoint: How many error-free lines did you key?

62C

Language Arts

Read the rule in the box at the right.

Then key each numbered sentence, supplying quotation marks and underscores where needed.

Check your work with the key in Appendix B.

Goal: To review use of quotation marks 8'

Use quotation marks to set off definitions from the word or words being defined.

Examples:

The verb <u>affect</u> means "to have an influence on."
The term <u>foregone conclusion</u> is defined as "an end regarded as inevitable."

1. The suffix osis also means a diseased or abnormal condition.
2. In phonetics, the phrase glottal stop refers to speech sounds.
3. The phrase touch and go means a precarious state of affairs.
4. The word justify means make all lines end at the same point.
5. The term buffer refers to a temporary storage area for data.
6. The word scroll refers to moving text displayed on a monitor.

Lesson 8

8A

Warmup

Key each line twice.

DS after each pair of lines.

Goal: To strengthen keyboarding skills 5'

1 all an are at do for has he his if in it
2 we should; we would; we think; we shall;
3 new no not of one our should than the is
4 Jane John Jennifer June Jewell Jill Jake

| 1 | 2 | 3 | 4 | 5 | 6 | 7 | 8 |

8B

Need to Know

Goal: To learn about word scales 3'

In keyboarding, every five strokes—including spaces—count as a "word." The drill lines in these lessons are 40 strokes long. That is, they contain a total of 40 letters, spaces, and punctuation marks. To figure the number of "words" in a line, divide the number of strokes in the line (40) by the number of strokes in a word (5). In this case, the result is 8 words (40 ÷ 5 = 8). So each 40-stroke line in these lessons equals 8 words.

The word scales below the Warmup drill lines divide the lines into 5-stroke (1-word) groups. By using these word scales, you can quickly see how many words you have keyed in a line.

8C

Technique Timing

Take a 1-minute timing on each line. Work on improving the technique shown.

DS after each timing.

Goal: To improve keyboarding techniques 12'

Do not pause between letters or words; keep the cursor/carrier moving.

1 few get need later least head note offer
2 seen shall she sheet soon sure used wish
3 jest dealer feel file free here high and

Tap the space bar with a down-and-in motion of the right thumb.

4 an at do if in is it no of to we go his;
5 all are has his new not one our the two;
6 than that were will with good note seen;

Keep your wrists low and almost motionless.

7 arrange asked finest needed offer during
8 friend furnish indeed reading sound than
9 through ordered later annual around does

| 1 | 2 | 3 | 4 | 5 | 6 | 7 | 8 |

Take two 2-minute timings on the paragraph.

¶ A ~~3rd~~ *third* choice is bond (a)(p)per, often sold in a quality   11 | 6

known as ~~twenty~~ *20* pound we(i)ght. Two thousand sheets of this   22 | 11

paper weigh(s) 20 ~~lbs~~ *pounds*. you can buy this high-quality ~~paper(s)~~   33 | 17

paper in *most* office supply stores(,) ~~I~~n 100-sheet quantities.   45 | 23

It is the kind of paper most comp(n)(a)ies ~~will find~~ use(ful).   55 | 27

61D

Keyboard Composition

Default or DS

Key as much as you can in 5 minutes.

Do not correct errors.

Goal: To compose at the keyboard   7′

Choose one sentence to complete, and use it as the beginning of a short paragraph.

1 One place I would like to visit is ____ because . . .

2 One thing I look for in a friend is ____ because . . .

3 One of my favorite hobbies is ____ because . . .

4 The book I like best is ____ because . . . .

5 As a future career, ____ sounds interesting because . . .

61E

Need to Know

Refer to the illustration at the right as you read about the format to use for continuing pages of unbound reports.

Goal: To learn the format for continuing pages   5′   *61-1*

The second and all remaining pages of the report body, called *continuing pages,* are keyed in the same format.

1. Side margins: 1 inch.
2. Top margins: 1 inch.
3. Page number: Placed on line 4, 2 columns/spaces before the right margin. The 2 spaces are needed on typewriters to keep the margin from locking. Set a tab so that the numbers on all pages of your report will be aligned.
4. Body of the report: Begins on line 7 and is double spaced.
5. Bottom margin: 1 inch.

61F

Application: Reports

Full sheet
DS

Goal: To key page 2 of an unbound report   15′

M *Microcomputers*

Retrieve L60H. Use the appropriate command to express move the cursor to the last line of keyed text. Then continue the report in 60H.

(Continued next page)

Technique Timing

Review proper arm position.

Then take two 2-minute timings.

Key each line once. If you finish before time is called, start again.

DS after each timing.

Goal: To improve keyboarding techniques 12'

For proper arm position, let your hands hang loosely at your sides. This is the distance you should keep your elbows from your body as you key.

Now, bend your arms at the elbows without changing the position of your upper arms. If you can't place your fingers comfortably in home-key position, move your chair forward or backward.

1 John wants work at two in the afternoon.
2 I do not go along with the higher rents.
3 Joe thought the letter was sent in June.
4 Let the student find the food she needs.
5 Logan is the town doing the water tests.

Checkpoint: Are your elbows and arms in the position illustrated?

Review the correct technique for operating the enter/return key.

Reach the **sem** finger to the enter/return key, keeping your **j, k,** and **l** fingers in home-key position. Tap the enter/return key lightly and release it quickly.

Take two 2-minute timings.

Enter/return when you see E/R. If time allows, start again.

DS after each timing.

Quickly return to home-key position after striking enter/return.

List all the orders. E/R He left three deals. E/R John leads in sales. E/R Here is the new one. E/R Let her send a note. E/R I went to the store. E/R John sent her a note.

Checkpoint: Did you release the enter/return key quickly?

M **Default Settings**
T SS   SM 1½" (12); 1" (10)   Tab ¶

61A

Warmup

Key each line twice.
DS after each pair.

"ite" combinations

Goal: To strengthen keyboarding skills 5'

1 finite kite bite site mite white item infinite dynamite item
2 Fly the white kite at a site away from the dynamited fields.
3 This item has an infinite value in eliminating the termites.

| 1 | 2 | 3 | 4 | 5 | 6 | 7 | 8 | 9 | 10 | 11 | 12 |

61B

Speed Practice

Take a 12- or 10-second timing on each line. If you complete a line in the time allowed, go on to the next one.

Goal: To build keyboarding speed 5'

GWAM

	12"	10"
1 Does your music reflect your moods?	35	42
2 Do you listen to songs that have a beat?	40	48
3 Do you listen to the words or just hum along?	45	54
4 Does the music keep you company when you're alone?	50	60
5 Does the music you choose change any when you're tense?	55	66

| 1 | 2 | 3 | 4 | 5 | 6 | 7 | 8 | 9 | 10 | 11 |

61C

Comparison Copy

Default or DS

Take two 2-minute timings on each paragraph.

Try to increase your speed on the second timing.

Try to keep your speed on the handwritten and rough-draft copy as high as your straight-copy speed.

Goal: To build keyboarding speed on a variety of copy 13'

	1'	2'
Are you aware of the various qualities of paper that	11	5
you can buy? One kind is an inexpensive, thin paper that	22	11
offers quantity at a low price. However, even careful	33	17
corrections are visible on this paper. It is suitable for	45	23
drill and rough—draft copy, but not for reports.	55	27

1' | 1 | 2 | 3 | 4 | 5 | 6 | 7 | 8 | 9 | 10 | 11 | 12 |
2' | 1 | 2 | 3 | 4 | 5 | 6 |

	1'	2'
A second choice is erasable bond paper. It is expen-	11	6
sive, but it is popular with students. It makes correcting	23	12
errors quick and easy since ink is not absorbed into the	34	17
paper. One major problem with its use, however, is that the	47	23
ink is easily smeared and smudged.	53	27

(Continued next page)

Language Arts

Read the rule in the box at the right.

Then key each numbered sentence, supplying capitalization where needed.

Check your work with the key in Appendix B.

Goal: To review capitalization rules 8′

> Capitalize the first word of a complete sentence.
>
> **Examples:**
>
> Tell them to begin work soon. Tell them also to see me.
> We want to do the job right. You want the same, I'm sure.
> Liz returned today. She will be a positive influence.

1 let Ned sign the letter. he will do it.
2 Katie will do it faster than Ned or Ken.
3 just write Helen; he will write her too.
4 it takes too long. use a different one.
5 look in here first. look there in June.
6 now I write songs. let Jewell sing one.

8F

Keyboard Practice

Key each line 3 times.

DS after each group of lines.

Goal: To practice proper keystroking techniques 10′

1 few sat was wag were fate drag wade dare
2 kin oil ink nil look join junk link hook
3 heir also worn usual jangle island shelf
4 fee fund her how join late loss lot rent
5 we are; we will; we want; we think that;
6 write a letter; let us take; here is the
7 Ken and Jana do take their dog downtown.

Lesson 9

M	**Default Settings**
T	SS SM 2″ (12-pitch), 24–78; 1½″ (10-pitch), 15–70

9A

Warmup

Key each line twice.

DS after each pair of lines.

Goal: To strengthen keyboarding skills 5′

1 the of to and in for we that is this our
2 of the; in the; to the; for the; on the;
3 it is; with the; of our; and the; it is;
4 I want to. He is here. Just tell Jude.

| 1 | 2 | 3 | 4 | 5 | 6 | 7 | 8 |

Need to Know   Goal: To learn top margin settings for continuing pages   2'

Most software programs require all pages of a document to be printed by the same format commands. For example, when you set a top margin of 12 lines, all pages of the document must use that same top margin. All pages of a report, however, do not have a 2-inch top margin. The text begins on line 7 on the second and continuing pages of a report.

An easy way to allow for different top margins is to use the default top margin. Then enter/return the number of times necessary to leave the appropriate top margin for that page.

60H

Application: Reports   Goal: To key page 1 of a two-page report   12'   *60-1*

File name: L60H   DS   SM: 1 inch

Key page 1 of this two-page report. Use the unbound report format.

Cue: Center and key the title on line 13.

Where Are The Jobs?

(Your Name)

When people think of computer jobs, they usually think first of programmers. However, that is only one of many jobs that are available in the computer field. Have you ever heard of jobs such as systems analyst, data entry operator, computer operator, or tape librarian. What do people in these jobs do? What are the job qualifications?

Let's look at the familiar job of computer programmer. At the beginning of the 1980's, more than 225,000 people were employed as programmers, and that number continues to increase rapidly. Large companies usually have several levels of programmers: trainee, junior, senior, and lead programmers. Most of these jobs require a college education and/or specialized training in data processing or computer science. Programmers must enjoy working with details; they must be persistent as they work to "debug" a system. They must be patient and be able to communicate effectively.

Systems analysts must have a college degree in computer science. Their primary job is to get quality performance from the computer at the lowest cost. Systems analysts are more involved with planning for the total business than with day-to-day computer operations. Since they work with all levels of employees, they also must have the ability to communicate effectively.

Another interesting job is that of data entry. There are three primary kinds of data entry jobs. Data entry operators enter data from source documents at various locations throughout the company. Keypunch operators enter data on punched cards while the on-line terminal operators enter data directly into the computer. All of these jobs require rapid and accurate keyboarding skills.

Another job group involves those persons who actually operate the computer. The computer operator uses the video display terminal (VDT). The peripheral equipment operator runs the input/output devices. Often, computer operators work with programmers and analysts to improve throughput—the amount of work the computer does. Computer operators must have high school diplomas and specialized training.

Tape librarians function much the same as a traditional librarian. They catalogue, file, and maintain all magnetic media, such as tapes and disks. They label all media and check it in and out of a central location. Tape librarians must be well organized and must enjoy working with details.

Technique Timing

Take a 2-minute timing on each group of lines. Work on improving the technique shown.

Key each line once. If you finish before time is called, start again.

DS after each timing.

Goal: To improve keyboarding techniques 5′

Key easy letter combinations more rapidly. Slow down to key difficult letter combinations.

1 like had his work use two than who their

2 when take new do should other there send

3 due line then wish those sure here shall

4 In this; I want; In our; I would; Is it;

Keep your arms in correct position: elbows slightly forward of your body and arms close to but not touching your body.

5 into would further where note list until

6 sent own high life total first shall few

7 last within week offer while long thinks

8 One of; Is the; I will; It was; It will;

New-Key Orientation

1. Locate the new key on the keyboard chart.
2. Next, locate the key on your keyboard.
3. Before keying the practice lines, read the instructions for each new key.
4. Practice the first line, returning to home-key position after making the reach to the new key.
5. Practice the second line for 2 minutes or until you can key it without looking at your hands.

Goal: To learn the location of Ⓟ Ⓓ and right ⬛SHIFT⬛ 13′

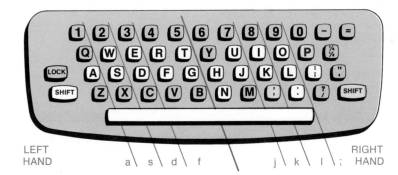

LEFT HAND   a   s   d   f   j   k   l   ;   RIGHT HAND

P Practice the reach to Ⓟ with the **sem** finger. Keep your other fingers in home-key position.

1 ;p ;p ;p ;p ;p ;p ;p ;p ;p ;p ;p ;p ;p

2 up; pat lap pal tape wipe soap; please

, Practice the reach to Ⓓ with the **k** finger. The **j** finger may lift slightly, but keep your other fingers in home-key position.

3 k, k, k, k, k, k, k, k, k, k, k, k, k,

4 kit, kid, kin, ink, rink, ring, kings,

SHIFT Practice the reach to the right shift key with the **sem** finger. Keep your other fingers in home-key position.

5 So So So So So So So So So So So So So

6 To Ron; Ed; Sal; Fred; Don; Dean; Sue;

The page layout at the right uses the default settings listed on page 151.

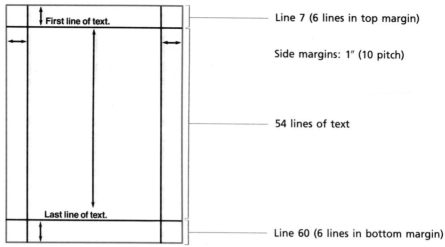

First line of text.

Line 7 (6 lines in top margin)

Side margins: 1" (10 pitch)

54 lines of text

Last line of text.

Line 60 (6 lines in bottom margin)

Page Layout

When the software's default settings are not the same as the format you want for a document, change the default settings so the document will print in the desired format.

> **60E** M

Read and Do   Goal: To give page layout commands for an unbound report 5'

Depending on your software, you may give page layout commands before or after you key the document. If your program allows you to give page layout commands before you key the document, complete the format commands listed below. Then key 60H. If your program requires you to give page layout commands when the document is ready to print, key 60H. Then complete the following format commands:

1. Determine the command to display page layout/print options on your software.
2. Key in the following settings. If these settings are default settings on your program, it is not necessary to rekey them.

a. Left margin: 10 (10 pitch); 12 (12 pitch)
b. Right margin: 75 (10 pitch); 90 (12 pitch) If your program requires line length, use 65 characters (10 pitch), 78 characters (12 pitch).
c. Top margin: 6 lines
d. Bottom margin: 6 lines
e. Page length: 54 lines
f. Line spacing: 2

Top margin, bottom margin, and page length must always total 66 lines for an 8½" × 11" page.

> **60F** M

Need to Know   Goal: To learn to determine the number of lines to fit on a page 3'

Many software programs display a status line. The status line tells you the line on which the cursor is positioned. At times, the status line is misleading—for example, when line spacing is set for DS and the program does not count the blank lines between the lines of text. If your status line ignores blank lines, use the following chart to determine the number of lines of double-spaced text that will fit on each page of a report with the margins shown.

Page 1	Continuing Pages
Top margin: 12 lines	Top margin: 6 lines
Bottom margin: 6 lines	Bottom margin: 6 lines
Actual text lines: 23	Actual text lines: 27

9D

Technique Timing

Take a 1-minute timing on each line. Work on improving the technique shown.

DS after each timing.

Goal: To improve keyboarding techniques 12′

Return to home-key position after making reaches to the new keys.

1 pet pen past pep pug proper prior praise
2 life, like, hike, sit, seek, sake, fits,
3 Find Take Dear Send All We Eat Run There

Keep your eyes on the textbook copy.

Repeat lines 1–3.

Quickly release the shift key and return the **sem** finger to home-key position.

4 Do it, Repair pens, Wipe pots, Sell soap
5 That is, Therefore, Well, Then, And thus
6 Tape this, Ask Sarah, We paid, Send help

9E

Keyboard Practice

Key each line 3 times.

DS after each group of lines.

Goal: To practice proper keystroking techniques 8′

Cue: Use the **a** finger for the left shift, the **sem** finger for the right shift.

1 Send the letter to Susan, the president.
2 Take an airplane to Dallas on the first.
3 The site of their new deal is Salt Lake.
4 Tell Paul to plan their trip to Newport.
5 Please take George, Dean, Helga, and Ed.
6 Please stop in San Jose and Los Angeles.
7 S. J. South and F. L. West are the ones.
8 Andrew worked with John throughout June.

9F

Technique Timing

Take a 2-minute timing.

Key each line once. If you finish before time is called, start again.

DS after each timing.

Goal: To improve keyboarding techniques 7′

Keep your other fingers in home-key position as you make the reaches to the shift keys.

1 F. Freddie, K. Karl, S. Sarah, A. Arthur
2 We hope to hear that Red is now at work.
3 Washington, Florida, Illinois, Tennessee

(Continued next page)

60B

Goal Writing

Default or DS

Take two 3-minute goal writings.

If you finish before time is called, start again.

Record your speed and accuracy.

Goal: To measure timed-writing progress 10'

	1'	3'
Keyboarding at a visual display terminal may cause	10	3
high fatigue in office workers. These suggestions may help	22	7
relieve the strain of working at a terminal.	31	10
You can avoid back strain by sitting in a chair de-	42	14
signed for keyboarding. Try to keep work periods at the	53	18
terminal short by alternating the tasks that require you to	65	22
sit at the terminal with those that do not. Prevent eye-	77	26
strain by looking away from the terminal every two or three	89	30
minutes and focusing on something far away. Be sure to	100	33
blink every now and then to keep eyes moist, and try to	111	37
remember to breathe properly.	117	39

1'	1	2	3	4	5	6	7	8	9	10	11	12	AWL
3'	1		2		3		4						5.7

60C

Language Arts

Read the rule in the box at the right.

Then key each numbered sentence, supplying underscores where needed.

Check your work with the key in Appendix B.

Goal: To review use of the underscore 8'

> Underscore terms, words, letters, and numbers used as words.
>
> **Examples:**
>
> Terry had never heard of the word <u>mastoid</u> before taking this course.
> Please write clearly. I can't tell whether this is an <u>e</u> or an <u>i</u>.

1. The words affect and effect are very frequently used wrongly.
2. Recently, the term information processing has been used more.
3. Practice reaches to numbers 6 and 7 using only your j finger.
4. Lee still isn't sure whether to write take or to write bring.
5. Sandy will be asked to define the term scrolling.

> 60D M

Need to Know

Refer to the illustration on page 152 after you read about page layout.

Goal: To learn more about page layout 5'

As you know, your software has certain default settings. If you printed a document using the default settings, your document would be formatted according to those settings. For example, let's assume that your software has the default settings shown at the right and that you are using a 10-pitch print size.

```
Left Margin = 10
Right Margin = 75
Top Margin = 6
Bottom Margin = 6
Page Length = 54
Line Spacing = 1
```

When a document is printed using these settings, the **page layout** looks like the one on the next page.

(Continued next page)

Take a 2-minute timing on each group of lines.

DS after each timing.

Avoid pauses when shifting for capitals by using a one-two count.

4 Pat said that Andrew sent this in April.

5 E. Edward, J. Johnson, T. Tessie, L. Lee

6 Idaho Falls, Atlanta, Logan, West Jordan

Keep your eyes on the textbook copy as you depress the shift keys.

7 She is sending us two letters for Lorna.

8 She hopes we plan to send Nedra to town.

9 Let us know when the order gets to Kate.

> **Checkpoint:** Did you look at your hands *Not at all, Once or twice, Several times* when you operated the shift keys?

Lesson 10

M Default Settings
T SS   SM 2″ (12-pitch), 24–78; 1½″ (10-pitch), 15–70

10A

Warmup

Key each line twice.

DS after each pair of lines.

Goal: To strengthen keyboarding skills 5′

1 paid following where full general period

2 Regarding Life Total Will Past Write Set

3 As the, I hope, That I, To take, The new

4 We will not see Jane; Paul will see her.

| 1 | 2 | 3 | 4 | 5 | 6 | 7 | 8 |

10B

Technique Timing

Take two 3-minute timings.

If you finish before time is called, start again.

DS after each timing.

Goal: To improve keyboarding techniques 7′

Keep your eyes on the textbook copy as you depress the right shift key.

1 Done Weep Going Group Did Sell Right The

2 Glad Gone Show Thanks Field Find Whether

3 Where Fill Gear Dot Fiddle Row Sand Wish

4 With this, Then the, There are, The past

5 When the, As there, And the, For we know

6 We heard Ralph and Frank are interested.

> **Checkpoint:** Did you remember to use the **sem** finger on the shift key?

Keyboard Composition

Goal: To compose at the keyboard 5′

Use each of the words or phrases listed in a complete sentence.

Do not correct errors.

1. cafeteria food
2. after school
3. pay day
4. summer job
5. exercise

6. Monday night football
7. space travel
8. home computer
9. Saturday morning television
10. breakfast

59F

Application: Reports

Goal: To key page 1 of an unbound report 16′

File name: L59F   Full Sheet   DS   SM: 1″
Top margin: 2″

PREPARING REPORTS

(Your Name)

Perhaps you have heard the saying, "First impressions are lasting ones." When you prepare a report, you can make that first impression a favorable one by putting the right amount of effort and care into the preparation of the report. A first impression is formed by the report's appearance.

An acceptable and recognized format is necessary when you prepare a report. Side, top, and bottom margins should frame the finished work so that the report has an attractive appearance. The title section must be properly capitalized with correct spacing between the parts.

A quality paper should be selected for the report. The paper should always be clean, white bond. If you use a microcomputer printer, select a better-quality paper than you use for ordinary jobs.

Once you have keyed your report, proofread it carefully. If you use a microcomputer, proofread the text before you print a hard copy. If you use a typewriter, proofread the text before you remove the paper from the typewriter. Correct all misstrokes or errors in context. Use your dictionary to verify any spellings of which you are not certain. Your completed report should be attractive and free of errors.

Lesson 60

M Default Settings
T SS   SM 1½″ (12); 1″ (10)   Tab ¶

60A

Warmup

Goal: To strengthen keyboarding skills 5′

Key each line twice. DS after each pair of lines.

Speed	1	The auto firm owns the big signs by the downtown civic hall.
Accuracy	2	Are you aware that their union has asked for a new contract?
Number/Symbol	3	My policy (#L–48356–G) for $50,000 was paid up May 27, 1982.
Data Entry	4	20 PRINT "COMPUTER LOCATIONS WITHIN THE STATE OF WASHINGTON"

| 1 | 2 | 3 | 4 | 5 | 6 | 7 | 8 | 9 | 10 | 11 | 12 |

New-Key Orientation

1. Locate the new key on the keyboard chart.
2. Next, locate the key on your keyboard.
3. Before keying the practice lines, read the instructions for each new key.
4. Practice the first line, returning to home-key position after making the reach to the new key.
5. Practice the second line for 2 minutes or until you can key it without looking at your hands.

Goal: To learn the location of Ⓜ Ⓑ and Ⓒ 12′

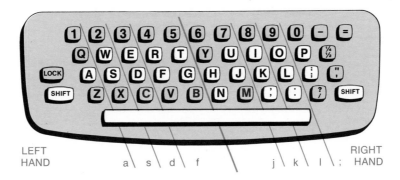

 Practice the reach to Ⓜ with the **j** finger. Keep your other fingers in home-key position.

1 jm jm jm jm jm jm jm jm jm jm jm jm jm

2 jam mud map met mad mum from time some

 Practice the reach to Ⓑ with the **f** finger. Keep your other fingers in home-key position.

3 fb fb fb fb fb fb fb fb fb fb fb fb fb

4 fob fib bit bid rib jab both been best

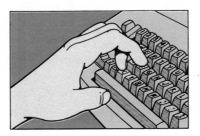

Practice the reach to Ⓒ with the **d** finger. The **f** finger may lift slightly, but keep your other fingers in home-key position.

 5 dc dc dc dc dc dc dc dc dc dc dc dc dc

6 cod cad cot cut cup cow such deck once

Technique Timing

Take a 1-minute timing on each line. Work on improving the technique shown.

DS after each timing.

Goal: To improve keyboarding techniques 11′

Return to home-key position after making reaches to the new keys.

1 most memo meet must form same month mail

2 able business board bill blue book banks

3 office course call stock cash cost local

Keep your eyes on the textbook copy.

Repeat lines 1–3.

(Continued next page)

59B

Speed Practice

Take a 12- or 10-second timing on each line. If you complete a line in the time allowed, go on to the next one.

Goal: To build keyboarding speed 5'

1 I try to keep my mind on what I do.   35 | 42
2 My accuracy comes from my concentration.   40 | 48
3 The concentration comes naturally and easily.   45 | 54
4 I will work better and faster by paying attention.   50 | 60
5 Always keeping my eyes on my book helps me concentrate.   55 | 66

| 1 | 2 | 3 | 4 | 5 | 6 | 7 | 8 | 9 | 10 | 11 |

59C

Technique Timing

Default or DS

Take two 2-minute timings on each technique.

Work on improving the technique shown.

Goal: To improve keyboarding techniques 10'

Keep your eyes on the textbook copy as you key this paragraph.

When using electric typewriters, end-of-line decisions are made by the user. When the bell rings, a certain number of spaces is available before the margin locks. On all microcomputers and on most electronic typewriters, the end of line is determined for you. A default "hot zone," which usually varies from five to eight spaces, determines whether words are placed at the end of a line or are moved to the next line. Since it is not necessary to use the enter/return key, keyboarding speeds increase.

Move to the beginning of the paragraph as quickly as you can. Proofread and correct as many misstrokes as possible.

59D

Language Arts

Read the rule in the box at the right.

Then key each numbered sentence, supplying the correct number style.

Check your work with the key in Appendix B.

Goal: To review rules for numbers 9'

> Use figures for pages, chapters, volumes, and so on.
>
> **Examples:**
>
> Frank found the information on page 116, Volume 2, Chapter 16.
> Your assignment was to complete Lessons 25–32 in Part 7.

1. Mr. Williamson assigned the problems from Chapter 43, page sixteen.
2. In Volume two, Chapter four, page 116, he found the secret formula.
3. Yesterday, Mrs. Henrique asked us to complete Lessons one and two.
4. Did Mrs. Ridley say the answer to the question was on page sixteen?
5. Judy said that the outline for Chapter nineteen required 5 pages.
6. Franklin read 4 passages from Volume six, Chapter nine, page 43.

Take a 1-minute tim-
ing on each line.

DS after each timing.

Keep your **a** finger in home-key position as you reach for Ⓑ and Ⓒ.

4 be bet came con comb cram crab brim balm
5 calm beam back bombs basic bricks beckon
6 cab cob mince crime cable crib clam much

> **Checkpoint:** Do you make finger reaches *Always, Frequently, Occasionally,* or *Seldom*?

10E

Keyboard Practice

Key each line twice.

DS after each pair of lines.

Goal: To practice proper keystroking techniques 7′

> **Cue:** Speed up for easy-to-key letter combinations.

1 One of the men will be able to sing now.
2 Marge would like Bob to sign the letter.
3 From the first, Carla did the job right.
4 I should be able to send the order soon.
5 Bill appreciates the time that we spent.
6 Right now is the time to finish the job.
7 Carole and Brendon canceled the meeting.
8 Mara called me, but she called too late.

10F

Technique Timing

Take a 2-minute tim-
ing on each group of
lines. Work on im-
proving the technique
shown.

Key each line once. If
you finish before time
is called, start again.

DS after each timing.

Goal: To improve keyboarding techniques 8′

Keep your wrist from turning outward as you strike Ⓒ with the **d** finger.

1 continue contain consult consist consent
2 combines combination combined completion
3 conduct companies conclude comment costs

Keep your **sem** finger in home-key position as you reach for Ⓜ.

4 making manner market master matter means
5 might among home mammoth him making seem
6 more them make from claim blame cream me

Keep your **a** finger in home-key position as you strike Ⓑ with the **f** finger.

7 Barbara is the best captain on the team.
8 Bob bought the better color combination.
9 He did bring the best batch to the game.

> **Checkpoint:** Were you able to keep your **a** finger anchored as you reached for Ⓑ?

Application: Reports

Goal: To key page 1 of an unbound report 18′

JOB 1   File name: L58F1   Full Sheet   DS
SM: 1″ (10- and 12-pitch)   Top margin: 2″

Key the report in unbound format.

Cue: Use your name as author of the report.

KEYBOARDING JOINS THE BASICS

The computer age, with space vehicles, home computers, and computerized factories, is upon us; and with it the very fabric of the way we live is changing. Even our educational system is affected. Traditional teaching methods are being supplemented by electronic courseware, allowing greater individualization inside and outside the classroom. One of the most significant changes, however, may be the addition of a new basic skill: Keyboarding.

Keyboarding is as important in this age of computers as reading and writing were to society 100 years ago! Ever since mass education began in the nineteenth century, reading, writing, and arithmetic have allowed people to communicate with one another, to conduct human affairs, and to live in the industrial age. Today, in the computer age, there is a fourth essential skill: the ability to communicate with the computer.

Almost every phase of our society has been touched by computer technology. Keyboarding, the way to communicate with the computer, is becoming as basic to the American way of life as being able to use a credit card. Indeed, keyboarding is the "key" to survival in our high-tech world.

JOB 2

M E If you are using electronic equipment with storage/memory capabilities, retrieve File L58E. Proofread and correct all errors. Print the document in unbound report format.

T On your hard copy of the document, use proofreader's marks to indicate corrections that you need to make. Use your rough-draft copy to rekey the document in final form. Proofread and correct all errors on the final copy.

Checkpoint: Did you correct all errors so your final copy is perfect?

Lesson 59

M Default Settings
T SS   SM 1½″ (12); 1″ (10)   Tab ¶

Warmup

Goal: To strengthen keyboarding skills 5′

Key each line twice.
DS after each pair.

"in" combinations

1 inside indoors insights begin beginning sing mind tin finals
2 Bring the tin ring into the bin and wind the vine in a line.
3 The line of pine design is a fine sign to bring to the city.

| 1 | 2 | 3 | 4 | 5 | 6 | 7 | 8 | 9 | 10 | 11 | 12 |

11A

Warmup

Key each line twice.

DS after each pair of lines.

Goal: To strengthen keyboarding skills 5′

1 much since cost could school price being
2 with this, and that, we do not, could be
3 Please see, We would like, Let them know
4 Colorado, California, Montana, Nebraska,

| 1 | 2 | 3 | 4 | 5 | 6 | 7 | 8 |

11B

Technique Timing

Take a 2-minute timing on each line. Work on improving the technique shown.

DS after each timing.

Goal: To improve keyboarding techniques 14′

Keep your eyes on the textbook copy as you depress the right shift key.

1 Action Doctor Bonds Below Bring Director
2 Dealer Cash Summer Agent Electric Remain
3 Catalogs Estate Standard Getting Showing

> **Checkpoint:** Did you keep your eyes on the copy *Always, Usually,* or *Infrequently*?

Quickly return to home-key position after depressing the left shift key.

4 Plants Include Understand Labor Programs
5 Policies Materials Post Persons Herewith
6 Opinion House Outstanding Prepared Lines

> 11C **M**

Need to Know

Goal: To learn how to print a document 6′   *11-1*

In Units 1 and 2, you are to print your documents using the software program's default settings. Determine the basic print procedure for your software program. Many programs use a procedure similar to the one that follows:

1. Store the document. Some programs require that documents be stored before printing. Others suggest storing documents to guard against accidental loss.

2. Select the print **option** from the main or opening menu.
3. Key in the file name.
4. Bypass the **format** options of the print menu and use the default settings. Most software programs use a key such as Escape (ESC) or Enter for this purpose. Use the key required by your program.
5. Use the print command to begin printing.

Need to Know

Refer to the illustration at the right as you read the instructions for keying an unbound report.

Goal: To learn the format for page 1 of an unbound report   5'   58-1

1. Side margins: 1 inch.
2. Top margin: 2 inches.
3. Bottom margin: 1 inch.
4. Title: Centered in all caps on line 13.
5. Name of author: Centered in initial caps a DS below the title. (If a title page is used with a report, the name of the author is on the title page instead of here.)
6. Body of the report: Begins a TS after the name of the author and is DS.

Note: A page with a title or a centered heading is not numbered.

The format for the continuing pages of a report is shown in 61E.

Project Preview

File name: L58E

DS

SM: 1″ (10-pitch and 12-pitch)

Key as much of page 1 as you can in 5 minutes.

Use your name as the author's name.

If you finish before time is called, start again.

Ignore misstrokes.

Store the document or save the hard copy to use in 58F, JOB 2.

Goal: To key page 1 of an unbound report   7'

A COMPUTER IN EVERY HOME? DS ↓line 13

Author's Name TS

Just a few years ago, the idea of having a computer in every home would have been labeled "ridiculous." Yet computers are increasingly completing tasks that once seemed impossible.

Already, computers are available to regulate the temperature of a room, to turn lights on and off, and to control home-security systems. Through electronic systems, one can shop, pay bills, access reference services, play games, or learn a foreign language. Even the familiar telephone is experiencing the changes of computerization. It is predicted that in the next few years a person will be able to use a home phone number to call people all over the world—regardless of where they may be when they place the call.

Technique Timing

Goal: To improve keyboarding techniques 6'

Keep your eyes on the textbook copy as you enter/return.

Take two 2-minute timings.

Enter/return when you see E/R . If you finish before time is called, start again.

DS after each timing.

Please send the letter. E/R See me soon. E/R We want their business. E/R I am going to Chicago. E/R With luck, we will finish soon. E/R The check has been mailed. E/R Please write. E/R Let us know what we should do. E/R The order has been sent.

11E

Need to Know

Goal: To learn how to use word scales 6'

11-2

You can use word scales to see how many words you keyed or to determine your keyboarding speed. Keyboarding speed is measured in gross words a minute, or GWAM. To determine your GWAM:

1. Count the number of *complete* lines you keyed.
2. Multiply the number of complete lines by the number of "words" in the line. The number of words in a line is the last number shown in the bottom word scale.
3. If you didn't finish a line, use the bottom word scale to determine the number of words keyed.
4. Add the number of words for the incomplete line (Step 3) to the number of words for the complete lines (Step 2). The total of the two represents your GWAM for 1 minute.

To save time, word scales that list cumulative GWAM, line by line, have been developed. These word scales are printed to the right of the copy. To determine GWAM with this kind of scale, find the cumulative word count in the side word scale for the last complete line you keyed. Then, using the bottom word scale, determine the number of words keyed in any incomplete line. Add these two numbers; the answer is your 1-minute GWAM.

If you are timed for longer than 1 minute, you can still use the 1-minute scales to figure your GWAM. Simply divide the word count you get using the 1-minute scales by the number of minutes in the timing. If you keyed 60 words in 3 minutes, for example, your GWAM is 20 ($60 \div 3 = 20$).

11F

Self-Check

Goal: To review word scale use 5'

Use the illustration at the right to answer the questions that follow.

Handwrite the number of the question and your answer on a sheet of paper.

Check your answers in Appendix C.

		1'
1	To do the job right, we need their help.	8
2	He would like to share the results soon.	16
3	She got the letter concerning the order.	24
4	Call the department as soon as possible.	32

| 1 | 2 | 3 | 4 | 5 | 6 | 7 | 8 |

1. If you key all of line 1, what is your GWAM?
2. If you key all four lines, what is your GWAM?
3. If you key all of line 1 and up through **th** in the word *the* in line 2, what is your GWAM?
4. If you key lines 1, 2, and 3 and up through the space after the word *department* in line 4, what is your GWAM?

58A

Warmup

Key each line twice.
DS after each pair.

"de" combinations

Goal: To strengthen keyboarding skills 5′

1 Debby's debts described in the deluxe deposit destroyed her.
2 Depau's decentralized department demanded deferred payments.
3 Much design and detail were demanded in his desk decoration.

| 1 | 2 | 3 | 4 | 5 | 6 | 7 | 8 | 9 | 10 | 11 | 12 |

58B

Goal Writing

Default or DS

Take two 3-minute
goal writings.

If you finish before
time is called, start
again.

Record your speed
and accuracy.

Goal: To measure timed-writing progress 10′

	1′	3′
The telephone is a very important tool in the business	11	4
world today. Every worker needs to know how to answer the	23	8
telephone in a proper way. You must always answer promptly	35	12
and courteously. Identify yourself and your department.	46	15
Keep message forms and a pen or pencil near the telephone so	59	20
you can record accurate and complete messages.	68	23
It is essential to be accurate. Do not hesitate to ask	79	26
the caller to spell out an unusual name. You may also want	91	30
to repeat the caller's telephone number to make sure that	103	34
you have recorded it accurately.	109	36

1′ | 1 | 2 | 3 | 4 | 5 | 6 | 7 | 8 | 9 | 10 | 11 | 12 | AWL
3′ | 1 | 2 | 3 | 4 | 5.7

58C

**Technique
Timing**

Default or DS

Take a two-minute
timing on each
technique.

Work on improving
the technique shown.

Goal: To improve keyboarding techniques 5′

Keep your eyes on the textbook copy as you key this paragraph.

One way to use time efficiently is to organize your day.
Make a list of what you want to accomplish. Working from
your list, decide which tasks are the most important and
begin with the task that has top priority. Whenever possible,
complete one task before another. This gives you a sense of
achievement and allows you to focus all your attention on the
next task when you begin it.

Move to the beginning of the paragraph as quickly as you can. Proofread
and correct as many misstrokes as possible.

Keyboard Practice

Key each line 3 times.

DS after each group of lines.

Goal: To practice proper keystroking techniques 8′

> **Cue:** Keep your eyes on the textbook copy as you operate the shift keys.

1 Claims South Lands Hear Funds North West
2 To take, We would like for our, She will
3 Senator Cramer will come to Idaho Falls.
4 Finance Congress Lake East Commerce Risk
5 President Sims went to East High School.
6 Ohio, Florida, Utah, and Iowa abstained.
7 Marta will go to Toronto or to Montreal.

Lesson **12**

M Default Settings
T SS   SM 2″ (12); 1½″ (10)

12A

Warmup

Key each line twice.

DS after each pair of lines.

Goal: To strengthen keyboarding skills 5′

1 The office is open. We want to see Jed.
2 The information is what Jo asked to see.
3 main range truck union file charges come
4 Trucking Charging Coming Clearing Filing

| 1 | 2 | 3 | 4 | 5 | 6 | 7 | 8 |

12B

Technique Timing

Take two 2-minute timings on each group of lines. Work on improving the technique shown.

Key each line once. If you finish before time is called, start again.

DS after each timing.

Goal: To improve keyboarding techniques 10′

Keep all other fingers in home-key position as you reach to the left shift key with the **a** finger. Release the shift key quickly.

1 Montana Utilities; Mutual Insurance Inc.
2 Northwest Petroleum Plant; Nebraskan Oil
3 Northern Illinois Products; North Kansas

Keep all other fingers in home-key position as you reach to the right shift key with the **sem** finger. Release the shift key quickly.

4 Christmas Shop; Coal Distribution Center
5 Eastern; Southern; Western; Southeastern
6 California Storage Area; Austin Electric

---

move directly to the beginning or end of a document. A command or a combination of keystrokes is used for each of these express cursor moves.

For example, one program uses the Code + Arrow (directional key) to move the cursor to the top of the text. Another program uses CTRL B to move the cursor to the beginning of a document.

Determine the commands for express cursor moves for your software. Using the copy keyed in 57A–D, carry out the following cursor moves:

1. Move the cursor to the first column of text on the left of the screen.
2. Move the cursor to the top line on the screen.
3. Move the cursor to the last column on the right of the screen.
4. Move the cursor to the last line of text at the bottom of the screen.
5. Move the cursor to the last character in the line. Enter/return to begin the next activity.

57F

Application: Rough Draft

File name: L57F1

Default or DS

Read the copy before you begin keying. Then key the paragraphs making the changes indicated by the proofreader's marks.

Store the document for use in JOB 2.

Do not remove your paper from the typewriter. Go on to JOB 2.

Goal: To key rough-draft copy 18'

JOB 1

Some years ago a very popular book encouraged people to say to each other: Think positive! While the saying is not said often today, it is still true that a positive attitude is the one of most important habit you can now develop in preparing for your future. You may have several years of schooling ahead of you; you may be looking forward to your first job. In either case, a good attitude maybe the difference between failure and success.

You too can become a Positive Thinker. Think of a person who has a positive attitude. Isn't it fun to be with that person? Doesn't that person make you feel better when things are not going well? develop the habit of saying "I'll do better next time" when you have not done well. Above all, think positively.

JOB 2

If you are using electronic equipment with storage/memory capabilities, retrieve File L57F1. If your equipment does not have storage/memory, use the correction key or correction paper. Make the following changes in JOB 1.

Paragraph 1

1. "some years" to "many years"
2. "is not said" to "is not used"
3. "years of schooling" to "years of education"
4. "failure and success" to "success and failure"

Paragraph 2

1. "person" to "friend"—in all instances
2. "think positive." to "think positive!"

12C

New-Key Orientation

1. Locate the new key on the keyboard chart.
2. Next, locate the key on your keyboard.
3. Before keying the practice lines, read the instructions given for each new key.
4. Practice the first line, returning to home-key position after making the reach to the new key.
5. Practice the second line for 2 minutes or until you can key it without looking at your hands.

Goal: To learn the location of Ⓨ Ⓠ and Ⓧ 12'

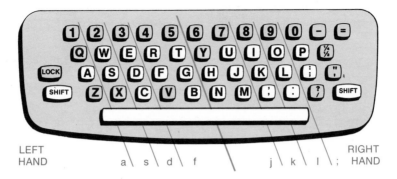

LEFT HAND   a s d f   j k l ;   RIGHT HAND

Practice the reach to Ⓨ with the **j** finger. Keep your other fingers in home-key position.

1 jy jy jy jy jy jy jy jy jy jy jy jy jy

2 joy jay gym many myth yoyo mayor youth

Practice the reach to Ⓠ with the **a** finger. Keep your other fingers in home-key position. Keep your wrist from turning as you strike Ⓠ.

3 aq aq aq aq aq aq aq aq aq aq aq aq aq

4 aqua quit quip queen quick squid quart

Practice the reach to Ⓧ with the **s** finger. The **a** finger may lift slightly, but keep your other fingers in home-key position.

5 sx sx sx sx sx sx sx sx sx sx sx sx sx

6 six axe lax exit next oxen taxed exist

12D

Technique Timing

Take a 1-minute timing on each line. Work on improving the technique shown.

DS after each timing.

Goal: To improve keyboarding techniques 12'

Return to home-key position after making the reach to the new keys.

1 years yearly you yard yellow yield young

2 quota squad quote request quart requires

3 next tax index mix mixed mixture sixteen

Keep your eyes on the textbook copy.

Repeat lines 1–3.

Do not pause while keying. Try to keep the cursor/carrier moving.

4 Yes, the tax men did your taxes quickly.

5 Tex quickly found her a new yellow rose.

6 Que is the quiet young Texan who called.

> **57E** **M**

57B

Accuracy Practice

DS after each group of lines.

Goal: To build keyboarding accuracy 5′

Take a 3-minute accuracy timing on the lines in 57A. If you make an error, start again. Stay on a line until you have keyed it without error.

> **Checkpoint:** How many error-free lines did you key?

57C

Language Arts

Read the rule in the box at the right.

Then key the paragraph supplying correct capitalization where needed.

Check your work with the key in Appendix B.

Goal: To review rules for capitalization 8′

> Capitalize the first word of a sentence and the first word of a complete, direct quotation (a person's exact words).
>
> **Examples:**
>
> Computers can increase productivity. (first word of sentence)
> The man said, "Keyboarding skill is essential for this job." (direct quotation)
> "Can you finish the job," she asked, "in time for the mail?" (direct quotation)

"what new software do you have to show to this group today?" asked Mr. Jones. "well," said Miss Conway, "we have a spelling verifier that will certainly improve the spelling on all your letters and reports." as Mr. Jones and the team watched, Miss Conway showed them how a spelling verifier checked the spelling of every word in several letters and reports. "it will show you which words are misspelled so you will be able to correct them," said Miss Conway. "isn't that amazing?" asked Mr. Jones. as heads nodded, he tossed his dictionary aside.

57D

Self-Check

Default or DS

Key the statement number and your answer: True or False.

Check your answers in Appendix C.

Goal: To review proofreader's marks 5′

1. Use ⤲ to indicate that a letter, word, or sentence is to be inserted into the copy.
2. Use # to indicate that a space should be added in the copy.
3. Use ≡ under a letter to indicate that the letter should be capitalized.
4. Use ⊐ to indicate that copy should be moved to the left.
5. Use ∧ to indicate that a letter, word, or sentence is to be deleted from the copy.
6. When keying the word schedule, you would capitalize every letter in the word.

M Note: Keep this activity on the screen. Go on to 57E.

Read and Do

Goal: To learn to express move the cursor through text 10′   *57-1*

In Lesson 20C, you learned to move the cursor up, down, left, and right one space or one line at a time. In this lesson, you will learn to express move the cursor directly to the top, bottom, far left, and far right of the text. Some programs also have **express cursor moves** that allow you to

(Continued next page)

12E

Goal Writing

Take two 1-minute goal writings.

Key each line once. If time allows, start again.

Determine your GWAM.

Goal: To measure timed-writing progress 4′

12-1

Cue:	Key at a pace that is comfortable for you.

1′

```
1 Please explain that print queue to them.    8
2 Rex Young ran the quiet ink jet printer.   16
3 The computer expert quietly did her job.   24
  |  1  |  2  |  3  |  4  |  5  |  6  |  7  |  8  |
```

12F

Keyboard Practice

Key each line 3 times.

DS after each group of lines.

Goal: To practice proper keystroking techniques 7′

```
1 liquid require bequest technique conquer
2 sixth expanse taxes expire taxed expired
3 easy equity except equal yearly equipped
4 for your exempt expense, you may inquire
```

Lesson 13

M Default Settings
T SS SM 2″ (12); 1½″ (10)

13A

Warmup

Key each line twice.

DS after each pair of lines.

Goal: To strengthen keyboarding skills 5′

```
1 hand member try welcome air men box firm
2 I would like, We feel, I would be, It is
3 January; July; February; August; October
4 Thank you for the order; we are pleased.
  |  1  |  2  |  3  |  4  |  5  |  6  |  7  |  8  |
```

13B

Technique Timing

Take a 2-minute timing.

Key each line once. If time allows, start again.

Goal: To improve keyboarding techniques 5′

Strike each key with a quick, sharp stroke.

```
1 exceed excellent excess exhibit existing
2 equality questionnaire require equipment
3 early yearly yield yourself youths yeast
```

(Continued next page)

Unit 5 / Unbound Reports

Your keyboarding skills may be used to prepare reports for your school classes or for business purposes. You will learn one format for preparing reports. Once you have learned this format, you may easily learn to use other formats.

In this unit, Lessons 57–70, you will learn to:

1. Increase your keyboarding speed and accuracy.
2. Use express cursor moves to move through keyed text.
3. Format and key reports in unbound format.
4. Enter page layout commands for an unbound report.
5. Determine the number of lines to use on a page.
6. Key subscripts and use them within text.
7. Key superscripts and use them within text.
8. Format and key short and long quotations.
9. Key endnotes, bibliography, and title pages for an unbound report.
10. Assemble parts of a report in correct order.

Micro Dictionary

express cursor moves	a command or a combination of keystrokes that allows the user to move through blocks of text
page layout	the vertical and horizontal arrangement of a document on a page. Page layout is determined by the margins, line spacing, and pitch.
status line	a line of information displayed on the microcomputer screen. The status line usually indicates the line and column position of the cursor.
subscripts	characters that appear one-half line below the line of print
superscripts	characters that appear one-half line above the line of print

Lesson 57

M Default Settings

T SS   SM 1½" (12); 1" (10)   Tab ¶

57A

Warmup

Goal: To strengthen keyboarding skills 5′

Key each line twice.
DS after each pair.

Confusing words:
principal and principle

1 As head of your school, your principal may also be your pal.
2 When it's used as a noun, <u>principle</u> is a fundamental belief.
3 The topic of Principal Hale's talk was "Principles of Life."

| 1 | 2 | 3 | 4 | 5 | 6 | 7 | 8 | 9 | 10 | 11 | 12 |

Take a 2-minute timing.

Key each line once. If time allows, start again.

Keep your other fingers in home key position as you reach to Ⓠ and Ⓧ.

4 I will try a quick stop on my next trip.

5 The quests for that extra exhibit ended.

6 The sixth technique is an excellent one.

13C

New-Key Orientation

1. Locate the new key on the keyboard chart.
2. Next, locate the key on your keyboard.
3. Before keying the practice lines, read the instructions for each new key.
4. Practice the first line, returning to home-key position after making the reach to the new key.
5. Practice the second line for 2 minutes or until you can key it without looking at your hands.

Goal: To learn the location of Ⓥ and Ⓩ 8'

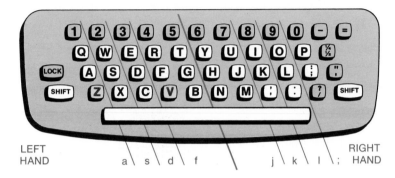

LEFT HAND   a s d f   j k l ;   RIGHT HAND

 Practice the reach to Ⓥ with the **f** finger. Keep your other fingers in home-key position.

1 fv fv fv fv fv fv fv fv fv fv fv fv fv

2 five cave vain favor value haven every

 Practice the reach to Ⓩ with the **a** finger. The **s** finger may lift slightly, but keep your other fingers in home-key position.

3 az az az az az az az az az az az az az

4 zap fez zoo lazy zero zone dozen graze

13D

Technique Timing

Take a 1-minute timing on each line. Work on improving the technique shown.

Then take a 2-minute timing on the pair of lines for the technique that needs the most improvement.

DS after each timing.

Goal: To improve keyboarding techniques 10'

Return to home-key position after making the reach to the new keys.

1 five given however service above provide

2 zest zigzag zoom zip zinc zippers zodiac

Keep your eyes on the textbook copy.

Repeat lines 1 and 2.

Space between words without pausing. Use a quick, down-and-in motion.

3 With great zeal, Victor studied zoology.

4 Virginia gave the zebra to the Zulu Zoo.

> **Checkpoint:** Did you key with *No, Few, Several,* or *Many* pauses?

56A

Goal Writing

Warm up on 55A for 5 minutes.

Default or DS

Take two 3-minute goal writings.

If you finish before time is called, start again.

Record your speed and accuracy.

Goal: To measure timed-writing progress 15′

	1′	3′
Jobs as word processing operators do not have to be	11	4
limited to the traditional, full-time job within the same	22	7
company. Some temporary agencies now regularly ask for	33	11
trained persons. Also, a whole new world is opening up for	45	15
those word processing operators who can and want to work at	57	19
home. As the communications features of word processors are	70	23
refined, this will be an even greater opportunity. A person	82	27
will be able to work at home and send the completed work to	94	31
his or her office by electronic means without leaving home.	106	35

1′	1	2	3	4	5	6	7	8	9	10	11	12	AWL
3′		1		2		3			4				5.7

56B

Production Measurement

Goal: To measure formatting skills 35′

JOB 1 File name: L56B1 Full sheet DS Center vertically and horizontally.

Good Health Practices

Get adequate amounts of sleep.
Exercise regularly.
Eat nutritious meals.
Think positive thoughts.
Take time for relaxing activities.

JOB 2 File name: L56B2 Full sheet DS Spaces between columns: 10 Center vertically and horizontally.

COMPUTER PROGRAMMING ENROLLMENTS		
ASSEMBLY	29	10.1
BASIC	115	39.9
FORTRAN	63	21.9
PASCAL	81	28.1

JOB 3 File name: L56B3 Full sheet 3a,t DS Spaces between columns: 8 Center vertically and horizontally.

Southeast State Birds and Trees		
Alabama	Yellowhammer	Pine
Arkansas	Mockingbird	Pine
Florida	Mockingbird	Sabal palm
Georgia	Thrasher	Live oak
Kentucky	Cardinal	Coffee tree
Louisiana	Pelican	Cypress
Mississippi	Mockingbird	Magnolia
North Carolina	Cardinal	Pine
South Carolina	Wren	Palmetto
Tennessee	Mockingbird	Poplar
Virginia	Cardinal	Dogwood
West Virginia	Cardinal	Sugar maple

13E

Need to Know Goal: To learn about tabs 3′

In keyboarding, you will often need to indent paragraphs or arrange text in columns. You could use the space bar to move the cursor/carrier to the point where you want to begin keying. However, it is much more efficient to set and use tabs. The tab moves the cursor/carrier directly to a tab stop.

The **tab key** is operated by the finger closest to it. On most equipment, the tab key is located on the left side of the keyboard and is operated by the **a** finger. To operate the tab key properly, strike the tab key quickly and return the **a** finger immediately to home-key position. Your other fingers should remain in home-key position as you operate the tab key.

Reach to the tab key with the **a** finger.

On some microcomputers you may have to depress a combination of keys to instruct the cursor to move to specific tab stops.

13F

Need to Know Goal: To learn to set tabs 3′

M *Microcomputer*

Most software packages have **default tabs** (preset tab stops) every so many spaces across a line. For example, tab stops may be preset every 5 or 8 spaces. Determine what default tab settings, if any, your software has. Use them whenever possible.

For those software packages that require you to set tab stops before you begin to key, use the space bar to move the cursor to the correct position. Using the appropriate key or command, set a tab stop.

T *Typewriter*

Before you set a tab, clear any **tab stops** that are already set. Determine the appropriate method for clearing tabs on your equipment. (See *About Your Equipment* in the front of this book.)

Once you have cleared all tab stops, use the space bar to move the carrier to the correct position. Using the appropriate key or command, set a tab stop.

13G

Read and Do Goal: To learn how to indent paragraphs 4′

Beginning with Lesson 14, suggested tab settings for each lesson will be shown in the color band in the lesson opener. The most common tab setting will be "Tab ¶." This symbol (¶) stands for paragraph indent. The first line of a paragraph is usually indented 5 spaces.

M *Microcomputer*

1. Using the tab key or command, move the cursor to the first default tab stop. If your software does not have a default tab, space over 5 spaces and set a tab stop.
2. Begin keying the paragraph in 13H at this point.

T *Typewriter*

1. Using the appropriate method for your equipment, clear all tab stops and operate the return.
2. Space over 5 spaces and set a tab stop. Then operate your return.
3. Press the tab key to check the tab setting. If the tab is correct, begin keying the paragraph in 13H at this point.

55C

Language Arts

Read the rule in the box at the right.

Then key each numbered sentence, supplying the correct number style.

Check your work with the key in Appendix B.

Goal: To review rules for numbers 10′

> Use figures when stating an exact time or when using the abbreviations a.m. or p.m. Spell out approximate times and times using the word o'clock.
>
> **Examples:**
>
> All students are expected to be at their desks by nine o'clock.
> The telephone rang at 7:45 a.m.; I got to work at exactly 8:30.

1. It was about 9 o'clock when Jack and Sarah finally arrived.
2. Madeline's work started at 8:15 a.m.; she arrived at eight a.m.
3. The party was supposed to begin around 2 and end around 6.
4. My class began at ten fifteen a.m. and ended much later at 3:15 p.m.
5. The factory's last shift begins work at exactly 4:30 each day.
6. I will have to hurry to catch the 9 o'clock commuter train.
7. It was almost 12 o'clock before they finished the project.
8. Complete that letter by three p.m. to get it in the mail at 4 p.m.

55D

Application: Tables

Goal: To center and key tables 25′

JOB 1 File name: L55D1 Full sheet DS Spaces between columns: 12 Center vertically and horizontally.

Professors and Courses Taught

Langton Stuart	Calculus
Ching Lau Chang	Ethics
Maria Juarez	Accounting
Peter von Heyre	Economics
Patrick Monahan	Programming
Joanna Cohen	Management
Ludwig Strauss	Law
Abduh Amman	Supervision
Georgene Colbert	Packaging

JOB 2 File name: L55D2 Full sheet DS Spaces between columns: 8 Center vertically and horizontally.

Today's Meetings and Fees

OIS	4:00 p.m.	$18.00
AMMA	4:30 p.m.	7.50
Sales Executives	5:00 p.m.	13.25
Beauty, Inc.	5:30 p.m.	8.75
Sunbelt Investors	6:00 p.m.	10.00
Gulfcoast Golf	6:00 p.m.	9.75
Florida Electric	6:00 p.m.	14.25

JOB 3 File name: L55D3 Full sheet DS Spaces between columns: 10 Center vertically and horizontally.

Locations of Computer Terminals

Accounting	Room 215	8 users
Administration	Plaza Suite	2 users
DPR	Subplaza 1	21 users
Personnel	Room 440	4 users
Purchasing	Room 1203	3 users
Receiving	Shipping Dock	1 user
Reception	Lobby	1 user
Sales	Room 305	6 users

Checkpoint: Did you center and key the title in all caps?

JOB 4 File name: L55D4 Full sheet DS Spaces between columns: 6 Center vertically and horizontally.

Key the information given in JOB 1. Use Computer Terminal Users as the title.

Lesson 55

13H

Keyboard Practice

Default or DS.

Tab: ¶

Key the paragraphs. If time allows, start again.

13-1

Goal: To practice proper keystroking techniques 6′

Cue: Use the tab to indent paragraphs.

Thank you for your recent order and letter of explanation.

We will ship your order in one week if the strike is over. We cannot assure shipment any sooner.

Please let us know at your earliest convenience whether you prefer the items to be shipped by overnight express.

13I

Goal Writing

Take two 2-minute goal writings.

Key each line once. If time allows, start again.

Determine your GWAM.

Goal: To measure timed-writing progress 6′

Cue: Key at a pace that is comfortable for you.

1′

1 Please send the letters to him tomorrow.   8
2 We want their business to buy our goods.   16
3 She will be able to mail the order soon.   24
4 Dan and I will go to the city next week.   32

| 1 | 2 | 3 | 4 | 5 | 6 | 7 | 8 |

Lesson 14

M **Default Settings**
T SS   SM 2″ (12); 1½″ (10)   Tab ¶

14A

Warmup

Key each line twice.

DS after each pair of lines.

Goal: To strengthen keyboarding skills 5′

1 If you have any questions, write to him.
2 Have Jody Pinckle bring me five quizzes.
3 Give your ideas to Gene, the supervisor.
4 Enclosed is a form; please mail it soon.

| 1 | 2 | 3 | 4 | 5 | 6 | 7 | 8 |

JOB 2

Computer Software Usage

File name: L54G2
Full sheet

DS
Spaces between
columns: 10

Center vertically and
horizontally.

Computer Software Usage	
Word Processing	63.5%
Computer Aided Instruction	52.1%
Spreadsheets	44.3%
Data Bases	27.6%
Integrated Packages	33.2%
Entertainment	32.7%
Telecommunications	18.0%
Income Tax Management	14.3%
Graphics	7.3%

Lesson 55

M Default Settings
T SS   SM 1½" (12); 1" (10)   Tab ¶

55A

Warmup

Key each line twice.
DS after each pair.

One-hand words.

Goal: To strengthen keyboarding skills 5'

1 monopoly greatest opinion exaggerated pupil reserves minimum
2 estate nylon taxes pupil rested union staffed linkup drafted
3 aluminum decorated symptoms extractions expressed ceremonial
4 eliminated improvements purposeful innovations manufacturers

| 1 | 2 | 3 | 4 | 5 | 6 | 7 | 8 | 9 | 10 | 11 | 12 |

55B

**Comparison
Copy**

Default or DS

Take two 2-minute
timings on each para-
graph.

Try to key at the
same rate of speed
on the handwritten
copy as you did on
the straight copy.

Goal: To build keyboarding speed on a variety of copy 10'

	1'	2'
Decimal alignment is a feature of most microcomputers	11	6
and electronic typewriters. When you use the decimal tab	23	11
feature, you do not have to manually align columns of fig—	34	17
ures. Some software programs also align columns of figures	46	23
that contain commas. Once you discover how easy decimal	58	29
tabs are to use, you can save time and effort in keyboarding.	70	35

1' | 1 | 2 | 3 | 4 | 5 | 6 | 7 | 8 | 9 | 10 | 11 | 12 |
2' | 1 | 2 | 3 | 4 | 5 | 6 |

When you use decimal tabs, digits appear to the left of	11	6
the tab setting until the decimal point is keyed. The	22	11
remaining digits appear to the right of the decimal point.	34	17
As a result, the figures in each column line up at the	45	23
decimal point, regardless of the number of digits in the	57	28
figures.	58	29

14B

Need to Know   Goal: To learn about line endings   3′

Beginning in this lesson, the drill lines contain 50 characters.

Equipment with Word Wrap

On equipment with an automatic word wrap feature, any word that is too long to fit within a set line length is automatically moved down to the next line. When using automatic word wrap, operate the enter/return key only at the end of a paragraph or at the end of a short line.

In the next activity, key the lines continuously without operating the enter/return at the end of each line. Enter/return at the end of each timing.

Equipment without Word Wrap

On equipment without word wrap, a margin signal sounds as copy nears the end of a line. This signal may be either a beep or a bell. When you hear the signal, you need to decide how much more copy you can key before you enter/return. If you are unable to complete a word before the margin locks, use the margin release.

The margin release enables you to key beyond the right margin. You may also use the margin release to move outside the left margin. Release the left margin and backspace to keep numbers in a list aligned on the right.

In the next activity, enter/return at the end of every line. "Tune" your ears to listen for the margin signal as you approach the end of a line. With practice, you will learn to enter/return shortly after hearing the margin signal.

14C

Technique Timing

Take two 2-minute timings on each group of lines. Work on improving the technique shown.

Key each line once. If time allows, start again.

DS after each timing.

Goal: To improve keyboarding techniques   19′

Release the shift keys quickly and return your fingers to home-key position.

1 I am sure; At this time; You will find; Along with
2 Do not hesitate; You will be; This company; I have
3 Enclosed is a; He would be; We believe; As soon as

Keep wrists from moving up and down as you strike the keys.

Repeat lines 1–3.

Sit in proper position at the keyboard.

4 We will congratulate you on the feasibility study.
5 We need a consensus on the format of the pamphlet.
6 Thank you for the opportunity to accommodate them.

Do not pause between letters or words.

7 absence concede explanation opportunity possession
8 pamphlet familiar accessible congratulate parallel
9 feasibility consensus practical consistent fulfill

Checkpoint: Did you key with *No, Few,* or *Several* pauses?

Project Preview

File name: L54E
Full sheet

Use the margins and decimal tabs set in 54D.

Key as much as you can in 3 minutes. If you finish, start again.

Goal: To key a table that contains decimals 5′

STATIONERY SALES TS

Sandra Larson	54 boxes	59.40 DS
John Durham	72 boxes	79.20 DS
Ellen Janell	18 boxes	19.80 DS
Ron Hastings	9 boxes	9.90 DS
Janet Wheller	110 boxes	121.00 DS
Jordan Anderson	172 boxes	189.20

Apply the Rule

Decimal Tabs: 3 spaces; 20 spaces; 20 spaces.

Regular Tabs: Every 20 spaces.

Key all three parts using the spacing indicated.

Key the *Application* section in three columns as shown. Line up the decimals in each column.

Goal: To review decimal alignment   8′

Rule DS

When keying numbers in columns, line up the decimal points one under the other in a straight line. TS

Example DS

155.62
 88.88
  1.98
672.19 TS

Application DS

22.75	68.94	53.16
7.11	2.80	46.35
.49	1.98	223.23
1.87	189.95	114.88
318.70	23.10	.22
.65	5.95	.99

Application: Tables

Goal: To center and key tables   16′

JOB 1 File name: L54G1 Full sheet DS Spaces between columns: 8
Center vertically and horizontally.

METRIC MEASUREMENTS

1 mm	millimeter	.04	inches
1 kg	kilogram	2.20	pounds
5 ml	milliliters	1.00	teaspoon
4 l	liters	1.06	gallons
1 l	liter	1.06	quarts
1 km	kilometer	.62	miles
1 m	meter	1.09	yards
1 g	gram	.04	ounces

(Continued next page)

14D

Goal Writing

Goal: To measure timed-writing progress 5'   *14-1*

Take two 2-minute goal writings.

Key each line once. If time allows, start again.

Determine your GWAM.

| **Cue:** Key at a pace that is comfortable for you. | 1' |

1 We are able to accommodate your request for parts. 10
2 Thank you for the recent opportunity to serve you. 20
3 We appreciate your order for the revised pamphlet. 30
4 At your convenience, please give us a second call. 40

| 1 | 2 | 3 | 4 | 5 | 6 | 7 | 8 | 9 | 10 |

14E

Need to Know

Goal: To learn to identify misstrokes 6'

All people who use keyboards make misstrokes. The important thing is to be able to find the misstrokes and correct them. Initially, you will need to identify the kinds of misstrokes that you make. Study the four kinds of misstrokes in the example to learn what some of the common kinds of misstrokes are.

Omitted Letter(s)   Plese let us know; he migt write Jack.

Omitted Word(s)   The members the board were all there.

Added Letter(s)   Please let use know; he might writes Jack.

Added Word(s)   The members of the of the board were all there.

14F

Keyboard Practice

Goal: To practice proper keystroking on handwritten copy 6'

Key each line twice.

DS after each pair of lines.

1 If you are able, please come; however, call first.
2 Ford Zoo is open; you are invited to go with them.
3 F. J. Rogerson, of course, will do the conducting.
4 We plan to attend. We hope they will also attend.

14G

Technique Timing

Goal: To improve keyboarding techniques 6'   *14-2*

Default or DS

Tab: ¶

Take two 2-minute timings.

If time allows, start again.

Return to home-key position after tabbing to indent paragraphs.

    The feasibility study was completed by Miss
Mary Cash. Our consensus is that it is well done.
    Since you are familiar with the study, will
you please congratulate her as soon as you can.
Your personal copy is in her possession.
    I will be available at the end of May.

54B

Speed Practice

Take a 12- or 10-second timing on each line. If you complete a line in the time allowed, go on to the next one.

Goal: To build keyboarding speed 5'

1 We will ship your orders in a week.   35 42

2 Take me to the leaders of the group now.   40 48

3 Your company is in a good financial position.   45 56

4 I would like to thank you for the fine time I had.   50 60

5 Contact the personnel manager if you want the position.   55 66

| 1 | 2 | 3 | 4 | 5 | 6 | 7 | 8 | 9 | 10 | 11 |

54C

Keyboard Composition

Answer each question with a complete sentence.

Do not correct errors.

Goal: To compose at the keyboard 5'

1. Which day of the week do you like the best?
2. What is your best subject in school?
3. When is your next birthday and how old will you be?
4. What are some of your favorite foods?
5. Would you rather work indoors or outside?
6. Do you like to work alone or with other people?
7. What jobs would you like to try?
8. How could you improve your keyboarding skills?
9. How will being able to keyboard help you?
10. If you could go anywhere in the world, where would it be?

54D

Read and Do

Goal: To learn how to set decimal tabs 6'

54-1

Columns of figures that contain decimals are usually aligned at the decimal point. Many microcomputers and electronic typewriters have a decimal tab (dec tab) feature that automatically aligns numbers at the decimal point.

M E *Microcomputer/Electronic Typewriter*

1. Determine the procedure for clearing and setting decimal tabs for your software/equipment.
2. Determine the key line for the table.
3. Set a decimal tab at the decimal position for each column of figures containing decimals. If the first column is figures with decimals, space in the necessary columns/spaces to set a tab at the decimal position for that column.
4. Set a decimal tab at the first space after the whole number for columns of figures without decimals.
5. Use a regular tab for a column that contains words without numbers.

T *Typewriter*

If you are using electric typewriters or equipment without the decimal tab feature, set regular tabs for keying columns of figures. Space forward or backward from the tab to align the numbers at the decimal.

Use the key line in the following illustration to set margins and decimal tabs for the Project Preview in 54E. Leave 4 spaces between columns.

```
                          Dec          Dec
LM                        Tab          Tab  RM
Jordan Anderson1234172  boxes1234189.20
```

M Default Settings
T SS   SM 2″ (12); 1½″ (10)   Tab ¶

15A

Warmup

Key each line twice.

DS after each pair of lines.

Goal: To strengthen keyboarding skills 5′

1 We shall; We may; At our; You were; Please let us;
2 practical, possession, parallel, pamphlet, fulfill
3 If you have the information we need, please phone.
4 council put quality why accept never juror thought

| 1 | 2 | 3 | 4 | 5 | 6 | 7 | 8 | 9 | 10 |

15B

Technique Timing

Take a 2-minute timing on each line. Work on improving the technique shown.

DS after each timing.

Goal: To improve keyboarding techniques 18′

Release the shift keys quickly and return fingers to home-key position.

1 The curriculum is easy. His criticism is helpful.
2 The taxes are deductible. Your procedure is good.
3 Analyze the grammar. Help with the new alignment.

Do not pause between letters or words.

4 file page shipment hearing times labor lines paper
5 manager store things health sale enough hand found

Keep your eyes on the textbook copy as you enter/return.

6 acquisition criticism grammar prejudice curriculum
7 alignment grateful privilege procedures deductible
8 analyze height apparent defendant proceed argument

15C

Goal Writing

Take two 2-minute goal writings.

Key each line once. If time allows, start again.

Determine your GWAM.

Goal: To measure timed-writing progress 5′

Cue: Key at a pace that is comfortable for you.

1′

1 We are grateful for your acquisition of the truck. 10
2 The procedure for alignment of districts is great. 20
3 His procedure is to analyze every deductible cost. 30
4 The reason is apparent; voting is their privilege. 40

| 1 | 2 | 3 | 4 | 5 | 6 | 7 | 8 | 9 | 10 |

Application: Tables
Goal: To center and key tables 27'

JOB 1   File name: L53E1   Full sheet   DS   Spaces between columns: 10   Center vertically. Use the key line for horizontal centering.

Cue: Use correct spacing below titles.

Big Ten Athletic Conference

Michigan State University	East Lansing
Northwestern University	Evanston
Ohio State University	Columbus
Purdue University	South Bend
University of Illinois	Champaign
University of Indiana	Bloomington
University of Iowa	Iowa City
University of Michigan	Ann Arbor
University of Minnesota	Minneapolis
University of Wisconsin	Madison

JOB 2   File name: L53E2   Full sheet   SS   Spaces between columns: 14   Center vertically and horizontally.

Birthdates of Famous Americans

Louis Armstrong	Musician	1900
Clara Barton	Nurse	1821
Leonard Bernstein	Composer	1918
Shirley Chisholm	Politician	1924
Walt Disney	Showman	1901
Stephen Foster	Songwriter	1826
Amelia Earhart	Aviator	1897
Ernest Hemingway	Novelist	1899

JOB 3   File name: L53E3   Full sheet   DS   Spaces between columns: 8   Center vertically and horizontally.

Principal Mountains of the United States

Mount Mckinley	Alaska	20,320 feet
Mount Whitney	California	14,494 feet
Mount Elbert	Colorado	14,433 feet
Mount Rainier	Washington	14,410 feet
Mount Shasta	California	14,162 feet
Pikes Peak	Colorado	14,110 feet
Gannett Peak	Wyoming	13,804 feet
Maunea Kea	Hawaii	13,796 feet
Kings Peak	Utah	13,528 feet
Boundary Peak	Nevada	13,143 feet
Lassen Peak	California	10,457 feet

Checkpoint: Did you use all caps in the title?

JOB 4   File name: L53E4   Full sheet   DS   Spaces between columns: 10   Center vertically and horizontally.

Key the information given in JOB 2. Use the formatting instructions given for JOB 4.

Lesson 54

M Default Settings
T SS   SM 1½" (12); 1" (10)   Tab ¶

Warmup
Goal: To strengthen keyboarding speed 5'

Key each line twice.
DS after each pair.

"pre" combinations

1 precisely pretend appreciate president predecessor premature
2 The pretty, preppy reporter from the press was very precise.
3 Don't pretend to appreciate the president's predecessor now.

| 1 | 2 | 3 | 4 | 5 | 6 | 7 | 8 | 9 | 10 | 11 | 12 |

15D

Need to Know

Goal: To learn to identify misstrokes 5′

The following examples show five additional kinds of misstrokes commonly made when keyboarding.

Extra Space   The (nex t) order will reach (you in) August.

No Space   I checked (theorder;) the goods (arehere.)

Misstroke   Please (wrote) us if you need (informarion.)

Transposition   Take (em) to the leaders of his (gruop) now.

T Strikeover   I am (familar) with the study (thg) wrote.

15E

Keyboard Practice

Goal: To key from handwritten copy 12′

Key each line twice.

DS after each pair of lines.

1   As a prominent person, she was very helpful to us.
2   Every defendant lost the argument about procedure.
3   We hope that keyboarding is in the new curriculum.
4   Her criticism was definite and very helpful to us.
5   The new tax assignment showed their keying skills.
6   Yes. I helped analyze the apparent grammar errors.
7   He is your liaison with Beneficial Life Insurance.
8   My note about the interference benefited everyone.
9   He will disappoint me; he cannot develop the film.
10   I believe that he plans to implement her decision.
11   Proceed with the new procedure to avoid criticism.
12   Those defendants accepted the practical arguments.

15F

Technique Timing

Goal: To improve keyboarding techniques 5′

Default or DS

Tab: ¶

Take two 2-minute timings.

If you finish before time is called, start again.

Keep your eyes on the textbook copy as you operate the tab.

      We are grateful to you, Mr. Long, for the helpful advice you gave about deductible taxes.

      We are hopeful that you will excuse whatever prejudice you saw at the height of your analysis. Our reasoning should now be apparent to you.

> **Checkpoint:** Did you keep your eyes on the copy *Always, Usually,* or *Seldom*?

Goal Writing

Default or DS

Take two 3-minute goal writings.

If you finish before time is called, start again.

Record your speed and accuracy.

Goal: To measure timed-writing progress 10′

	1′	3′
A very powerful feature of the electronic spreadsheet	11	4
is that it can make instant calculations once you enter	22	7
values and formulas. You can make changes or corrections in	35	12
one value and the spreadsheet will instantly recompute all	46	15
other values that are related to the one you changed.	57	19
With a spreadsheet, it is very easy to make forecasts.	68	23
The spreadsheet allows people in business to see the effects	80	27
of a price change. It may also help them to avoid problems	92	31
and be able to reach the best decisions about how to manage.	104	35

1′ | 1 | 2 | 3 | 4 | 5 | 6 | 7 | 8 | 9 | 10 | 11 | 12 | AWL
3′ | 1 | | 2 | | 3 | | 4 | | 5.7

Need to Know

Goal: To learn how to key tables 3′

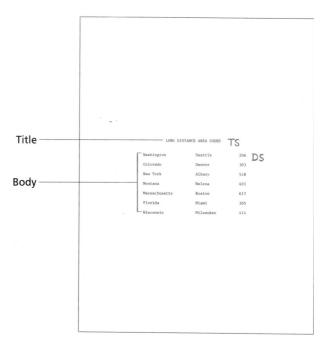

Title

Body

Tables are used in reports, letters, and memos to present a large amount of information in a little space.

1. Center tables vertically and horizontally on the page.
2. Center the title and key it in all caps. TS after the title.
3. Format the body of the table in columns. SS or DS the body.
4. Center the columns horizontally, leaving the same amount of space between columns—usually 4–12 spaces.
5. Line up word columns on the left. Line up figures on the right or at the decimal points.

Self-Check

Key the statement number and your answer: True or False.

Check your answers in Appendix C.

Goal: To review the keying of tables 5′

1. The title of a table is centered and keyed in all caps.
2. The body of a table may be single or double spaced.
3. The spaces left between the columns of a table varies within a table.
4. Columns of words are usually aligned on the left.
5. Columns of figures are usually aligned on the right or at the decimal.
6. A double space follows the title of a table.

M Default Settings
T SS   SM 2″ (12); 1½″ (10)   Tab ¶

16A

Warmup

Key each line twice.

DS after each pair of lines.

Goal: To strengthen keyboarding skills   5′

1 page correspondence directly discussed next family
2 dependent implement questionnaire attendance label
3 He will receive a questionnaire at the restaurant.
4 I believe that Zeke benefited from our attendance.

| 1 | 2 | 3 | 4 | 5 | 6 | 7 | 8 | 9 | 10 |

16B

Technique Timing

Take a 3-minute timing on each group of lines. Work on improving the technique shown.

Take another 3-minute timing on the lines for the technique that needs the most improvement.

Key each line once. If time allows, start again.

DS after each timing.

Goal: To improve keyboarding techniques   16′

Shift for capital letters with a one-two count.

1 He believes that; You will develop; Your reference
2 At the restaurant; She can describe; The label was
3 Our liaison is; Her dependents are; They benefited

Keep your elbows at your side and your arms parallel to the keyboard.

Repeat lines 1–3.

Strike the space bar with a quick, down-and-in motion.

4 lines dozen six lot proper ten terms near tell try
5 hand level once using found item major bring doing
6 entire least title welcome air final men box means

16C

Goal Writing

Take two 2-minute goal writings.

Key each line once.

If time allows, start again.

Determine your GWAM.

Goal: To measure timed-writing progress   5′

Cue: Key at a pace that is comfortable for you.

1′

1 I need to have your description of each dependent. 10
2 They will receive the new questionnaire very soon. 20
3 We recommend that you open the restaurant at noon. 30
4 Beginning in August, their attendance is required. 40

| 1 | 2 | 3 | 4 | 5 | 6 | 7 | 8 | 9 | 10 |

52G

Application: Columns

File name: L52G1

Full Sheet

DS

Goal: To center columns vertically and horizontally   18'

JOB 1

Key the columns in 52E. You have already selected the key line and determined your margins and tab stops. Determine the starting line to vertically center the columns.

JOB 2   File name: L52G2   Full sheet   DS   Spaces between columns: 4   Determine the key line. Center vertically and horizontally.

> **Cue:**   Clear tabs before setting new ones.

farther	further	quiet	quite
effect	affect	clothes	cloths
casual	causal	device	devise
desert	dessert	formally	formerly
fair	fare	feet	feat
four	for	here	hear
aisle	isle	altar	alter
brake	break	cent	sent
hole	whole	its	it's

> **Checkpoint:**   Did you use the key line to determine the margins and tab stops?

JOB 3   File name: L52G3   Full sheet   DS   Spaces between columns: 10   Center vertically and horizontally.

poet	poem	pen
painter	painting	brush
writer	novel	typewriter
lyricist	song	piano
playwright	play	stage
reporter	story	CRT
flautist	music	flute
producer	movie	theatre
potter	ceramics	wheel
mechanic	car	wrench
printer	books	press
tailor	clothes	machine

Lesson 53

M Default Settings

T SS   SM 1½" (12); 1" (10)   Tab ¶

53A

Warmup

Goal: To strengthen keyboarding skills   5'

Key each line twice. DS after each pair of lines.

Speed   1 The names of everyone who works at the site should be known.
Accuracy   2 Victor Covey received five invoices for convention services.
Number/Symbol   3 Invoices 22–348 and 23–902 (10/8 and 10/19) total $1,104.70.
Data Entry   4 2600 PRINT N;" SEAT(S) CONFIRMED ON FLIGHT ";F;" ON";M;"/";D

| 1 | 2 | 3 | 4 | 5 | 6 | 7 | 8 | 9 | 10 | 11 | 12 |

Need to Know

Goal: To learn how to identify misstrokes 6′

Proofreading, or finding misstrokes, is as important as keying accurately. You must be able to find your errors before you can correct them.

In the last two lessons you learned the most common kinds of misstrokes. From now on, identify your misstrokes when directed to do so.

After you complete a timed writing, you need to proofread your keyed text for misstrokes. Use the following guidelines when you are asked to record your speed and accuracy rates. (Practice using 16C.)

1. Count only one misstroke per word. That is, if a word has two or more misstrokes in it, count the word only once as one misstroke.

2. Treat the spacing and punctuation that follow a word as part of the word. If the spacing or punctuation after a word is incorrect, count the word as a misstroke.

Screen Copy

1. Proofread the copy on your screen.
2. Identify and record on a separate sheet of paper any words that have misstrokes.

Paper Copy

1. Proofread the copy on your paper.
2. Circle any word in which there is a misstroke. Circle the entire word, not just the letter or space that was keyed incorrectly.

Keyboard Practice

Key each line twice.

DS after each pair of lines.

Goal: To practice proper keystroking techniques 10′

1 quart quaint Quaker liquid request require quizzes
2 zero dizzy dozens frozen zoom zoological lazy whiz
3 extra next except exempt excessive exit text exams
4 brand brass brazier Brazil brave brag brace breaks
5 populate popular popcorn population poppy populace
6 attendance dependent implement questionnaire label
7 beginning describe interference receive restaurant
8 believe description benefited recommend beneficial
9 disappoint judgment reference bookkeeper embarrass

Technique Timing

Default or DS

Tab: ¶

Take two 3-minute timings.

If time allows, start again.

Goal: To improve keyboarding techniques 8′

16-1

Tab in to begin each paragraph without pausing.

In reference to your questionnaire, I believe you need to label the sections. In my judgment, the heading you use should describe each section.

I also recommend that you try to give better directions at the beginning. If the directions are not clear, you might be disappointed with the responses you receive.

settings to the ends of the scale and insert a piece of scrap paper.

2. Clear all tabs. Return the cursor/carrier.
3. Key the longest line in column 1—February.
4. Key the numbers 123456—the number of spaces to be left between columns 1 and 2.
5. Key the longest line in column 2—August.

6. Key the numbers 123456—the number of spaces to be left between columns 2 and 3.
7. Key the longest line in column 3—September.

You have now prepared a key line. When a key line has ten or more spaces between columns, key the numbers through 9; then key 0 for 10, 1 for 11, and so on until you have the desired number of spaces.

52E

Application: Key Line

File name: L52E

Determine the longest line in each column.

Input the key line. Leave 4 spaces between columns.

Goal: To prepare a key line to use in centering columns 3'

address	accessory	embarrass
accessible	happiness	assessment
suppress	occurrence	committee
accommodate	assassin	balloon
commission	misspell	repossess
burglary	belief	chaos
develop	endorse	envelope
grammar	height	perceive

Keep the document on the screen or in your typewriter for use in the activity in 52F.

> 52F

Read and Do

Goal: To learn how to use the key line to center columns 6' *52-1*

```
Left                                     Right
margin          Tab           Tab        margin
accommodate1234occurrence1234assessment
```
Key line in 52E.

1. Use one of these methods to set a left margin or a tab setting for the first column.

M *Microcomputer*

Use the automatic centering function to center the key line in 52E. Note the column/space where the left edge of the key line begins. Set a tab at this point. Column 1 starts at the "a" in accommodate. (Note: You may need to write down the tab settings as you space in from the left edge. Then use the format or layout function to set tabs.) Remember to delete the key line after you have set the tabs.

E *Electronic Typewriter*

Use the automatic centering function to center the key line in 52E. Set the left margin at the position where the centered key line begins. Column 1 starts at the "a" in accommodate.

T *Typewriter*

Move the carrier to the center of the page. Backspace once for every two characters in the key line in 52E. Set the left margin at this point. Column 1 begins at the "a" in accommodate.

2. From the position where column 1 begins, move the cursor/carrier forward once for each character in the first column of the key line, including the 4 spaces to be left between columns. Set a tab at the "o" in occurrence. Column 2 begins at this point.
3. From the tab stop for column 2, move the cursor/carrier forward once for each character in the second column of the key line plus 4 spaces. Set a tab at the "a" in assessment. Column 3 begins at this point.
4. Space to the first space after the "t" in assessment. Set the right margin at this point.

The beginning point of column 1 and the tabs for the other columns are now set.

Unit 2 / Number and Symbol Keys

Now that you have learned to key the alphabetic keys by touch, you are ready to become acquainted with the rest of the keyboard. While you continue to improve your skills on the alphabetic keys, you will learn to use the number and symbol keys.

In this unit, Lessons 17–32, you will learn to:

1. Increase your keyboarding speed and accuracy.
2. Key all number keys by touch.
3. Key the most frequently used symbol keys by touch.
4. Locate additional machine parts and use them correctly.
5. Improve techniques associated with proper keystroking and efficient use of various machine parts.
6. Figure your speed on 3-minute timed writings.
7. Continue to identify misstrokes.
8. Use correction techniques to correct misstrokes.

Micro Dictionary

cursor movement keys	special keys that allow you to move the cursor up, down, left, or right on the display screen
delete	the process of removing or omitting copy from text that has already been keyed
edit	the process of making changes in text by inserting, deleting, rearranging, or correcting errors
embedded command	an instruction that is given to a computer and often does not appear on the display screen. The instruction is usually carried out when the text is printed.
insert	the process of adding new copy to text that has already been keyed

Lesson 17

M Default Settings
T SS   SM 2" (12); 1½" (10)   Tab ¶

17A

Warmup

Key each line twice.
DS after each pair.

Identify misstrokes.

Goal: To strengthen keyboarding skills 5'

1 This is a good time of day to sit alone and dream.
2 bookkeeper eligible library separate license brief
3 We have canceled; The enclosure is; For a brochure
4 The new bookkeeper is a former employee from here.

| 1 | 2 | 3 | 4 | 5 | 6 | 7 | 8 | 9 | 10 |

52A

Warmup

Key each line twice. DS after each pair.

Confusing words: two and too

Goal: To strengthen keyboarding skills 5'

1 <u>Two</u> is the number that follows one, as in "One, two, three."
2 <u>Too</u> means more than needed, as in "Norman paid me too much."
3 <u>Too</u> can mean as well or also, as in "Vi paid too much, too."

| 1 | 2 | 3 | 4 | 5 | 6 | 7 | 8 | 9 | 10 | 11 | 12 |

52B

Accuracy Practice

DS after each group of lines.

Goal: To build keyboarding accuracy 5'

Take a 3-minute accuracy timing on the lines in 52A. If you make an error, start again. Stay on a line until you have keyed it without error.

> **Checkpoint:** How many error-free lines did you key?

52C

Technique Timing

DS

LM: 10 (10-pitch); 18 (12-pitch)

Tabs: Every 10 spaces

Key as many lines as you can in 5 minutes.

If you finish before time is called, start again.

Goal: To improve keyboarding techniques 8'

Use the tab key to move from one column to the next.

algebra	books	writing	computer
science	pencil	speech	teacher
lockers	homeroom	counselor	notebook
swimming	credits	subjects	homework
reports	reading	math	friends
principal	library	spelling	sports

52D

Read and Do

Goal: To learn how to determine and use the key line 5'

January	May	September
February	June	October
March	July	November
April	August	December
Key line February123456August123456September		

To horizontally center columns of words or figures, begin by determining the **key line.** The key line is made up of the longest line in each column and the spaces to be left between columns. Follow these steps to determine the key line.

1. Move the cursor/carrier to the left of the screen/paper. On a typewriter, move the margin

(Continued next page)

Technique Timing

Take two 3-minute timings. Work on improving the technique shown.

DS after each timing.

Goal: To improve keyboarding techniques 8′

Do not pause as you move from one line to the next.

1 similar library separate brief license serviceable
2 eligible brochure employee summarize miscellaneous
3 maintenance calendar enclosure canceled enterprise
4 mortgage superintendent careful envelope necessary

17C

New-Key Orientation

1. Locate the new key on the keyboard chart.
2. Next, locate the key on your keyboard.
3. Before keying the practice lines, read the instructions for each new key.
4. Practice the first line, returning to home-key position after making the reach to the new key.
5. Practice the second line for 2 minutes or until you can key it without looking at your hands.

Goal: To learn the location of : and ? 9′   *17-1*

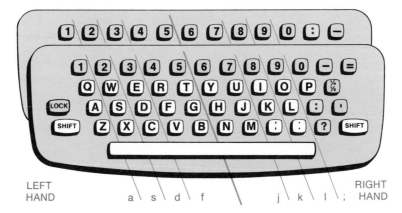

LEFT HAND   a   s   d   f   j   k   l   ;   RIGHT HAND

: Practice striking the : with the **sem** finger. On some keyboards, you have to depress the left shift key while striking the :. If so, quickly release the shift key and return the **a** finger to home-key position. Space twice after a colon used as a mark of punctuation.

1 ;: ;: ;: ;: ;: ;: ;: ;: ;: ;: ;: ;: ;:
2 Dear Sir: Dear Ms. Chin: as follows:

? Practice the reach to ? with the **sem** finger while depressing the left shift key. Quickly release the shift key and return the **a** finger to home-key position. Space twice after a question mark at the end of a sentence.

3 ;? ;? ;? ;? ;? ;? ;? ;? ;? ;? ;? ;? ;?
4 They are? She is? It is? Why? Who?

17D

Technique Timing

Take a 1-minute timing on each line. Work on improving the technique shown.

DS after each timing.

Goal: To improve keyboarding techniques 7′

Return to home-key position after making reaches to new keys.

1 Key these words: separates, eligible, enterprise.
2 Can Sue conduct? Can Wes sing? Can Rex practice?

(Continued next page)

4. Press enter/return to move the cursor to the line on which the document is to begin.
5. Key the information across the page. Use the tab key to move from one column to the next.

T *Typewriter*

1. Set the paper guide at 0.
2. Move the margin stops to the ends of the scale.

3. Clear all tab stops.
4. Set the left margin as instructed.
5. Move the carrier to the required tab positions and set tab stops.
6. Tab across the page to make sure all tabs are set.
7. Key the information across the page. Use the tab key to move from one column to the next.

51E

Project Preview

Full sheet

DS

Left margin: 10 (10-pitch); 18 (12-pitch)

Tabs: every 20 spaces

Key as much as you can in 3 minutes. If time allows, start again.

Goal: To key columns of words 5′

line 13 ↓half	Tab → moon	Tab → ward	Tab → robe
home	work	whip	lash
rain	drop	door	stop
snow	boot	golf	club
cook	book	fish	bowl

51F

Application: Columns

Goal: To key centered columns 20′

JOB 1   File name: L51F1   Full sheet   DS   Left margin 10 (10-pitch); 18 (12-pitch)   Tabs: Every 20 spaces   Center vertically.

moon	beam	road	way
kitchen	table	salt	shaker
hair	comb	bow	tie
water	bottle	freeze	ice
cowboy	boots	plastic	wrap
weather	balloon	pine	tree
wrist	watch	call	phone
yell	shout	sun	shine

JOB 2   File name: L51F2   Full sheet   DS   Left margin: 10 (10-pitch); 18 (12-pitch)   Tabs: Every 22 spaces   Center vertically.

23	234	34	432
78	789	89	987
56	567	76	765
45	456	54	543
78	432	89	398
88	887	98	987
98	988	39	398

JOB 3

File name: L51F3
Full sheet
SS

Key the information given in the PROJECT PREVIEW, 51E. Center the information vertically.

> **Checkpoint:** Is there equal space between the columns?

Take a 1-minute timing on each line.

DS after each timing.

Quickly release the shift key and return to home-key position.

3 Will Chuck attend? Will he write? Will he speak?

4 Spell these words: calendar, embarrass, mortgage.

5 Was the test: too long, too short, or just right?

> **Checkpoint:** Did you leave two spaces after the colon and question mark?

17E

Read and Do

Goal: To learn to operate the backspace key 6′   17-2

Strike the backspace key with the **sem** finger.

If your keyboard has a backspace key, it is located at the far right on the top row. The backspace key moves the cursor/carrier back one space each time it is depressed. On some microcomputers and electronic typewriters, the backspace key deletes characters as you move back through text. Follow these steps to learn to operate the backspace key.

1. Move your cursor/carrier to the left margin.
2. Key: at end
3. With the **sem** finger, strike the backspace key four times. Notice how the cursor/carrier moves back to **d**, then to **n**, next to **e**, and finally to the blank space between the two words. (These characters may be deleted by your equipment.)
4. Strike Ⓣ. Rekey the letters end, if necessary. The two words at end are now the word attend.
5. Enter/return and repeat steps 1–4.

17F

Goal Writing

Default or DS

Take two 2-minute goal writings.

Key at a pace that is comfortable for you.

If time allows, start again.

Determine your GWAM.

Goal: To measure timed-writing progress 6′

17-3
1′

Computers are playing a role of importance in	9
all our lives. Computers are used in car engines,	20
robots, home appliances, and even toys and games.	29
They are used in hospitals, banks, airports,	39
and stores. They may even be found in many of our	49
homes today.	51

| 1 | 2 | 3 | 4 | 5 | 6 | 7 | 8 | 9 | 10 | AWL 5.7 |

17G

Keyboard Practice

Key each line 3 times.

DS after each pair of lines.

Goal: To practice proper keystroking techniques 9′

1 Are these they: enclosure, similar, and separate?

2 Can you spell these words: maintenance, employee?

3 Is calendar right? Are library and license right?

4 He spelled enterprise; then he spelled bookkeeper.

5 Did you rekey: eligible, canceled, and mortgages?

51B

Speed Practice

Take a 15- or 12-second timing on each line. If you complete a line in the time allowed, go on to the next one.

Goal: To build keyboarding speed 5′

		15″	12″
1	Five managers completed the course.	28	35
2	The members of the board were all there.	32	40
3	They used three reams of paper to do the job.	36	45
4	He and Les think you are all ready to do the work.	40	50
5	The workers are expected to be at their desks by eight.	44	55

| 1 | 2 | 3 | 4 | 5 | 6 | 7 | 8 | 9 | 10 | 11 |

51C

Language Arts

Read the rule in the box at the right.

Then key each numbered sentence, supplying the correct number style.

Check your work with the key in Appendix B.

Goal: To review rules for numbers 10′

> For sums of money less than $1, use figures and the word <u>cents</u>. Use figures and a dollar sign for sums of money of $1 or more. Do not use a decimal point and ciphers (.00) with whole dollar amounts unless they appear with other sums that include both dollars and cents.
>
> **Examples:**
>
> For every dollar contributed, 10 cents is added by the company.
> Our bill was $17.30; including the tip, Phyllis paid $25.00.
> Mary received a check for $10; she bought a gift for $8.

1. Billy charged ten cents a glass for his lemonade; Ava, $.09.
2. The architect charged $10,000.00 for the drawings of the mansion.
3. Of the $300 collected, $275.28 will be used for publishing.
4. My utility bill was $131.75 this month and $300 last month.
5. A strip of stamps that costs $22 today used to cost $16.50.
6. If you collect fifteen cents from each person, we will have $23.10.
7. Mary said the bill was for ten dollars; I wrote a check for $10.75.
8. Fees for jogging are $4.00; for racquetball, $8.00; for tennis, $10.

> 51D

Need to Know

Goal: To learn how to key columns of information 5′

Information is often arranged in column format. Columns provide a more attractive format and make the copy easier to read.

M *Microcomputer*

1. Move the cursor to the first column/space on your screen.
2. Clear all tab stops, using the procedure for your software program.
3. Use the method required by your program to set new tab stops. The two most common methods of setting tab stops are:

a. Access the ruler/format line. Move the cursor to the first desired tab position. Press the appropriate key for setting tabs (usually the tab key or the letter **T**). Repeat this procedure to set the remaining tab stops.

b. Give the tab set command. When the prompt asks for a column number, key in the column number for the first tab setting. Repeat this procedure to set the remaining tab stops.

(Continued next page)

M Default Settings
T SS   SM 2" (12); 1½" (10)   Tab ¶

18A

Warmup

Key each line twice. DS after each pair.

Identify misstrokes.

Goal: To strengthen keyboarding skills 5′

```
1 Jane is apt to fix the torn flap if she can do it.
2 These withholding rates supersede all former ones.
3 Spell these words:  withholding, excellent, yield.
4 That omission was not noticeable to Zelda Jackson.
```
| 1 | 2 | 3 | 4 | 5 | 6 | 7 | 8 | 9 | 10 |

18B

New-Key Orientation

1. Locate the new key on the keyboard chart.
2. Next, locate the key on your keyboard.
3. Before keying the practice lines, read the instructions for each new key.
4. Practice the first line, returning to home-key position after making the reach to the new key.
5. Practice the second line for 2 minutes or until you can key it without looking at your hands.

Goal: To learn the location of ' **and** - 10′

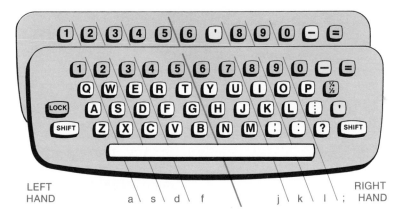

 KEYBOARD 1: Practice the reach to ' with the **sem** finger. Keep your other fingers in home-key position.

```
1 ;' ;' ;' ;' ;' ;' ;' ;' ;' ;' ;' ;' ;'
2 it's she's you're can't don't couldn't
```

KEYBOARD 2: Practice the reach to ' with the **j** finger while depressing the left shift key. Quickly release the shift key and return the **a** finger to home-key position.

```
3 j' j' j' j' j' j' j' j' j' j' j' j' j'
4 won't don't I'm can't shouldn't you're
```

 Practice the reach to - with the **sem** finger. Keep your other fingers in home-key position. Do not lift your wrist as you strike -.

```
5 ;- ;- ;- ;- ;- ;- ;- ;- ;- ;- ;- ;- ;-
6 up-to-date four-page one-way well-read
```

5. Start keying on the 27th line from the top edge of the screen/paper. If you are using a microcomputer, remember to include the default top margin as a part of your count down to the 27th line.

50F

Self-Check

Default or DS

Key the statement and your answer: True or False.

Check your answers in Appendix C.

Goal: To review vertical centering 5′

1. The first step in determining the correct starting line is to count the number of used lines.
2. A standard sheet of paper is 11½″ long.
3. To leave one blank line between printed lines, double space.
4. Disregard fractions when subtracting used lines from available lines.
5. There are 65 lines available on a standard sheet of paper.
6. To leave 10 blank lines for the top margin, begin keying text on line 11.

50G

Application: Centering

Goal: To center lines vertically and horizontally 15′

JOB 1   File name: L50G1   Full sheet   DS

Key the example in 50E for which you determined the starting line. Center each line horizontally.

JOB 2   File name: L50G2   Full sheet   DS
          Center vertically and horizontally.

The Executive Management Club
Is Pleased to Announce
the Appointment of
John L. Quincy, III
to the Office of President
Effective July 1, 19--

JOB 3   File name: L50G3   Full sheet   DS
          Center vertically and horizontally.

Office Automation, Inc.
invites you to interview for
expanded employment opportunities
in information processing
Greater Boston Technical Plaza
Suites 1001 and 1005
May 15-18, 19--
Appointments necessary
Telephone 675-4003 before May 10

Lesson 51

M Default Settings

T SS   SM 1½″ (12); 1″ (10)   Tab ¶

51A

Warmup

Key each line twice. DS after each pair.

Two- and three-letter combinations

Goal: To strengthen keyboarding skills 5′

1 as an am if it is to do go so no on of or we he me us up bee
2 all see any fee too gee the few was for add sad aid did toes
3 now who out are not can one but may two use day per due pays

| 1 | 2 | 3 | 4 | 5 | 6 | 7 | 8 | 9 | 10 | 11 | 12 |

Technique Timing

Take a 1-minute timing on each line. Work on improving the technique shown.

DS after each timing.

Goal: To improve keyboarding techniques   9'

Return to home-key position after making reaches to new keys.

```
1 don't won't isn't wouldn't wasn't hadn't shouldn't
2 six-page memo; up-to-date report; well-read person
```

Keep your eyes on the textbook copy.

Repeat lines 1 and 2.

Do not move your wrist up as you reach to ⊝.

```
3 easy-to-read papers; simple-to-complex assignments
4 The sales quota is a do-or-die effort on his part.
5 The red-faced woman is Kate's part-time secretary.
```

| 1 | 2 | 3 | 4 | 5 | 6 | 7 | 8 | 9 | 10 |

18D

Apply the Rule

Read the rule and the example.

Then key the sentences in the *Application* section. As you key them, use the correct spacing before and after the hyphen.

Goal: To learn the spacing around the hyphen   7'

Rule

1. Do not space before or after the hyphen.
2. A dash is made by keying two hyphens. Do not space between the hyphens or before and after the dash.

Example

```
His hat--an out-of-date style--was not attractive.
```

Application

```
1 The up-to-date report--as you know--was completed.
2 That day--Monday--is a happier-than-ever occasion.
3 Your two-page memos have been found--to my relief.
4 Mr. Tree--the mild-mannered diplomat--met Marilyn.
```

18E

Read and Do

Do each activity to the right as you read it.

Goal: To learn to key in all capital letters   4'

To key a series of letters or words in all capital letters (ALL CAPS), use the caps lock or shift lock key. On some software, ALL CAPS is a special command.

1. Locate and depress the caps lock or shift lock key (usually to the left of Ⓐ)) or use the ALL CAPS command.
2. Key: FBLA
3. Release the caps lock or shift lock key or end the ALL CAPS command. Then, enter/return.

(Continued next page)

Need to Know   **Goal: To learn about page layout** 5′   *50-1*

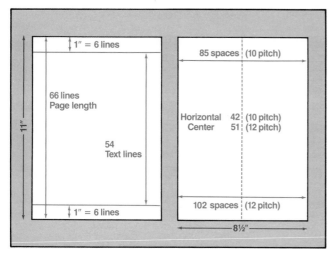

Vertical layout   Horizontal layout

Before a document can be printed, certain decisions must be made about the **page layout** or the placement of the document on the page. The decisions involve vertical and horizontal placement of the document.

Vertical Layout

A standard sheet of paper is 8½″ wide and 11″ long. Total page length includes 66 lines. With 1-inch top and bottom margins, a total of 12 lines, the number of lines available for text is 54.

Horizontal Layout

In 10 pitch, there are 85 spaces from the left edge of the paper to the right edge. In 12 pitch, there are 102 spaces available. A margin setting of 10-75 (10 pitch) or 12-90 (12 pitch) gives 1-inch side margins or a **line length** of 65 characters (10 pitch); 78 characters (12 pitch). The center of the page is 42 for 10 pitch and 51 for 12 pitch.

M *Microcomputer*

With many software programs, a **ruler line** is displayed across the top or the bottom of the screen while you are keying or editing a document. This line may show the current left and right margins and tab settings. To make changes in these settings, use the keys or appropriate **format commands** required by your program.

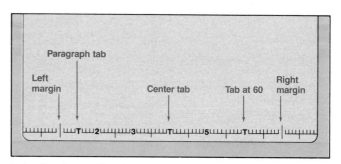

Ruler line for an 80-column screen.

Read and Do   **Goal: To learn how to vertically center lines** 5′   *50-2*

1 Astor Industries
2
3 Extends a
4
5 Welcome to
6
7 OUR LEADERS OF
8
9 TOMORROW
10
11 Redfern's
12
13 Graduates

1. Count the number of printed and blank lines in the copy to be keyed at the left (1 blank line is left when you DS lines).

   13 used lines

2. Subtract the total number of used lines from 66.

   66
   −13 used lines
   ‾‾53 unused lines (top/bottom margin)

3. Divide by 2. Disregard any fraction.

   53 ÷ 2 = 26 blank lines

4. Add 1 line. (The first line of text will be on line 27, leaving 26 blank lines for the top margin.)

   26 + 1 = 27 (first line of text)

(Continued next page)

Do each activity to the right as you read it.

4. Depress the caps lock or shift lock key or use the ALL CAPS command.
5. Key: DATA PROCESSING, Seventh Edition, releasing the caps lock or shift lock key or ending the ALL CAPS command to key Seventh Edition.
6. Key: I can key ALL CAPS. Depress the caps lock or shift lock key or use the ALL CAPS command to key ALL CAPS.
7. Release the caps lock or shift lock key or end the ALL CAPS command. Then, enter/return.

18F

Keyboard Practice

Key each line 3 times.

DS after each group of lines.

Goal: To practice proper keystroking techniques 8′

> Cue: Use the caps/shift lock or ALL CAPS command.

1 She plans to attend meetings of UNICEF and UNESCO.
2 The WAAC, the WAF, and the WAC were in the parade.
3 The well-equipped truck's problems are noticeable.
4 Jared's none-too-competent committee was thorough.
5 The top-rated team in the NBA is from Judy's town.

18G

Technique Timing

Default or DS

Take two 3-minute timings.

If time allows, start again.

Goal: To improve keyboarding techniques 7′   *18-1*

Do not pause as you move from one paragraph to the next.

    The meeting was not canceled but was held in the library. I will summarize it in a brief manner as a separate enclosure in this letter.

    As a new employee, do not be embarrassed about missing the meeting. Company bookkeepers were not eligible to attend.

Lesson 19

M Default Settings
T SS   SM 2″ (12); 1½″ (10)   Tab ¶

19A

Warmup

Key each line twice. DS after each pair.

Identify misstrokes.

Goal: To strengthen keyboarding skills 5′

1 Can he handle the problem if she is not with them?
2 The jury--as you predicted--did high-quality work.
3 Vice-President Oveson's all-steel desk isn't here.
4 Sue's reason--and mine also--has to do with money.

| 1 | 2 | 3 | 4 | 5 | 6 | 7 | 8 | 9 | 10 |

50A

Warmup

Goal: To strengthen keyboarding skills 5′

Key each line twice. DS after each pair of lines.

Speed 1 The key social work may end if they turn down the usual aid.
Accuracy 2 Cass tried various copiers to find one that suits her needs.
Number/Symbol 3 He's sure questions 36–40 are from Chapter 29 (pp. 481–508).
Data Entry 4 The math student was certain that A < B and C < D and J > K.

| 1 | 2 | 3 | 4 | 5 | 6 | 7 | 8 | 9 | 10 | 11 | 12 |

50B

Goal Writing

Default or DS

Take two 3-minute goal writings.

If you finish before time is called, start again.

Record your speed and accuracy.

Goal: To measure timed-writing progress 10′

	1′	3′
The role of a manager is about the same in any type of	11	4
organization and requires special talents that have to be	23	8
developed through a lot of practice. A manager will bring	35	12
together the efforts of employees to reach the goals of the	47	16
organization. Reducing costs may be one of the goals the	58	19
organization wants to reach. In order to reach that goal, a	70	23
good manager must direct the employees. A good manager will	83	28
know how to motivate the employees. Good communication is	95	32
also essential if the manager is to be effective.	104	35

1′ | 1 | 2 | 3 | 4 | 5 | 6 | 7 | 8 | 9 | 10 | 11 | 12 | AWL
3′ | 1 | 2 | 3 | 4 | 5.7

50C

Keyboard Composition

Answer each question with a complete sentence.

Do not correct errors.

Goal: To compose at the keyboard 5′

1. How many words can you key in a minute?
2. Which do you like more, Technique Timings or Goal Writings?
3. What other business classes are you enrolled in now?
4. Are you keyboarding on a microcomputer or a typewriter?
5. What are some of the objects in your classroom?
6. What ways do you plan to use your keyboarding skills?
7. How would you describe your school?
8. How many people are in your family?
9. Would you like to be younger or older than you are now?
10. If you could meet a famous person, who would it be?

Technique Timing

Take two 2-minute timings.

Key each line once. Repeat if time allows.

Goal: To improve keyboarding techniques 5′

Keep your eyes on the textbook copy.

1 supersede category equivalent noticeable temporary

2 equipped committee occasion occurrence comparative

3 competent exaggerate excellent withholding yielded

4 envelope necessitate thoroughly carefully omission

> **Checkpoint:** Did you look up fewer times on the second timing?

New-Key Orientation

1. Locate the key on the keyboard chart.
2. Next, locate the key on your keyboard.
3. Before keying the practice lines, read the instructions for each new key.
4. Practice the first line, returning to home-key position after making the reach to the new key.
5. Practice the second line for 2 minutes or until you can key it without looking at your hands.

Goal: To learn the location of " and _ 8′

19-1

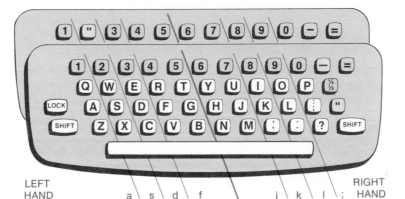

LEFT HAND a s d f j k l ; RIGHT HAND

 KEYBOARD 1: Practice the reach to " with the **sem** finger while depressing the left shift key. Keep your other fingers in home-key position.

1 ;" ;" ;" ;" ;" ;" ;" ;" ;" ;" ;" ;" ;"

2 "his" "was" "the" "she" "duty" "water"

KEYBOARD 2: Practice the reach to " with the **s** finger while depressing the right shift key. Keep your other fingers in home-key position.

3 s" s" s" s" s" s" s" s" s" s" s" s" s"

4 "she" "new" "way" "run" "stay" "asked"

 KEYBOARD 1: Practice the reach to _ with the **sem** finger while depressing the left shift key. Keep your other fingers in home-key position. For line 6, key the word, backspace to the beginning of the word, and then underscore it. Note: If you have automatic word underscore or if you need a special command to underscore, skip lines 5 and 6 and go on to 19D.

5 ;_ ;_ ;_ ;_ ;_ ;_ ;_ ;_ ;_ ;_ ;_ ;_ ;_

6 I; is; no; yes; can; okay; joke; your;

Self-Check

Goal: To review line spacing 4'

1. When you DS lines of text, ____ blank line is left between the printed lines.
2. When you QS lines of text, ____ blank lines are left between the printed lines.
3. When you SS lines of text, ____ blank lines are left between the printed lines.
4. When you TS lines of text, ____ blank lines are left between the printed lines.

49F

Application: Centering

Goal: To center lines horizontally 18'

JOB 1

M

File name: L49F1
Default top margin

T

Full sheet
1-inch top margin

Center each line horizontally.

Cue: Follow the spacing indicated to set off the information contained in the document.

PROFESSIONAL COMPUTER USER SEMINAR TS

Parsons Business Institute

4500 Amplex Avenue

Des Moines, IA 50316 DS

July 10–11, 19––

9 a.m.–5 p.m. DS

Cost: $150 per participant DS

Reservations: (515) 363–1200

JOB 2 **M** File name: L49F2   Default top margin
T Full sheet   1-inch top margin / DS
Center each line horizontally.

(FEATURES OF THE₃ DICTIONARY)

A style manual
A Guide ᴸᶜ To Pronunciation
Biographical Entries
Geographical
Entries
Common Abbreviations
A guide to word division
Listing of colleges and universities

JOB 3 **M** File name: L49F3   Default top margin
T Full sheet   1-inch top margin / DS
Center each line horizontally.

American Athletes

Tyrus Raymond Cobb
Robert Bruce Mathias
Wilma Glodean Rudolph
George Herman Ruth
James Francis Thorpe
Mildred Ella Zaharias

Checkpoint: Did you TS after the title?

Read and Do   Goal: To learn to underscore using commands 5'   *19-2*

M *Microcomputer*

Underscoring may require an embedded command to the printer on some software packages. To underscore, begin the command before keying the first letter to be underscored, and end the command after the last letter to be underscored. The underscore may not show on your screen, but it will appear in the printed copy.

For example, when you key text to be underscored, it may appear on the screen as: *Gone with the Wind*. However, the same line will print: Gone with the Wind.

Determine the appropriate method to underscore for your equipment. Then do the following:

1. Key the following, inserting the underscore commands at the beginning and end: The Wall Street Journal.
2. Look at your screen. Notice whether or not the codes for the underscore appear.
3. Print the keyed line. It should appear as: The Wall Street Journal.

E *Electronic Typewriters*

Some electronic typewriters have an automatic underscore feature. By pressing a key or using a special command, a word or series of words will be underscored automatically as you key text.

Determine the appropriate method to underscore on your equipment. Then do the following:

1. Key the following, inserting the underscore commands at the beginning and end: The Wall Street Journal.
2. Look at the line on your paper. It should appear as: The Wall Street Journal.

19E

Technique Timing   Goal: To improve keyboarding techniques 8'

Take a 1-minute timing on each line. Work on improving the technique shown.

DS after each timing.

Return to home-key position after making the reach to the new keys.

1 "Yes," said Michael, "we have need for a new car."
2 We hope to get an order; we shall ship it by rail.

Keep your eyes on the textbook copy.

Repeat lines 1 and 2.

Use a one-two count when using the shift keys.

3 The supervisor said, "Get this in the mail today."
4 Janet will surely have to read Gone with the Wind.

19F

Need to Know   Goal: To learn how to use double word scales 3'

Beginning with this lesson, you will take 3-minute goal writings. The word scales shown are *double* word scales; that is, they give GWAM for both 1-minute and 3-minute timings. Look at the word scales in 19G. The 1-minute scales at the side and bottom are printed in blue. The 3-minute scales are printed in black.

On 3-minute goal writings, use the 3-minute side and bottom word scales. First, find the cumulative word count in the *3-minute* side word scale for the last complete line you keyed. Then, use the *3-minute* bottom word scale to determine the number of words in any incomplete line. Add these two numbers for your 3-minute GWAM.

Need to Know
Goal: To learn about spacing between lines of text 3′

Single-Spaced Lines	Double-Spaced Lines	Triple-Spaced Lines	Quadruple-Spaced Lines
1 Rushmore School SS 2 Football Jamboree 3 October 9, 1 p.m. 4 Rushmore Stadium	1 Rushmore School DS 2 3 Football Jamboree 4 5 October 9, 1 p.m. 6 7 Rushmore Stadium	1 Rushmore School TS 2 3 4 Football Jamboree 5 6 7 October 9, 1 p.m. 8 9 10 Rushmore Stadium	1 Rushmore School QS 2 3 4 5 Football Jamboree 6 7 8 9 October 9, 1 p.m. 10 11 12 13 Rushmore Stadium
When you SS, *no blank lines* are left between the printed lines.	When you DS, *one blank line* is left between the printed lines.	When you TS, *two blank lines* are left between the printed lines.	When you QS, *three blank lines* are left between the printed lines.

Read and Do
Goal: To learn how changing margins affects text 15′

Line lengths or left and right margins determine the amount of white space that frames your printed document. As you know, line lengths and margins may be changed to fit the format you are using. In the exercises that follow, you will see how text is affected by margin changes.

M *Microcomputer*

Your software program has default margin settings that may be changed in one of two ways:

1. By entering a left or right margin command.
2. By accessing the print menu.

Determine the appropriate method of changing margins on your equipment. Then complete the three exercises in the second column. Print the documents when you have completed Exercise 3.

On some equipment, the changes in line length may not appear on the screen. You will see the results only when you print the document.

T *Typewriter*

Determine the appropriate method of changing left and right margins on your equipment. (See page xiv.) Then, complete the following exercises.

Exercise 1: File name: L49D1
Set SM: 25(L), 75(R). Key the following text.

To set microcomputer margins is easy once you have mastered the language of the prompts. Such terms as "column" and "mode" may seem very confusing at first.

Exercise 2: File name: L49D2 (if needed)
Set SM: 30(L), 70(R). Key the following text.

Don't let the language confuse you. Use the manual that comes with your equipment. You will refer to it less often as you become more familiar with your equipment.

Exercise 3: File name: L49D3 (if needed)
Set SM: 35(L), 65(R). Key the following text.

The more you use the equipment, the more functions you will want to learn. Using your computer becomes a habit!

Your copy should look similar to the following illustrations.

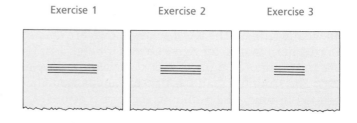

Exercise 1   Exercise 2   Exercise 3

Goal Writing

Goal: To measure timed-writing progress 10'

Default or DS

Take two 3-minute goal writings.

Key at a pace that is comfortable for you.

If time allows, start again.

Determine your GWAM.

		1'	3'
Finding just the right software for the job		9	3
to be done can be quite challenging. Dozens of		19	6
programs are now available for each of the most		28	9
popular applications. A number of magazines and		38	13
other print items rate software. You may want to		48	16
consult one or more of them when you choose a new		58	19
program. You certainly should review the program		68	23
thoroughly before you buy it.		74	25

1' | 1 | 2 | 3 | 4 | 5 | 6 | 7 | 8 | 9 | 10 | AWL
3' | 1 | 2 | 3 | 5.7

19H

Keyboard Practice

Goal: To practice proper keystroking techniques 6'   19-3

Default or DS

Key the two paragraphs. If time allows, start again.

Identify misstrokes.

> **Cue:** Keep your eyes on the textbook copy when operating the enter/return.

Writers often must determine if they should use the word affect or the word effect in their writing.

The simplest procedure to follow in choosing the correct word is to determine the part of speech needed. Do you require a noun or a verb? The word effect is appropriate if a noun is needed. If a verb is needed, affect is usually correct.

Lesson 20

M Default Settings
T SS   SM 2" (12); 1½" (10)   Tab ¶

20A

Warmup

Goal: To strengthen keyboarding skills 5'

Key each line twice. DS after each pair.

Identify misstrokes.

1 The usual penalty paid by the audit firm is small.
2 The effect--as I predicted--was a four-page issue.
3 James said, "Wasn't one group affected--the NLRB?"
4 Its effects are two: one-day service and quality.

| 1 | 2 | 3 | 4 | 5 | 6 | 7 | 8 | 9 | 10 |

Application: Centering

Goal: To key centered projects with headings 14'

JOB 1 **M** File name: L48G1   Default top margin
T Full sheet   1-inch top margin / DS
Center each line horizontally.

> **Cue:** Center and key the title in all caps. TS after the title.

Sources of College Information

Letters of inquiry
Library copies of college catalogs
Alumni among family and friends
Teachers and guidance counselors
Attendance at college nights
Campus visits
College recruiting films

JOB 2 **M** File name: L48G2   Default top margin
T Full sheet   1-inch top margin / DS
Center each line horizontally.

Reinforcing Keyboarding Techniques

Arrange desk and work area
Place copy to right of keyboard
Keep eyes on copy
Keep arms close to sides
Keep feet flat on floor
Curve your fingers
Proofread copy or screen display carefully

> **Checkpoint:** Did you center and key the title in all caps with a TS after it?

Lesson 49

M Default Settings
T SS   SM 1½" (12); 1" (10)   Tab ¶

49A

Warmup

Key each line twice.
DS after each pair.

Confusing words: its and it's

Goal: To strengthen keyboarding skills 5'

1 It's is the contraction that can be used to replace "it is."
2 Its is a pronoun indicating possession or "belonging to it."
3 If it's not the contraction for it is, it's the pronoun its.

| 1 | 2 | 3 | 4 | 5 | 6 | 7 | 8 | 9 | 10 | 11 | 12 |

49B

Accuracy Practice

DS after each group of lines.

Goal: To build keyboarding accuracy 5'

Take a 3-minute accuracy timing on the lines in 49A. If you make an error, start again. Stay on a line until you have keyed it without error.

> **Checkpoint:** How many error-free lines did you key?

20B

Technique Timing

Take two 2-minute timings on each group of lines. Work on improving the technique shown.

If time allows, start again.

DS after each timing.

M Keep 20B on the screen to use in 20C.

Goal: To improve keyboarding techniques 14′

Keep your eyes on the copy as you key hyphens and dashes.

1 I will advise you when our open—stock sale begins.
2 Our advice——and it is advice only——is to sell now.
3 I advise you to seek high—level advice from Jones.

Keep wrists low, but not touching the keyboard.

4 The jeep is serviceable, but it needs maintenance.
5 That license is similar, but it has been canceled.
6 The bookkeeper sent this mortgage to that library.

Key easy stroke combinations rapidly; slow down for difficult stroke combinations.

7 manual method nature road save checks machines its
8 teachers told worked brought code enjoyed valuable
9 informed indeed move persons release accounts late

| 1 | 2 | 3 | 4 | 5 | 6 | 7 | 8 | 9 | 10 |

> 20C **M**

Read and Do

Goal: To learn to move the cursor through text 6′   20-1

Cursor movement keys are found on most microcomputers. These keys are usually marked with arrows. Cursor movement may also be a special software function requiring the use of keys other than those marked with arrows. Cursor movement keys allow you to move the cursor up, down, left, or right. These keys also allow you to scroll through text.

Determine the cursor movement keys for your software or equipment. Then, using the last two lines of text in 20B, complete these activities:

1. Move the cursor up to the i in informed.
2. Move the cursor right to the i in indeed.
3. Move the cursor up to the t in told.
4. Move the cursor left to the s in teachers.
5. Move the cursor down and to the right across the line to the space after the e in late.
6. Operate your enter/return two times.

20D

Keyboard Practice

Key each line 3 times.

DS after each group of lines.

Goal: To practice proper keystroking techniques 8′

> **Cue: Use correct spacing after punctuation marks.**

1 Do you think the best gymnast is Jon, Cal, or Lee?
2 Is F. K. Simmons here? What about Ray M. Western?
3 We are finished. They can do the report tomorrow.
4 Tell Harris to see me; I will advise him properly.
5 Who won? Who lost? I don't know; ask the others.

M **E**

Automatic centering

T

Tab: Center

DS

Take two 3-minute timings.

If you finish before time is called, start again.

Goal: To improve techniques for centering copy   8′

Cue: Key *p.m.* without spacing.

Future Business Leaders of America

Requests the Honor of Your Presence

at the

Fourth Annual Employer Appreciation Banquet

Wednesday, April 23

6:30 p.m.

Country Dinner Playhouse

Arapahoe Road and Clayton Lane

Portland, Maine

48E

Need to Know

Refer to the illustration at the right as you read about the format for headings and titles.

Goal: To learn how to format headings and titles   3′

A heading or title identifies the information that it introduces.

1. Center the heading or title horizontally.
2. Key the heading or title in all caps.
3. Triple space (TS) after the heading or title.
4. Double space (DS) or single space (SS) between the other lines as indicated in the directions.

48F

**Project
Preview**

 M

File name: L48F
Default top margin

 T

Full sheet
1-inch top margin

Center each line horizontally.

Goal: To key a centered project with a heading   7′   48-1

Key as much as you can in 5 minutes. If you finish before time is called, start again.

THE CARE AND HANDLING OF DISKETTES TS

Do not touch the surface DS

Do not bend diskette DS

Avoid smoke and excessive dust DS

Avoid using paper clips DS

Maintain a constant temperature DS

Keep away from magnetized items DS

Use only felt tip pens to write on diskettes

20E

Apply the Rule

Read the rule and the example.

Then key the sentences in the *Application* section. As you key them, use the correct spacing.

Goal: To learn the spacing before and after quotation marks 8′

Rule

1. Do not space between quotation marks and the copy within them.
2. When quotation marks follow punctuation, use the spacing that applies to the mark of punctuation.

Example

He said, "I will." "I am unable to go," she said.

Application

1 "The plan of action," he said, "is to do the job."
2 Joe said, "Get the job done." I did what I could.
3 "Buy low; sell high," said Sue. "That's my rule."
4 Put these in quotes: "few," "once," and "always."
5 Sarah was shocked. "You're kidding!" she shouted.
6 Barbara said, "My job is to get the project done!"
7 "When," Harry said, "do you plan to call Richard?"

20F

Technique Timing

Take two 1-minute timings on each line.

DS after each timing.

Goal: To improve keyboarding techniques 9′

Key handwritten copy without pausing.

1 Michelle is proficient in keying handwritten copy.
2 Twenty people made their last-minute reservations.
3 The blue-gray suit looks better than the rust one.
4 The up-to-date summary of your meeting is concise.

Lesson 21

M Default Settings
T SS   SM 2″ (12); 1½″ (10)   Tab ¶

21A

Warmup

Key each line twice. DS after each pair.

Identify misstrokes.

Goal: To strengthen keyboarding skills 5′

1 She said they wish to visit downtown and the lake.
2 Quinn said, "Has anyone read The Laughable Clown?"
3 Any one of the following will do: SE, SW, or SSW.
4 Is anyone's birthday on the same day as Cameron's?

| 1 | 2 | 3 | 4 | 5 | 6 | 7 | 8 | 9 | 10 |

Lesson 48

48A

Warmup

Key each line twice.
DS after each pair.

"th" combinations

Goal: To strengthen keyboarding skills   5'

1   Theola Thoma thanked the theater watchers for their therapy.
2   The thin, thankful thief escaped through the three thickets.
3   Throughout the third month Harold was thatching three roofs.

| 1 | 2 | 3 | 4 | 5 | 6 | 7 | 8 | 9 | 10 | 11 | 12 |

48B

Speed Practice

Take a 15- or 12-second timing on each line. If you complete a line in the time allowed, go on to the next one.

Goal: To build keyboarding speed   5'

GWAM

	15"	12"
1 Lorenzo received $137.00 from Lois.	28	35
2 Does she think that 92% is a good score?	32	40
3 The 60 units will be shipped to you on May 9.	36	45
4 On April 2, we sent you our order for 89 fixtures.	40	50
5 Mr. Johnson said he would need four 250-page notebooks.	44	55

| 1 | 2 | 3 | 4 | 5 | 6 | 7 | 8 | 9 | 10 | 11 |

48C

Language Arts

Read the rule in the box at the right.

Then key each numbered sentence, supplying the correct number style.

Check your work with the key in Appendix B.

Goal: To review rules for numbers   8'

> Use figures for decimals, fractions, and percentages. Use the percent symbol (%) or the word *percent*.
>
> **Examples:**
>
> The figure of 0.272765 was quoted by the bank as a guide.
> That store allows a 7 percent discount on all cash purchases.
> The partners had ⅓, ½, and ⅙ interests in the business.
> Municipal bonds may carry interest rates of 6%, 7%, 8%, and more.

1. We were told that the interest rate for savings was six percent.
2. Mary Lou was told to use 3.1416 in order to solve the problem.
3. The stock moved from 9⅜ to 16⅜ before dropping to four and ⅞.
4. Mrs. Ray said that over sixteen percent of the workers were absent.
5. We were quoted rates of six percent, 7%, eight %, and 9% by different banks.
6. To add one half and ³⁄₁₃, you must first find a common denominator.
7. Mr. Pang said the average time spent on the job was two point three years.
8. Nearly seventy % of the students in my class failed the test.

Speed Practice

Goal: To build keyboarding speed 6'

Take a 20- or 15-second timing on each line. If you complete a line in the time allowed, go on to the next one.

> **Cue:** Push to improve your speed. Don't be concerned about misstrokes.

GWAM

| | 20' | **15'** |

1 He is delivering a new copier.   18 | 24

2 He would like to buy eight of them.   21 | 28

3 We are pleased to sell you the new bike.   24 | 32

4 The train's engine will be shipped in August.   27 | 36

| 1 | 2 | 3 | 4 | 5 | 6 | 7 | 8 | 9 |

> **Checkpoint:** Were you able to concentrate on improving your keyboarding speed all of the time?

21C

Read and Do

Goal: To learn how to correct misstrokes 5'

21-1

Keying information accurately is important. Misstrokes and other input errors do happen, however. The important thing is to find these errors and correct them.

M Microcomputers

To correct misstrokes within a word, most software programs allow you to replace the incorrect characters by keying over them. Some programs may require you to *delete* the incorrect characters before or after keying the corrections. Review the delete instructions for your program. Then do the following:

1. At the left of your screen, key teh keyboard.
2. Position the cursor under the e in teh.
3. Strike the letter h.
4. The cursor will move to the letter h. At that point, strike the letter e.

T Typewriters with Correction Keys

To correct misstrokes on a typewriter with a backspace correction key, operate the backspace correction key to delete the incorrect characters. Then, rekey the correct characters.

1. At the left margin, key teh keyboard.
2. Use the backspace key to position the carrier to the right of the letter h (the carrier should be under the space).
3. Operate the backspace correction key to delete the letter h.

4. Operate the backspace correction key again to delete the letter e.
5. Key the letters h and e.

Note: With some backspace correction keys, it may be necessary to strike over the incorrect letters to delete them.

T Typewriters without Correction Keys

On typewriters without correction keys, use special correction paper to correct misstrokes.

1. At the left margin, key teh keyboard.
2. Position the carrier under the e in teh.
3. Place correction paper over the misstroke, chalky side against the paper.
4. Strike over the e.
5. Position the carrier under the h.
6. Place correction paper over the misstroke and strike over the h.
7. Remove the correction paper.
8. Backspace two times to the space beside the t.
9. Key the correct letters h and e.

Read and Do   Goal: To learn how to use an automatic centering function   10'

In Lesson 46, you learned the backspace method for centering words and lines horizontally. However, your equipment may have an **automatic centering** function.

M Microcomputer

1. Automatic centering may be done by one of two methods. Determine the appropriate method for your equipment:
   a. Enter a centering command. For example, one program uses ^ OC.
   b. Use a Code or Command key in combination with a dual-function key. For example, one program uses the Code + C.
2. Move the cursor to the left side of the screen.
3. Follow the steps for automatic centering on your equipment. Key the text that is to be centered.

E Electronic Typewriter

1. Make sure the paper guide is at 0.
2. Move the margin settings to the left and right edges of the paper.
3. Clear all tab stops.
4. Set a tab stop at center. The center of a standard-size sheet of paper is 42 for 10 pitch and 51 for 12 pitch.
5. Follow the steps required for automatic centering on your typewriter. The most common procedure includes these steps:
   a. Set left and right margins.
   b. Tab to center, if necessary.
   c. Use one of these methods: (1) Hold down the Center key; (2) Hold down the Code or Command key while depressing the key for centering, usually the **c**.
   d. Key the word or line to be centered.
   e. Press the return to print centered text.

47E

Application: Centering   Goal: To horizontally center and key lines   20'

JOB 1   File name: L47E1   Full sheet   DS
Center each line horizontally.

```
           Horizontal centering is easy
               Tab or space to center
         Backspace once for two characters
             Key when backspacing ends
             Keep your eyes on the copy
```

JOB 2   File name: L47E2   Full sheet   DS
Center each line horizontally.

```
         To become a superior employee
                Be a self-starter
         'Develop a positive attitude
             Assume responsibility
                  Be flexible
             Listen very carefully
```

JOB 3   File name: L47E3   Full sheet   DS
Center each line horizontally.

Developing decision-making ability involves
Identifying the problem
Gathering the facts
Determining possible solutions
Choosing the best solution
Evaluating the solution

JOB 4   File name: L47E4   Full sheet   DS
Center each line horizontally.

A job interviewer may ask you about
Your past work experience and education
Your absentee record from school or a job
Your ability to get along with others
Why you want the job

Checkpoint: Did you ignore single characters left at the end of a line?

Technique Timing

Take two 3-minute timings on each group of lines. Work on improving the technique shown.

DS after each timing.

Goal: To improve keyboarding techniques 14'

Keep your eyes on the textbook copy.

1 Everyone——and I mean everyone——is welcome to come.
2 Five-State Motor Lines can buy custom-built autos.
3 Has every one of the specifications been verified?
4 The discount that everyone got is not the maximum.
5 The principal's concern is that of low-cost books.

Key easy-stroke combinations rapidly; slow down for difficult combinations.

6 We will lose the game if anyone gets ill tomorrow.
7 Every one of us will lose a friend if John leaves.
8 If any one of the principles is unclear, see Mary.
9 Every one of the principles will be covered today.
10 Set him loose and I cannot lose the football game.

21E

Goal Writing

Default or DS

Take two 3-minute goal writings.

Key at a pace that is comfortable for you.

If time allows, start again.

Determine your GWAM.

Goal: To measure timed-writing progress 10'

	1'	3'
Computer disks should always be handled and	9	3
stored properly if they are to have long, useful	19	6
lives. When you label disks, don't write directly	29	10
on them. Write on the sleeve, or you may write on	39	13
a separate label.	43	14
Never leave disks in the drive when they are	52	17
not in use. Keep them away from electrical appli-	62	21
ances. Don't touch their surfaces. If at all	71	24
possible, store them in storage boxes.	79	26

1' | 1 | 2 | 3 | 4 | 5 | 6 | 7 | 8 | 9 | 10 | AWL
3' | 1 | 2 | 3 | 5.7

21F

Keyboard Practice

Default or DS

Key the paragraph to the right twice using word wrap or the margin signal to determine line endings.

Goal: To practice proper keystroking techniques 10'

Choosing between everyone as one word and every one as two words is relatively simple. Select two words, every one, if a prepositional phrase beginning with "of" follows it. For example, in the sentence, "Will every one of you attend," key every one as two words because "of you" follows every one.

(Continued next page)

Lesson 47

47A

Warmup

Goal: To strengthen keyboarding skills 5′

Key each line twice. DS after each pair of lines.

Speed 1 `If they make such a visit, it may end a fight for the title.`
Accuracy 2 `Violet reads the meters on the oil heaters in the warehouse.`
Number/Symbol 3 `Key:  #138 and (9%) and 15-lb. bag and 270 A-1 at $46/share.`
Data Entry 4 `1900 PRINT "PERCENTAGE IS";(N[1,1]+N[1,2]+N[1,3])/T*100;"%."`

| 1 | 2 | 3 | 4 | 5 | 6 | 7 | 8 | 9 | 10 | 11 | 12 |

47B

Goal Writing

Default or DS

Take two 3-minute goal writings.

If you finish before time is called, start again.

Record your speed and accuracy.

Goal: To measure timed-writing progress 10′

		1′	3′
One of the most useful types of software available now		11	4
is the spreadsheet. It uses many of the same principles as		23	8
tabulation and can help to arrange data into columns and		35	12
rows.		36	12
By using mathematical formulas fed into the computer,		47	16
you are able to get accurate totals. Also, you can use a		58	19
"what if" approach with a spreadsheet. In other words, you		70	23
can enter new data in rows or columns and the computer will		82	27
automatically make adjustments in the totals all the way		94	31
through the data, saving considerable time.		102	34

1′ | 1 | 2 | 3 | 4 | 5 | 6 | 7 | 8 | 9 | 10 | 11 | 12 | AWL
3′ | 1 | 2 | 3 | 4 | 5.7

47C

Self-Check

Default or DS

Key the statement number and your answer: True or False.

Check your answers in Appendix C.

Goal: To review the manual method of horizontal centering 5′

1. The center of a standard-size sheet of paper is 42 when you are using a 10-pitch printwheel or element.
2. Move the cursor/carrier to the center before backspacing.
3. Backspace once for each character to be centered.
4. Always begin centering from the left margin.
5. When centering the word *keyboarding*, do not backspace for the letter *g*.
6. Copy that is centered horizontally has equal side margins.
7. The center of a standard-size sheet of paper is 51 when you are using a 12-pitch printwheel or element.

Key each line twice.

DS after each pair of lines.

Repeat if time allows.

1 Buy two books: <u>Principles of Health</u> and <u>The King</u>.
2 Don't lose sight of their firm's annual objective.
3 Principal Hanson taught "botany principles" today.
4 "Yes, Red McGraw is loose again," said the warden.

Lesson 22

 M Default Settings
T SS   SM 2″ (12); 1½″ (10)   Tab ¶

22A

Warmup

Key each line twice.
DS after each pair.

Identify misstrokes.

Goal: To strengthen keyboarding skills 5′

1 Rod may wish to pay for the visit when he is paid.
2 If they do lose the game, will anyone be affected?
3 Her advice is good; every one of them understands.
4 I can't dispute any one of the principal findings.

| 1 | 2 | 3 | 4 | 5 | 6 | 7 | 8 | 9 | 10 |

22B

Accuracy Practice

DS after each group of lines.

Goal: To build keyboarding accuracy 5′   22-1

Take a 3-minute accuracy timing on the lines in 22A. If you make an error, start again. Stay on a line until you have keyed it without error.

Checkpoint: How many error-free lines did you key?

22C

Goal Writing

Default or DS

Take two 3-minute goal writings.

Key at a pace that is comfortable for you.

If time allows, start again.

Determine your GWAM.

Goal: To measure timed-writing progress 10′   1′ | 3′

     There are many uses of the computer in the   9 | 3
arts today. For example, authors more and more   18 | 6
are relying on the computer and word processing to   29 | 10
help them write. A computer may be a fine drawing   39 | 13
tool in the hands of an artist. Designers, car-   49 | 16
toonists, and illustrators find that a computer   58 | 19
can give them a new means of creative expression.   68 | 23
A growing number of musicians now use computers   78 | 26
in their work.   81 | 27

1′ | 1 | 2 | 3 | 4 | 5 | 6 | 7 | 8 | 9 | 10 | AWL
3′ | 1 | 2 | 3 | 5.7

Read and Do Goal: To learn a manual method of horizontal centering 5'

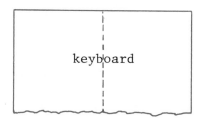

keyboard

When copy is centered horizontally, there are the same number of characters to the left and right of center.

Your equipment may have an automatic centering feature. However, you should learn a manual method for horizontal centering so that you have a skill that is appropriate for all kinds of equipment. Use the following guidelines to learn the backspace method of horizontal centering:

1. Use one of the following methods to move the cursor/carrier to the center.

M *Microcomputer*

a. Determine the center of the line. For example, if you have an 80-character/column screen display, the center is 40 characters from the left edge.

b. Use the space bar to move the cursor to the center of the line.

T *Typewriter*

a. Make sure the paper guide is at 0.
b. Move the margin settings to the ends of the scale.
c. Clear all tab stops.

d. Set a tab stop at center. The center of a standard size (8½" × 11") sheet of paper is 42 for 10 pitch and 51 for 12 pitch.
e. Tab to center.

2. Move the cursor/carrier to the left once for every two characters in the word *keyboard*. Do not key the word.

a. Say to yourself *ke* and move the cursor/carrier to the left one space.
b. Say to yourself *yb* and move the cursor/carrier to the left one space.
c. Say to yourself *oa* and move the cursor/carrier to the left one space.
d. Say to yourself *rd* and move the cursor/carrier to the left one space.

```
          ke yb oa rd

Move left  1  1  1  1
```

3. Begin keying the word *keyboard* at the point where the cursor/carrier is located.
4. If a single character is left at the end of a word, do not move the cursor/carrier for that character.
5. Use the same procedure for centering lines of text. Move the cursor/carrier to the left once for every two characters in the line, including spaces (#). For example:

```
         ce nt er in g# li ne s

Move left  1  1  1  1  1  1  1  0
```

Application: Centering Goal: To horizontally center and key a list of words 12'

Strike the enter/return key twice to DS these activities.

Center each word horizontally.

JOB 1	File name: L46G1	Full sheet

Cue: Move the cursor/carrier to the left once for every two characters.

```
characters
horizontal
proofreads
 material
  indent
production
  center
```

JOB 2	File name: L46G2	Full sheet

Cue: Do not move the cursor/carrier for a single character left at the end of a word.

```
manuscripts
 reproduce
keystroking
handwritten
 diskettes
 indicator
   pitch
```

Need to Know | **Goal: To learn how to edit text** 5′

Most software programs and some electronic typewriters allow you to **edit** (delete and **insert**) text. Follow these general guidelines.

Deleting Text

1. To delete unwanted text, move the cursor to where you want to begin deleting.
2. Using the appropriate delete key or delete command, delete all unwanted text. The text to the right automatically moves left to fill the space left by the deleted text.

3. When you have finished deleting, use the appropriate key or command to end the delete mode.

Inserting Text

1. To insert new text, move the cursor to where you want to begin inserting.
2. Using the appropriate insert key or insert command, key in the new text. The remaining text automatically moves right to make room for the new text.
3. Once you have finished inserting, use the appropriate key or command to end the insert mode.

22E

Keyboard Practice

Key each line 3 times.

DS after each group of lines.

Goal: To practice proper keystroking techniques 9′

1. The bookkeeper is not eligible to use the library.
2. An employee tried to embarrass the superintendent.
3. Their free-enterprise calendar is a separate item.
4. Be brief as you summarize the miscellaneous memos.
5. Send the mortgage papers as enclosures next month.
6. As a new office employee, she is eligible to vote.

22F

Self-Check

Key the statement letter and your answer: True or False.

Check your answers in Appendix C.

Goal: To review spacing rules 8′

a. Space once after a period within an abbreviation.
b. Always space before and after a hyphen.
c. Space twice after a semicolon within a sentence.
d. Space once after a period that ends a sentence.
e. When quotation marks follow punctuation, use the spacing that applies to the mark of punctuation.
f. Space once after a colon within a sentence.
g. A dash is made by keying hyphen, space, hyphen.

22G

Technique Timing

Take two 3-minute timings.

Key each line once. Repeat if time allows.

Goal: To improve keyboarding techniques 8′

Keep your eyes on the textbook copy.

1. acquisition apparent criticism prejudice summarize
2. alignment curriculum yield deductible interference
3. withholding privilege height helpful proceed brief
4. procedure recommend definitely defendant excellent

Accuracy Practice

DS after each group of lines.

Goal: To build keyboarding accuracy 5′

Take a 3-minute accuracy timing on the lines in 46A. If you make an error, start again. Stay on a line until you have keyed it without error.

Checkpoint: How many error-free lines did you key?

46C

Technique Timing

Take two 2-minute timings on each group of lines. Work on improving the technique shown.

If time allows, start again.

DS after each timing.

Goal: To improve keyboarding techniques 14′

Keep your eyes on the textbook copy.

1 Purchase order Nos. 357, 412, and 689 are missing.
2 If--and only if--you respond, will they too react.
3 The boys' and girls' departments are in the annex.

Key without pausing between words or lines.

4 The correct total for Invoice No. 556-1 is $99.23.
5 Leach & Jones ordered more 100# bags of bird seed.
6 Amy's new (unlisted) telephone number is 214-7689.

Keep hands and arms in correct position while keying.

7 Did Shirley actually negotiate for a 25% discount?
8 The asterisk (*) is used to denote multiplication.
9 His sales of $1,259.98 + 367.45 totaled $1,627.43.

Checkpoint: Were you able to keep your hands and arms in correct position? If necessary, review 8D.

46D

Keyboard Composition

Key the paragraph, filling each blank with a word or a short phrase.

Do not correct errors.

Goal: To compose at the keyboard 5′

Let me tell you about myself. I was born in ____ on ____. I have ____ brothers and ____ sisters. The oldest person living at home is ____, who is ____. The place we live is ____. My favorite room there is ____ because ____. If I could change one thing about where I live, it would be ____. I think it would be nice to give my family ____.

46E

Technique Timing

Take a 1-minute timing on each line.

DS after each timing.

Goal: To improve keyboarding techniques 4′

Try to key the numbers as smoothly as you key the letters.

Key lines 1–3 in 23D, page 62.

Checkpoint: Did you look at the keyboard as you made reaches to the number keys?

23A

Warmup

Key each line twice. DS after each pair.

Identify misstrokes.

Goal: To strengthen keyboarding skills   5'

1 The big quake did shake the dorm but it held firm.
2 The devices--all four of them--have been patented.
3 He said, "I must read <u>The Car--An Amazing Device</u>."
4 The device is new; Jane devised it in record time.

| 1 | 2 | 3 | 4 | 5 | 6 | 7 | 8 | 9 | 10 |

23B

Technique Timing

Take two 2-minute timings.

If time allows, start again.

DS after each timing.

Goal: To improve keyboarding techniques   6'

Key easy stroke combinations rapidly; slow down for difficult ones.

1 Their office staff has already completed the exam.
2 Bob and Lynn are all ready to attend the meetings.
3 Jack is all ready to review the contract tomorrow.
4 Nedra, Michael, and Rex will already be in Dallas.
5 They will lose that game if we modify our offense.

23C

New-Key Orientation

1. Locate the new key on the keyboard chart.
2. Next, locate the key on your keyboard.
3. Before keying the practice lines, read the instructions for each new key.
4. Practice the first line, returning to home-key position after making the reach to the new key.
5. Practice the second line for 2 minutes or until you can key it without looking at your hands.

Goal: To learn the location of ② ③ and ④   12'

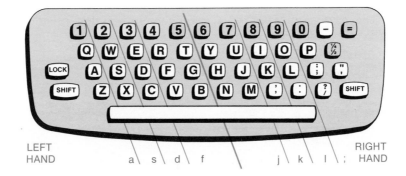

2   Practice the reach to ② with the **s** finger. Keep the **f** finger anchored in home-key position.

1 s2 s2 s2 s2 s2 s2 s2 s2 s2 s2 s2 s2 s2
2 2; 2 sets; 22 sides; 222 sums; 22 sips

(Continued next page)

Unit 4 / Horizontal and Vertical Centering

The appearance of a document is enhanced by its position on the page. Therefore, the ability to center documents vertically and horizontally is an important aspect of document formatting. Most microcomputer software packages and electronic typewriters have automatic centering functions. However, if your equipment does not have an automatic centering function, you may center a document manually. In this unit, Lessons 46–56, you will learn to:

1. Increase your keyboarding speed and accuracy.
2. Center words and lines of text using a manual method of horizontal centering.
3. Center words and lines of text using an automatic centering function.
4. Recognize single, double, triple, and quadruple spacing.
5. Change margins and line lengths.
6. Center copy vertically on the page.
7. Prepare centered columns and tables.
8. Set and use decimal (dec) tabs.

Micro Dictionary

automatic centering	a software or machine function that centers words or lines horizontally
decimal (dec) tab	a software or machine function that automatically aligns columns of figures at decimal points
format commands	commands that are used in arranging text on the screen. Format commands include margins, line spacing, and tab settings.
line length	the number of columns/spaces available between the left and right margin settings
page layout	the vertical and horizontal arrangement of a document on the page. Page layout is determined by the margins, line spacing, and pitch.
ruler line	usually displayed at the top or bottom of the screen to show the left and right margin settings and tab settings

Lesson 46

M Default Settings
T SS   SM 1½" (12); 1" (10)   Tab ¶

46A

Warmup

Key each line twice.
DS after each pair.

Confusing words:
whether and weather

Goal: To strengthen keyboarding skills 5'

```
1 April showers are a true indication of the weather in Texas.
2 Whether the weather will be sunny or not is anybody's guess.
3 Kenny knew the word whether was being used as a conjunction.
  | 1 | 2 | 3 | 4 | 5 | 6 | 7 | 8 | 9 | 10 | 11 | 12 |
```

Follow steps 1-5 on page 61 to learn the reaches to the new keys.

Practice the reach to ③ with the **d** finger. Keep the **a** finger anchored in home-key position.

3 d3 d3 d3 d3 d3 d3 d3 d3 d3 d3 d3 d3 d3

4 3; 3 days; 33 dogs; 333 dimes; 33 dice

Practice the reach to ④ with the **f** finger. Keep the **a** finger anchored in home-key position.

5 f4 f4 f4 f4 f4 f4 f4 f4 f4 f4 f4 f4 f4

6 4; 4 films; 44 facts; 4 fads; 444 furs

23D

Technique Timing

Take a 1-minute timing on each line. Work on improving the technique shown.

DS after each timing.

Goal: To improve keyboarding techniques   12′

Return to home-key position after making reaches to new keys.

1 Order us 2 books, 22 catalogs, and 22 price lists.
2 Please find 3 apples, 33 oranges, and 33 avocados.
3 Send 44 screws, 44 bolts, 44 nuts, and 44 washers.

Keep your eyes on the textbook copy.

Repeat lines 1–3.

Keep your **a** finger anchored in home-key position as you strike ③ and ④.

4 Their numbers are 23, 24, 42, 43, 32, 34, and 234.
5 We want Nos. 22, 33, 44, 234, 432, 23, 24, and 43.
6 Please total these numbers: 23, 443, 323, and 34.

23E

Apply the Rule

Read the rule and the example.

Then key the sentences in the *Application* section. As you key them, use the correct spacing.

Goal: To learn spacing for decimals and commas in numbers   7′

Rule

1. Do not space before or after a period used as a decimal point.
2. Do not space before or after a comma used to separate thousands and millions in numbers of four or more digits.

Example

In August, 2,342 cars, or 42.2 percent, were sold.
Janet Worth drove 233.33 of her 2,432 miles today.

(Continued next page)

Lesson 23

45A

Goal Writing

Warm up on 39A for 5 minutes.

Default or DS

If you finish before time is called, start again.

Record your speed and accuracy.

Goal: To measure timed-writing progress 15'

	1'	3'
If something is put in an envelope with a business let-	11	4
ter, you should add an enclosure notation to the letter.	23	8
The notation will let a reader know that something else is	35	12
in the envelope. An enclosure may be anything that will fit	47	16
in a large envelope. Usually it is mentioned in the body of	59	20
a letter. Enclosures may be tickets, invitations, cards,	71	24
forms, or checks.	74	25
The notation is keyed at the left margin only a double	85	29
space below your own initials. The notation will appear as	97	32
Enclosure.	99	33

1' | 1 | 2 | 3 | 4 | 5 | 6 | 7 | 8 | 9 | 10 | 11 | 12 | AWL
3' | 1 | 2 | 3 | 4 | 5.7

45B

Production Measurement

Goal: To measure formatting skills 35'

JOB 1   Personal Business Letter

File name: L45B1 / Full sheet   Block format
Supply necessary information.

Dr. Annette Thor / Dean of Admissions / Brynwood College / 10 Buckingham Place / Lexington, KY 40503 / I am a student majoring in business education. I plan to attend Brynwood College. Does Brynwood offer a major in court reporting? Is the course of study for two years, leading to an associate degree, or for four years, leading to a bachelor's degree? Are scholarships available for this area of study? ¶ Please send me a catalog and any other materials I may need to answer my questions. Also, please send application forms for any scholarships for which I should apply. / Sincerely / (your name and address)

Checkpoint: Proofread your work and correct errors.

JOB 2   Business Letter/Envelope

File name: L45B2 / Letterhead/Envelope
Block format   Supply necessary information.

Mr. Carl Closet / 8290 Red Lion Drive / Elko, NV 89801 / Personal skills and characteristics have a great impact on career success. Business people know that hiring a person's brain and skills also means hiring the person's personality. The current trend in hiring is to weigh personality along with grades, education, and work experience. Communication skills, "people skills," maturity, and motivation are all essential for success on the job. In fact, these attributes often determine who gets hired. ¶ I've enclosed a booklet that you might find interesting as you prepare to enter the job market. It contains ideas that may help you get ahead in the personality game: get a summer or part-time job, take writing and speech courses, and take part in school functions. / Sincerely / Russell Blackman / Career Specialist

Use correct spacing with the decimals and commas.

Application

1 Patrick lives 2.2 miles from the railroad station.

2 The new petroleum company created 22.434 new jobs.

3 Over 34.2 percent of the seniors already had jobs.

4 By March, they had added over 2.433 new customers.

5 John added the numbers 3,143 and 2,432 for Jackie.

6 The figure of 3.34 was obtained by the accountant.

23F

Keyboard Practice

Key each line 2 times.

DS after each group of lines.

Identify misstrokes.

Goal: To practice proper keystroking techniques 8′

> **Cue:** Use correct spacing with commas and decimals.

1 The percentage figures are 43.2, 232.4, and 324.3.

2 We sold 3,342 units this year and 2,443 last year.

3 Of the 4,442 calls, 23.4 percent are out of state.

4 Invoice No. 3,324 covers their order for 23 items.

5 Our plant is exactly 23.3 miles from Kay's office.

6 This segment has 3.4 percent, or 2,434 executives.

7 The order for 43 items is included in the invoice.

8 There are 3,442 employees which equals 32 percent.

9 The sales staff will be increased by 32.4 percent.

10 Order 34 of Item No. 2234, and 42 of Item No. 342.

> **Checkpoint:** If you used correct spacing, the periods align at the ends of the sentences.

Lesson 24

M Default Settings

T SS   SM 2″ (12); 1½″ (10)   Tab ¶

24A

Warmup

Key each line twice.
DS after each pair.

Identify misstrokes.

Goal: To strengthen keyboarding skills 5′

1 Eight firms wish to bid for the right to the land.

2 During the year just passed, we sold 443 new cars.

3 The council passed all 24 motions this past month.

4 On September 23, Brad's past-due account was paid.

| 1 | 2 | 3 | 4 | 5 | 6 | 7 | 8 | 9 | 10 |

Self-Check

Goal: To review letter parts 5'

Choose the word or phrase that correctly completes each statement.

Key the statement number and your answer.

Check your answers in Appendix C.

Answers:	writes	double space	open
	single spaced	date	courtesy title
	salutation	Ladies and Gentlemen	reference initials

1. Dear Ms. Ryan is an example of a ____.
2. The first item in a business letter printed on letterhead stationery is the ____.
3. The originator is the person who ____ the letter.
4. The body of a letter is ____.
5. In a block-format business letter, you usually ____ to indicate the beginning of a new paragraph.
6. The name used in the salutation of business letters usually consists of the addressee's ____ and last name.
7. With ____ punctuation, do not put a colon after the salutation.
8. When a letter is addressed to a company, an appropriate salutation to use is ____.
9. The ____ may be used to identify the person who prepared a letter.

Application: Letters

Goal: To prepare block-format letters 21'

JOB 1   File name: L44F1 / Letterhead/Envelope

> Cue: Supply an appropriate salutation and other missing information for the following letter.

Ms. Beverly Starcher / District Manager / Type-Master, Inc. / 6063 Franklin Avenue / Franklin Lakes, NY 07417 / As you requested, I have prepared some suggestions that may help your employees avoid back problems on the job. Too often, these problems are caused by sitting incorrectly. ¶ For maximum comfort, chairs should be low enough so you can place both feet on the floor. Knees should be higher than the hips. Sit firmly against the back of the chair with your back straight but not rigid. Do not slump. Sitting in chairs that are too high or too far from your work may cause unnecessary back strain. Pull your chair closer to your desk to avoid leaning forward and arching your back. ¶ I hope these suggestions will be beneficial to you and your employees. / Sincerely / Sonja Ellsberg / Health Care Director

JOB 2   File name: L44F2 / Full sheet

Key the following letter. Supply appropriate information to fill in the blanks.

Miss Jane Adams / Employment Counselor / Temporary Services, Inc. / 9706 Midway Boulevard / (Your city, state, and ZIP Code) / In response to today's advertisement in (your local newspaper), I wish to apply for employment as a ____. I will be available to begin work on ____. I am a responsible and a dependable person. My grade point average for the past year is ____. My teacher, ____, has offered to provide you with further information regarding my abilities. You may reach me at my home phone ____, after 5:00 p.m. I will be happy to come to your offices for an interview. / Sincerely / (Your name) / (Your address)

> Checkpoint: Were you able to compose the information needed to complete the letter while you were keying the document?

Technique Timing

Take two 3-minute timings on each group of lines. Work on improving the technique shown.

Key each line once. If you finish before time is called, start again.

DS after each timing.

Goal: To improve keyboarding techniques   15'

Keep your eyes on the textbook copy as you strike the number keys.

1 The latter figures, 3,243 and 23,324, are correct.
2 Later, we ordered 42, 24, 32, 34, 43, 23, and 342.
3 After selecting both 22 and 44, I like the latter.
4 Later in the day, they will deliver Order No. 333.
5 Flight 433 leaves too early; I'll take the latter.

Don't let your wrists "bounce" as you reach to the top row.

6 23 dogs; 32 birds; 234 cats; 2,344 mice; 43 snakes
7 43 pens, 32 pencils, 432 papers, 23 books, 3 desks
8 Jane is 34; Dennis is 43; Elvira is 23; Mike is 2.
9 Order 2 apples, 3 bananas, 4 oranges, and 4 plums.
10 These selected numbers are 23, 24, 34, 42, 32, 22.

24C

New-Key Orientation

1. Locate the new key on the keyboard chart.
2. Next, locate the key on your keyboard.
3. Before keying the practice lines, read the instructions for each new key.
4. Practice the first line, returning to home-key position after making the reach to the new key.
5. Practice the second line for 2 minutes or until you can key it without looking at your hands.

Goal: To learn the location of 7 8 and 9   12'

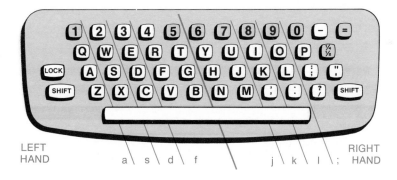

7 Practice the reach to 7 with the **j** finger. Keep the **sem** finger anchored in home-key position.

1 j7 j7 j7 j7 j7 j7 j7 j7 j7 j7 j7 j7 j7
2 7; 7 jokes; 77 jets; 7.77 jacks; 7,777

8 Practice the reach to 8 with the **k** finger. Keep the **sem** finger anchored in home-key position.

3 k8 k8 k8 k8 k8 k8 k8 k8 k8 k8 k8 k8 k8
4 8; 8 kites; 88 kinds; 8,888 kings; 8.8

9 Practice the reach to 9 with the **l** finger. Keep the **j** finger anchored in home-key position.

5 l9 l9 l9 l9 l9 l9 l9 l9 l9 l9 l9 l9
6 9; 9 lives; 99 lakes; 99.9 lots; 9,999

Language Arts

Read the rule in the box at the right.

Then key each numbered sentence, supplying the correct number style.

Check your work with the key in Appendix B.

Goal: To review rules for numbers 7'

> Spell out names of numbered streets up to and including ten. Use ordinal figures (*11th*, *12th*, *22nd*, and so on) for numbered streets over ten.
>
> **Examples:**
>
> Tom's store is on the corner of Third Avenue and First Street.
> Manuel built a house on 14th Street near the 32nd Avenue exit.

1. You may write to that company at their 7th Street address.
2. Stephanie's parents will live in Newburgh at East Fortieth Street.
3. The fires on 6th Avenue spread to the houses on 22nd Street.
4. Many cities have a 2nd Avenue, but few have a Hound Street.
5. The company's offices are located at 1 Hanover Place.
6. Marita joined a health club on East Thirty-sixth Street.

44D

Apply the Rule

Key all three parts using the spacing indicated.

In the *Application* section, key the lines of the address in the correct order. Key one address beneath the other.

Goal: To review the format for the inside address 7'

<u>Rule</u> _{DS}

The inside address of a business letter usually contains the following information keyed in the order given: (1) addressee's name, (2) addressee's title, (3) company name, (4) delivery address (street or post office box), and (5) city, state, and ZIP Code. _{TS}

<u>Example</u> _{DS}

Mr. David Marr
President
Fine Arts Council of Omaha
P. O. Box 1192
Omaha, NE 68105 _{TS}

<u>Application</u> _{DS}

1 Franklin Trust Company / Philadelphia, PA 19105 / 200 Broad Street / Ms. Margaret A. Gomez / Loan Officer _{DS}

2 P. O. Box 28 / Devon, DE 06460 / Mr. A. J. Garb / Treasurer / Future Business Leaders of America _{DS}

3 Atlanta, GA 30324 / 1844 North Piedmont Drive / Mr. Jon Takata / United Fund Campaign / Manager _{DS}

4 Mrs. Alice Hermann / 5102 Linwood Boulevard / Kansas City, MO 64128 / Designer / D'Agostino Design Studio _{DS}

5 Computer General Corporation / President / Boston, MA 02134 / 7123 Cambridge Street / Mr. Thomas Manning

---

24D

Technique Timing

Take a 1-minute timing on each line. Work on improving the technique shown.

DS after each timing.

Goal: To improve keyboarding techniques 12'

Return to home-key position after making reaches to new keys.

1 Mail an order for 7 mats, 77 blanks, and 77 rings.
2 Be sure you buy 88 kits, 88 boxes, and 888 covers.
3 Send 99 ovals, 99 boxes, 99 lights, and 99 rivets.
4 Patricia bought 77 beads, 88 strings, and 99 kits.

Keep your eyes on the textbook copy.

Repeat lines 1–4.

Do not turn your wrists as you strike the number keys.

5 Their numbers are 78, 79, 97, 98, 87, 89, and 789.
6 We want Nos. 77, 88, 99, 789, 987, 89, 79, and 98.
7 Help find these numbers: 7,789; 998; 878; and 89.
8 Can you add these numbers: 77, 789, 88, 789, 987?

24E

Speed Practice

Take a 20- or 15-second timing on each line. If you complete a line in the time allowed, go on to the next one.

Goal: To build keyboarding speed 6'

GWAM

		20″	15″
1 We are sending 32 more copies.		18	24
2 He would like to order 332 of them.		21	28
3 We are pleased to sell you 342 brackets.		24	32
4 We are not able to sell you another 44 units.		27	36

| 1 | 2 | 3 | 4 | 5 | 6 | 7 | 8 | 9 |

Lesson 25

M Default Settings
T SS   SM 2" (12); 1½" (10)   Tab ¶

25A

Warmup

Key each line twice. DS after each pair.

Identify misstrokes.

Goal: To strengthen keyboarding skills 5'

1 That lake is so clear that you can see the bottom.
2 Herb is the one who's there; whose name was heard?
3 Whose number does Que want—89, 28, 94, 39, or 27?
4 Who's going to referee: Beth, Tex, Zeke, or Fran?

| 1 | 2 | 3 | 4 | 5 | 6 | 7 | 8 | 9 | 10 |

Application: Letters

Goal: To key a block-format business letter with an envelope 13'

File name: L43G / Letterhead/Envelope

Cue: Key an envelope in OCR format.

Mr. Michael L. Williams / Agent / Astro Travel, Inc. / 13400 Ridgeway Road / Dallas, TX 75234 / Dear Mr. Williams / In response to your letter asking about the "rules of the air," I have compiled some information that may help you. ¶ Federal law requires that all passengers who ask for seats in the nonsmoking section of the plane be given such seats. If the nonsmoking section is full, you must designate the first row in the smoking section as a nonsmoking area. ¶ Another requirement is that all baggage must have the passenger's name clearly marked on the outside. Remind passengers to put their names inside their luggage and to carry all valuables (such as money, cameras, and jewelry) with them on board. ¶ I will be happy to answer any other questions you might have about "rules of the air." / Sincerely / Antoinette Ninghetti / District Manager

Checkpoint: Did you remember to supply an appropriate salutation?

Lesson 44

M Default Settings
T SS   SM 1½" (12); 1" (10)   Tab ¶

Warmup

Goal: To strengthen keyboarding skills 5'

Key each line twice. DS after each pair.

1 Business letters are usually sent out by companies or firms.
2 Business letters are usually keyed on letterhead stationery.
3 Letterhead has the company's name and address printed on it.
4 The typist's initials are at the end of the business letter.

| . 1 | 2 | 3 | 4 | 5 | 6 | 7 | 8 | 9 | 10 | 11 | 12 |

Speed Practice

Goal: To build keyboarding speed 5'

GWAM

Take a 15-or 12-second timing on each line. If you complete a line in the time allowed, go on to the next one.

		15"	12"
1	Have you chosen your future career?	28	35
2	Do you feel you have an aptitude for it?	32	40
3	Now, what background or training do you have?	36	45
4	What training or courses do you still need for it?	40	50
5	Be smart. Know yourself, and know what you want to be.	44	55

| 1 | 2 | 3 | 4 | 5 | 6 | 7 | 8 | 9 | 10 | 11 |

25B

Accuracy Practice

DS after each group of lines.

Goal: To build keyboarding accuracy 5′

Take a 3-minute accuracy timing on the lines in 25A. If you make an error, start again. Stay on a line until you have keyed it without error.

Checkpoint: How many error-free lines did you key?

25C

Goal Writing

Default or DS

Take two 3-minute goal writings.

Key at a pace that is comfortable for you.

If time allows, start again.

Determine your GWAM.

Goal: To measure timed-writing progress 10′

	1′	3′
Many career opportunities await the person	9	3
today who is excited about word processing. Each	19	6
position has unique qualifications, but the common	29	10
requirement is a willingness to change.	37	12
New equipment comes on the scene every day.	46	15
New capabilities are certain to be seen. There	55	18
are now products in research centers that we have	65	22
not even heard about yet. The one who can adapt	75	25
is the one who will be able to get the job.	84	28

AWL 5.7

25D

Keyboard Composition

Key each word at the right, followed by a colon. Then key at least three words that rhyme with each word.

Goal: To compose at the keyboard 5′

Example Cat: bat, rat, mat

1	Seat	4	Tire	7	Week
2	Pair	5	Pink	8	Ring
3	Hear	6	Bright	9	Date

25E

Keyboard Practice

Key each line three times.

DS after each group of lines.

Identify misstrokes.

Goal: To practice proper keystroking techniques 16′

1 Call me if you're positive about Engine No. 83492.
2 Your 34-minute call was your second one that week.
3 If you're the one with No. 44-999, please call me.
4 Your rooms, 839, 832, 878, and 889, are scheduled.
5 You're to call John at 373-8993 or 373-7899 today.
6 We already work later than all of the other crews.
7 You're sure to be all ready for my test by Monday.

(Continued next page)

Need to Know

Goal: To learn how to key envelopes in OCR format 5′   43-1

Use a No. 10 envelope keyed in **OCR** (Optical Character Recognition) format for business correspondence. Many businesses use printed envelopes with their return addresses in the upper left-hand corner.

The mailing address on the envelope should contain the same information that is in the inside address of the letter. That is, a four-line inside address is keyed as a four-line mailing address on the envelope.

M Before you begin, make these changes in default settings: set the top margin and the left margin at 0.

The following steps for keying envelopes are the same for all kinds of equipment.

1. If a plain envelope is used, key the return address in the upper left corner, 2 lines down from the top and 3 **columns**/spaces over from the left edge of the screen/envelope.
2. Key the mailing address as follows:

   Top margin: 2½ inches (line 15) from the top edge of the screen/envelope.

   Left margin: 4 inches (40 columns/spaces, 10-pitch; 48 columns/spaces, 12-pitch) from the left edge of the screen/envelope.

3. Single space the address in all capital letters. Use no punctuation except for the hyphen in the ZIP-Plus or nine-digit ZIP Code.
4. Key the city, two-letter abbreviation, and ZIP Code on the same line. Leave 2 spaces between the two-letter state abbreviation and the ZIP Code.

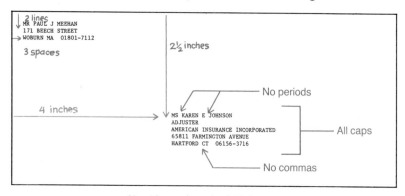

No. 10 envelope in OCR format

Need to Know

Read the copy to the right as you prepare to print an envelope.

Goal: To learn how to print envelopes 5′

If your printer does not have an automatic paper feed, you may be able to print envelopes on it. Read and do the following steps:

1. Name the document: Envelope.
2. Set the top margin at 0.
3. Set the left margin at 0.
4. Key the mailing address.

5. Insert an envelope in the printer.
6. Give the command to begin printing.

You may store the envelope format. When you are ready to prepare another envelope, retrieve the envelope, delete the previous address, key in the new address, and print your envelope.

Application: Envelopes

Goal: To key envelopes in OCR format 6′

Key an envelope for each of the addresses in 43C. Refer to 43D for correct placement.

8 Whose idea was it to market their lighting device?
9 He passed their examination on the latter attempt.
10 Your brother will devise a new system to consider.

25F

Technique Timing

Tab: ¶

Take three 2-minute timings.

For lines 1, 3, 5, and 7, depress the tab key.

If time allows, start again.

DS after each timing.

Goal: To improve keyboarding techniques 9'

Keep your eyes on the textbook copy as you use the tab.

1   We hope that they will attend.
2 We would like to hear from Ty soon.
3   Please let us serve them soon.
4 The department will open next week.
5   Enclosed are the eight copies.
6 We will be able to ship your order.
7   It will arrive before June 27.

> **Checkpoint:** Were you able to tab without having to look at the keyboard?

Lesson 26

M Default Settings
T SS   SM 2" (12); 1½" (10)   Tab ¶

26A

Warmup

Key each line twice. DS after each pair.

Identify misstrokes.

Goal: To strengthen keyboarding skills 5'

1 A big fish toyed with the line but would not bite.
2 Lakeview's City Council will appeal to OSHA today.
3 Please take Max's counsel; you'll be glad you did.
4 Is Elaine Olson head of the Council of Publishers?

| 1 | 2 | 3 | 4 | 5 | 6 | 7 | 8 | 9 | 10 |

26B

Technique Timing

Take a 2-minute timing.

Key each line once. If time allows, start again.

Goal: To improve keyboarding techniques 6'

Use a one-two count when shifting for capitals.

1 Bob Lake cited Dr. Ira West at the August meeting.
2 The Loyal Order of Moose's meeting site is Denver.
3 "A Sight for Sore Eyes" is Jennifer Riley's title.

(Continued next page)

Goal Writing

Default or DS

Take two 3-minute goal writings.

If you finish before time is called, start again.

Record your speed and accuracy.

Goal: To measure timed-writing progress   10'

	1'	3'
Computers can generate graphs, charts, and drawings	11	4
as well as various three-dimensional shapes with shading and	23	8
animation. The image on the computer screen is made up of	35	12
thousands of pixels, tiny boxes of light. How sharp the	46	15
image is on the screen depends on the numbers of pixels the	58	19
screen has.	60	20
You can create your own graphics, or you can use	70	23
graphics software. In selecting graphics programs, be	81	27
sure to consider how you will use them in your work.	92	31

1' | 1 | 2 | 3 | 4 | 5 | 6 | 7 | 8 | 9 | 10 | 11 | 12 | AWL
3' | 1 | | 2 | | 3 | | 4 | | 5.7

Apply the Rule

Key all three parts using the spacing indicated.

In the *Application* section, key the mailing addresses in OCR format. Key one address beneath the other.

Goal: To learn to key mailing addresses in OCR format   6'

Rule _{DS}

Key mailing addresses on envelopes in OCR (Optical Character Recognition) format. OCR format uses all capital letters and leaves out all marks of punctuation. That is, periods are not used with abbreviations or initials; commas are not used between the cities and states. However, a hyphen is used with ZIP-Plus or nine-digit ZIP Codes. _{TS}

Example _{DS}

MS MARY RHIA
MARKETING SPECIALIST
AMERICAN NATIONAL BANK
370 EAST 23RD STREET
ST PAUL MN 55101 _{TS}

Application _{DS}

1 Ms. Madelline Zeller
  Sales Representative
  Airflow Heating Systems
  324 Country Street
  Bennington, VT 05203 _{DS}

2 Mr. Dennis Clough
  Senior Buyer
  Winsome Fabrics, Inc.
  727 South East Second Avenue
  Springfield, MO 65811 _{DS}

3 Mr. J. T. Tillis
  Assistant Director
  Houston Energy Council
  P. O. Box 2106
  Houston, TX 77202 _{DS}

4 Mrs. Patricia L. Delmonte
  Attorney
  Carmichael, Winn, and Sumoto
  3830 Kelly Avenue
  Cleveland, OH 44114-0130

Take a 2-minute timing.

Key each line once. If time allows, start again.

Keep your eyes on the textbook copy as you strike the hyphen.

4 Their glasses give you sight-of-the-future vision.

5 The all-important site is near the east-side park.

6 Those sights were not-to-be-forgotten experiences.

26C

New-Key Orientation

1. Locate the new key on the keyboard chart.
2. Next, locate the key on your keyboard.
3. Before keying the practice lines, read the instructions for each new key.
4. Practice the first line, returning to home-key position after making the reach to the new key.
5. Practice the second line for 2 minutes or until you can key it without looking at your hands.

Goal: To learn the location of ① ⓪ and Ⓢ 12′

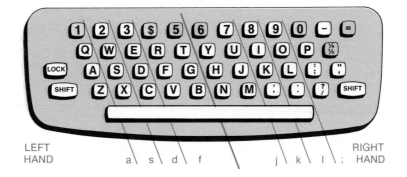

LEFT HAND   a s d f   j k l ;   RIGHT HAND

1 Practice the reach to ① with the **a** finger. Keep the **f** finger anchored in home-key position.

1 a1 a1 a1 a1 a1 a1 a1 a1 a1 a1 a1 a1 a1

2 1; 1 act; 11 ads; 111 dozen; 1.11 days

0 Practice the reach to ⓪ (zero) with the **sem** finger. Keep the **j** finger anchored in home-key position.

3 ;0 ;0 ;0 ;0 ;0 ;0 ;0 ;0 ;0 ;0 ;0 ;0 ;0

4 0; 20 laws; 300 dots; 7,000 years; 402

$ Practice the reach to the Ⓢ with the **f** finger while depressing the right shift key. Quickly release the shift key and return the **sem** finger to home-key position. Do not space after the dollar sign.

5 f$ f$ f$ f$ f$ f$ f$ f$ f$ f$ f$ f$ f$

6 $; $4; $78; $2.34; $33.97; $89.99; $42

26D

Technique Timing

Take a 1-minute timing on each line. Work on improving the technique shown.

DS after each timing.

Goal: To improve keyboarding techniques 12′

Return to home-key position after making reaches to new keys.

1 The fourth item is 1,719; it isn't 1,123 or 1,411.

2 The final dates are May 20, May 30, and August 20.

3 The sums were $4, $84, $94, $34, $24, $74, and $4.

Keep your eyes on the textbook copy.

Repeat lines 1–3.

(Continued next page)

**Application:
Letters**

Goal: To key block-format business letters 13′

JOB 1   File name: L42G1 / Full sheet

Key the document. Do not proofread and correct errors at this time. Store your document. Then print the document. Use the hard copy in JOB 2.

Ms. Karen Gilbert / American Insurance
Company / 6581 Farm Road / Hartford CT 06156 /
Dear Ms. Gilbert / Business letters are
usually printed ~~all typed~~ on letterhead stationery.
Stationery is high-quality bond paper
with the company's name and address pro-

fessionally printed on the top of each sheet. The letterhead may ~~include~~ also a tele-phone number, slogan, logo, or names of the executives of ~~of~~ the company. Enclosed is an invitation to the american management society's annual business show. Please be our guest at this ~~display~~ exhibit of inovative office supplies and products.
Sincerely / Neal Shultz / Sales Manager

JOB 2

Letterhead

Using the hard copy prepared in JOB 1, proofread and indicate any changes that are to be made—using proofreader's marks. Retrieve L42G1 and make corrections, or key a corrected document. In addition to correcting your errors, make the following changes in the document.

1. Change the inside address to:

   Mr. Walter Taff
   Purchasing Supervisor
   Automated Offices, Inc.
   4900 Billings Plaza
   Helena, MT 59601

2. Change the salutation to:

   Dear Mr. Taff

3. Change the show's name to:

   ABC Computer Users' Symposium

4. Change the originator's name and title to:

   Margarita Chavez / District Sales Coordinator

Lesson 43

M Default Settings
T SS   SM 1½″ (12); 1″ (10)   Tab ¶

Warmup

Goal: To strengthen keyboarding skills 5′

Key each line twice. DS after each pair of lines.

Speed	1	Take some personal copies with you when you go to the hotel.
Accuracy	2	Mr. Cox expected an experienced executive in Oaxaca, Mexico.
Number/Symbol	3	They cut the lumber into 10-foot lengths (6 3/4" x 10 3/4').
Data Entry	4	Within the binary number system, the letter "A" is 00100101.

| 1 | 2 | 3 | 4 | 5 | 6 | 7 | 8 | 9 | 10 | 11 | 12 |

Take a 1-minute timing on each line.

DS after each timing.

Quickly release the shift key and return the **sem** finger to home-key position.

4 For $44, I'll get 10 books, 10 keys, and 10 exams.
5 Order 141 is for $144; 142 for $841; 143 for $941.
6 Your Invoice No. 1001 covers 10 reels at $41 each.

26E

Goal Writing

Default or DS

Take two 3-minute goal writings.

Key at a pace that is comfortable for you.

If you finish before time is called, start again.

Identify misstrokes.

Determine your GWAM.

Goal: To measure timed-writing progress 10′

	1′	3′
A good software program will have proper docu-	9	3
mentation. Documentation will tell you what the	19	6
program offers and how you can use it very well.	29	10
With so many features, it could easily take you a	39	13
very long time to discover for yourself all its	48	16
capabilities. A complete documentation will tell	58	19
you all you need to know about the program. You	68	23
will be able to locate answers to all of your	77	26
questions accurately and without any great delay.	87	29

1′ | 1 | 2 | 3 | 4 | 5 | 6 | 7 | 8 | 9 | 10 | AWL
3′ | | 1 | | 2 | | 3 | | 5.7

26F

Keyboard Composition

Answer each question with a single word.

Do not correct errors.

Goal: To compose at the keyboard 5′

a. Do you own a bicycle?
b. Does your family have any pets?
c. Is Delaware larger than Texas?
d. Which do you prefer: Fall or Spring?

e. What month does school begin?
f. What is your favorite day of the week?
g. In what month were you born?
h. What color is your hair?

Lesson 27

M Default Settings
T SS   SM 2″ (12); 1½″ (10)   Tab ¶

27A

Warmup

Key each line twice. DS after each pair.

Identify misstrokes.

Goal: To strengthen keyboarding skills 5′

1 That tall elm tree has been in our yard for years.
2 She will not venture forth without NASA's consent.
3 Here is the fourth in every case: 47, 37, 98, 21.
4 "Go forth in style," said Tex, "or go not at all."

| 1 | 2 | 3 | 4 | 5 | 6 | 7 | 8 | 9 | 10 |

Language Arts

Read the rule in the box at the right.

Then key the numbered sentences, supplying correct capitalization where needed.

Check your work with the key in Appendix B.

Goal: To review rules for capitalization 7'

> When keying names of businesses, use the capitalization preferred by the business; refer to the company's stationery for the preferred capitalization. In other cases, generally capitalize the first and all important words.
>
> **Examples:**
>
> Henry bought typing paper at Pen and Pencil Stationery Shoppe.
> On separate evenings we ate at The Deli and Pier One-Oh-Eight.

1. My tennis team plays every day at racquets and nets unlimited.
2. Harvey went to work for aschetino, williams, and turnage, inc.
3. While on vacation, he stayed at a place called inn on the sea.
4. At an antique shop, the yankee traveler, we found an old desk.
5. She interviewed at whitcomb and sons as well as at mcKinley's.
6. We'd prefer to eat at either the big apple or at pete's patio.

42E

Need to Know

Goal: To learn additional proofreader's marks 5'

The last four proofreader's marks to be learned are shown in the following table. Study the table to learn what each mark means, how to use it, and what the corrected copy looks like.

Mark	Meaning	Example	Corrected Copy
/	lower case	many People were	many people were
⌐	move right	You will find	You will find
⌐	move left	You will find	You will find
¶	paragraph	lawn¶There are three	lawn. There are three

42F

Rough Draft

M

File name: L42F
Default settings

T

Full sheet
DS

Read the copy. Then key the paragraphs making the changes indicated.

Proofread and correct all errors.

Goal: To key rough-draft copy 10'

The computer has become a veery important part of our world today. You will find it in medicine, government, health care, science, law enforcement, busines, and they home. class-rooms throughout the country are also beginning use to the computer for many purposes--drill practice, and motivation. a few years ago, the computer was a large, inexpensive peice of equipment that performed limited number of tasks. Today, You can by a samll computer for less than $2,000; in fact, you may even be able to to purchase a very small com-puter for less than $400.

27B

Accuracy Practice

DS after each group of lines.

Goal: To build keyboarding accuracy 5′

Take a 3-minute accuracy timing on the lines in 27A. If you make an error, start again. Stay on a line until you have keyed it without error.

Checkpoint: How many error-free lines did you key?

27C

Technique Timing

Take two 2-minute timings on each group of lines. Work on improving the technique shown.

DS after each timing.

Goal: To improve keyboarding techniques 9′

Key short words as words rather than as separate letters.

1 Before proceeding, be sure you get the directions.
2 The procedures for that conference were not clear.
3 Ms. West thinks we need to revise Procedure No. 4.

Keep your eyes on the textbook copy and do not pause between letters or words.

4 The proceedings at the college won't be televised.
5 Before you proceed any further, stop by my office.
6 Mr. Court preceded Mrs. Court in death by a month.

| 1 | 2 | 3 | 4 | 5 | 6 | 7 | 8 | 9 | 10 |

27D

New-Key Orientation

1. Locate the new key on the keyboard chart.
2. Next, locate the key on your keyboard.
3. Before keying the practice lines, read the instructions for each new key.
4. Practice the first line, returning to home-key position after making the reach to the new key.
5. Practice the second line for 2 minutes or until you can key it without looking at your hands.

Goal: To learn the location of ⑤ ⑥ and ⑧ 13′

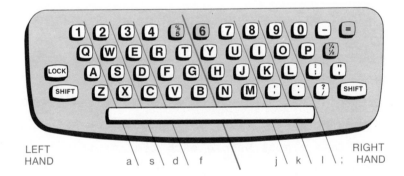

5 Practice the reach to ⑤ with the **f** finger. Keep the **a** finger anchored in home-key position.

1 f5 f5 f5 f5 f5 f5 f5 f5 f5 f5 f5 f5 f5
2 5; 5 fires; 55 fans; 5,555 hats; 55.55

6 Practice the reach to ⑥ with the **j** finger. Keep the **sem** finger anchored in home-key position.

3 j6 j6 j6 j6 j6 j6 j6 j6 j6 j6 j6 j6 j6
4 6; 6 jobs; 66 jabs; 666 gaps; 6.6 rugs

(Continued next page)

JOB 2 Doc. L41F2 / Letterhead

Ms. Ashley Prescott / 449 Sea Street / Cohasset, MA 02025 / (supply salutation) / We were pleased to receive your letter requesting information about our new health and exercise club, Fit-N-Trim. ¶ Our membership fee is $350 a year. The membership fee includes unlimited use of our facilities. These facilities include the regular fitness salon, weight-lifting equipment, swimming pool, and racquetball and tennis courts. Throughout the year, we offer our club members and their families many extra activities. You will receive information about all club activities in our weekly newsletter. ¶ If you would like to join our club, please fill out and return the enclosed membership application. Please enclose your membership fee with the application. If you need further information, please call me at 770-1080. / Sincerely / Alicia Thurman / Membership Director

---

Lesson 42

M Default Settings
T SS   SM 1½" (12); 1" (10)   Tab ¶

42A

Warmup

Key each line twice. DS after each pair.

"al" combinations

Goal: To strengthen keyboarding skills 5'

1 although always all altogether fall call sale mall calm lamp
2 Although the lamp would always fall, the male remained calm.
3 Clap after all the pals call the tall, pale males from Yale.

| 1 | 2 | 3 | 4 | 5 | 6 | 7 | 8 | 9 | 10 | 11 | 12 |

42B

Speed Practice

Take a 15- or 12-second timing on each line. If you complete a line before time is called, go on to the next one.

Goal: To build keyboarding speed 5'

GWAM

| | 15" | 12" |

1 This first line is very, very easy.   28   35

2 You can key this drill at faster speeds.   32   40

3 Give more effort to improve your skill level.   36   45

4 To strengthen your skill, practice with a purpose.   40   50

5 State a goal before each timing; then try to attain it. 44   55

| 1 | 2 | 3 | 4 | 5 | 6 | 7 | 8 | 9 | 10 | 11 |

42C

Keyboard Composition

Key the paragraph, filling each blank with a word or a short phrase.

Do not correct errors.

Goal: To compose at the keyboard 5'

Do you ever think about colors? Some colors have a special meaning. For example, a ___ traffic light tells you to stop. When it is safe to ___, the light turns ___. Sports cars are often ___. Brides and ___ usually wear white. Red, white, and ___ make many people think of ___.

Follow steps 1–5 on page 70 to learn the reaches to the new keys.

 Practice the reach to ⊛ with the **f** finger while depressing the right shift key. Quickly release the shift key and return the **sem** finger to home-key position. Do not space before the percent sign.

5 f% f% f% f% f% f% f% f% f% f% f% f% f%

6 %; 4%; 31%; 78%; 100%; 99%; 14.0%; 28%

27E

Technique Timing

Take a 1-minute timing on each line. Work on improving the technique shown.

DS after each timing.

Goal: To improve keyboarding techniques 13'

Return to home-key position after making reaches to new keys.

1 What is the sum of 5 and 55 and 555 and 55 and 55?

2 Should Mina buy 66 lids, 66 bottoms, and 6 labels?

3 He gave chain discounts of 7%, 4%, and 3% to them.

> **Checkpoint:** Did you return to home-key position *Always, Usually,* or *Seldom*?

Keep your eyes on the textbook copy.

Repeat lines 1–3.

Quickly release the shift key and return to home-key position.

4 About 56% of the Class of 1956 are at the meeting.

5 He is not sure whether 56 or 65 is the 50% figure.

6 These numbers represent 56%: 156, 56, 15, and 65.

| 1 | 2 | 3 | 4 | 5 | 6 | 7 | 8 | 9 | 10 |

27F

Keyboard Composition

Key the sentence number, followed by a period and two spaces. Then key each sentence and the word or number that best completes it.

Do not correct errors.

Goal: To compose at the keyboard 5'

> **Cue:** Don't be concerned about the format or misstrokes—just try to get your thoughts on paper.

1. The weather today is (hot, cool, warm, cold).
2. My favorite food is (spicy, sweet, tender, juicy).
3. I was born in the (north, south, east, west).
4. I usually get the news from the (newspaper, television, radio).
5. For a pet, I would most like to have a (dog, canary, cat, fish).
6. Each day I (ride, walk, skip, bike) to school.
7. The month after June is (May, July, September, December).
8. My favorite flavor is (chocolate, vanilla, coconut, strawberry).
9. I would rather (swim, read, sew, sleep).
10. The vegetable I like most is (squash, beans, lettuce, corn).

Mark	Meaning	Example	Corrected Copy
≡	capitalize	k̲eep	Keep
		k̳eep	KEEP
∽	change the order	⌐have/you⌐	you have
		mil͡ccocomputer	microcomputer
⋏	insert a comma	pause⋏your	pause, your
⊙	insert a period	equipment⊙Keep	equipment. Keep

41E

Rough Draft

File name: L41E
Default settings

Full sheet
DS

Read the copy before you begin keying. Then key the paragraphs making the changes indicated by the proofreader's marks.

Proofread and correct all errors.

Goal: To key rough-draft copy   10′

l̲earning to proofread is an impro̲tant part of developing your keyb̲oa̲rding skills. If you are using a micc͡orcomputer⋏you can save bt͡oh time and money if you proofread your document while it is on the screen and before you print it⊙ If you are using a typee͡writer⋏should/you proofread before you remove your paper from the machine. Errors are much easier to correct ⌐that/at⌐ time⊙

Develop the habit of reading your text twice. Read ⌐aech⌐ line very slowly the first time. a̲re all words ⌐correctly/spelled⌐? Did you use your Word Book or dictionary when needed? ⌐all/are⌐ det̲ia̲ls correct? s̲ome people suggest reading text fo͡rm right to left when checking spelling⊙ Perhaps this teh͡cnique will help you.

41F

Application: Letters

Goal: To key block-format business letters   18′

JOB 1   Doc. L41F1 / Letterhead

Mr. Wayne Howell / President   Howell Publishing Company / 47129 Eighth Street / New York, NY 10801 / (supply salutation) / Your letter requesting information about how to safeguard your computer operations has been referred to me. ¶ As you know, Mr. Howell, many computer crimes go undetected until it is too late to catch the criminal. A criminal may even be able to erase the evidence of fraud from the computer's memory. However, there are several safeguards that may help you to protect your computer operations. ¶ Some of the safeguards that we recommend are: change program passwords and user ID's frequently, build in security checks, leave an audit trail within the computer files, and watch persons who come to repair computers. ¶ I hope, Mr. Howell, that I have given you the information you need. If we can be of further assistance in helping you set up appropriate safeguards for your computer system, please let us know. / Sincerely / Diane Mulroone / Systems Analyst

(Continued next page)

| M | Default Settings |
| T | SS   SM 2″ (12); 1½″ (10)   Tab ¶ |

28A

Warmup

Key each line twice.
DS after each pair.

Identify misstrokes.

Goal: To strengthen keyboarding skills 5′

1 My job at home is to rake maple leaves every fall.
2 It's time for a quiz; we'll have it on January 15.
3 His book, <u>The 13th Day</u>, is in its fourth printing.
4 Bill said, "It's 23% profit on the $15.25 candle."

| 1 | 2 | 3 | 4 | 5 | 6 | 7 | 8 | 9 | 10 |

28B

Speed Practice

Take a 20- or 15-second timing on each line. If you complete a line in the time allowed, go on to the next one.

Goal: To build keyboarding speed 5′

GWAM

	20″	15″
1 She will order 20 more copies.	18	24
2 Please send us $932 by return mail.	21	28
3 The total is $865 more than we expected.	24	32
4 Can they help us locate 46 more usable tires?	27	36

| 1 | 2 | 3 | 4 | 5 | 6 | 7 | 8 | 9 |

28C

Goal Writing

Default or DS

Take two 3-minute goal writings.

Key at a pace that is comfortable for you.

If you finish before time is called, start again.

Identify misstrokes.

Determine your GWAM.

Goal: To measure timed-writing progress 10′

	1′	3′
Electronic mail is sending and receiving mes—	9	3
sages by computer. It is fast, direct, reliable.	19	6
Electronic mail can save a considerable amount of	29	10
time that would otherwise be wasted by someone not	40	13
being able to talk on the telephone at a time you	50	17
needed to talk with them. In some instances, a	59	20
letter can be transmitted electronically most of	69	23
the way, then printed and sent the rest of the way	79	26
by mail or courier to the addressee.	86	29

1′ | 1 | 2 | 3 | 4 | 5 | 6 | 7 | 8 | 9 | 10 |
3′ | 1 | 2 | 3 |

AWL
5.7

41A

Warmup

Key each line twice. DS after each pair.

Confusing words: complement and compliment

Goal: To strengthen keyboarding skills   5'

```
1 Joanne feels it is a compliment to be asked to talk to them.
2 Dessert of fresh fruit was a complement to Cal's heavy meal.
3 Rose received many compliments on the typed English reports.
```
| 1 | 2 | 3 | 4 | 5 | 6 | 7 | 8 | 9 | 10 | 11 | 12 |

41B

Accuracy Practice

DS after each group of lines.

Goal: To build keyboarding accuracy   5'

Take a 3-minute accuracy timing on the lines in 41A. If you make an error, start again. Stay on a line until you have keyed it without error.

> **Checkpoint:** How many error-free lines did you key?

41C

Language Arts

Read the rules in the box at the right.

Then key each numbered sentence, supplying commas where needed.

Check your work with the key in Appendix B.

Goal: To review use of the comma   8'

> Use commas to separate items in a series. When the last item in the series is preceded by *and, or,* or *nor,* place a comma before the conjunction as well.
>
> **Examples:**
>
> The cooking class will be held either on Monday, Wednesday, or Friday.
> Tom, Mary, Rudy, and Toni were selected to represent the club.
> He answers the phone, prepares letters, and files correspondence.

1. Mandy's three favorite colors are yellow brown and burgundy.
2. Now I know how to key columns business letters and reports.
3. The theatre will show the new movie at 7:30 10:00 and 11:30.
4. Did you strongly agree moderately agree or totally disagree?
5. Her pets included a dog a cat and a three-foot garter snake.

41D

Need to Know

Goal: To learn additional proofreader's marks   4'

Four proofreader's marks are shown on the next page. Study the table to learn what each mark means, how to use it, and what the corrected copy looks like.

(Continued next page)

Apply the Rule

Read the rule and the examples.

Then key the sentences in the *Application* section. As you key them, use the correct spacing after the colons.

Goal: To learn the spacing after a colon 7'

Rule

1. Space twice after a colon used as a mark of punctuation.
2. Do not space after a colon used to express time.

Examples

Order stationery as follows: [2] Nu—Tone and Scented.
He will be leaving Chicago at 6:15 in the morning.

Application

1 The following were fired: Fields, Jex, and Hanks.
2 The fire started at 1:20 a.m.; we arrived at 1:50.
3 Give them as follows: math, English, and science.
4 The truck leaves promptly at 9:45 a.m.--not 10:00.
5 The 8:35 bus stops in two cities: Vail and Aspen.
6 Be sure to bring two things: toothbrush and soap.
7 Arriving at 11:05 were: Betsy, Martin, and Trina.

28E

Technique Timing

Take two 3-minute timings.

DS after each timing.

Goal: To improve keyboarding techniques 8'

Return to home-key position after striking each number or symbol key.

1 $29.00 $286.57 $1,067.23 $450.05 $293.74 $1,134.89
2 29% 13% 65% 50% 36.84% 23.85% 45.62% 14.76% 45.99%
3 The new retail prices are $9.95, $7.50, and $5.40.
4 Did you check the high scores of 99%, 98% and 97%?
5 At least 49% of the items are priced below $19.95.

28F

Keyboard Composition

Key the sentence number, followed by a period and two spaces. Then key each sentence, completing it with a one-word answer.

Do not correct errors.

Goal: To compose at the keyboard 5'

1. My name is . . .
2. I am planning to be a . . .
3. A bicycle has two . . .
4. For plants to grow, they need . . .
5. The opposite of hot is . . .
6. Animals with feathers are called . . .
7. Some people wear glasses to help them . . .
8. A dollar contains ten . . .
9. I can keyboard faster than I can . . .
10. I have a friend named . . .

Rough Draft

Read the copy before
you begin keying.
Then key the para-
graphs making the
changes indicated by
the proofreader's
marks.

Proofread and correct
all errors.

Goal: To key rough-draft copy   10′

You can improve your keyboarding ability if you will do the
following things: At tend class regularrly; avoid looking at your
hands when using keys such as the enter/return key or the tab key;
and keep your hands in a "ready to key" position. Even when
you pause, your hands should stay in the correct position not
rest on the edge of the key board.

Keep a positive attitude about your progress. Set goals f or
for improving your key boarding speed. Once you have set that
sped goal, do your very best to reach it. Likewise, set
realistic goals for controlling your accuracy. If you feel
that you have made too many errors, then you should try to reduce
the errors a little at a time until you reach your goal.

Application:
Letters

Goal: To key block-format business letters   19′

JOB 1 File name: L40F1 / Letterhead   Store/Keep
the document for use in Job 2.

> **Cue:** Supply information indicated in parentheses.

Mr. Paul Perez / 1860 Lincoln Street / Boyle,
MS 38730 / (supply salutation) / You are wise
to begin your career planning early. According
to the U.S. Census Bureau, population is expected to grow over the next ten years. As
the population grows, so should opportunities
for employment. ¶ The Occupational Outlook
Handbook, published every two years by the
Department of Labor, forecasts probable
changes for the next ten years in each of 250
occupations. This book can be of great assistance to you in planning your career. It is available at any public library. / Sincerely / Don
Groves / Career Specialist

JOB 2

If you are using electronic equipment with storage/memory capabilities,
retrieve File L40F1. If your equipment does not have storage/memory, rekey
the letter. Make the following changes in the letter.

1. Change the inside address to:

   Ms. Rebecca Loeb
   1739 Rosemount Avenue
   Peabody, MA   01960

2. Change the complimentary close to:

   Sincerely yours

3. Change the originator's name to:

   Rhonda Samone

4. Change the originator's title to:

   Career Consultant

> **Checkpoint:** Did you proofread and correct your
> misstrokes?

28G

Keyboard Practice

Key each line 3 times.

DS after each group of lines.

Identify misstrokes.

Goal: To practice proper keystroking techniques 10′

1 practical concede explanation opportunity pamphlet
2 absence familiar occurrence accessible feasibility
3 convenience parallel consensus accommodate fulfill
4 acquaintance category envelope necessary supersede
5 equipped noticeable temporary committee equivalent
6 careful interference thorough serviceable eligible
7 proceeds criticism occasions compliments summarize
8 brief similar competent exaggerate yield mortgages

Lesson 29

M Default Settings
T SS   SM 2″ (12); 1½″ (10)   Tab ¶

29A

Warmup

Key each line twice.
DS after each pair.

Identify misstrokes.

Goal: To strengthen keyboarding skills 5′

1 The pears will be ready to be picked by next week.
2 "The Personnel Department," said Vic, "wants her."
3 Personal Finance I is scheduled; Lane can take it.
4 About 30% bought personal copies at $23.75 apiece.

| 1 | 2 | 3 | 4 | 5 | 6 | 7 | 8 | 9 | 10 |

29B

Technique Timing

Take two 2-minute timings on each group of lines. Work on improving the technique shown.

DS after each timing.

Goal: To improve keyboarding techniques 10′

Keep other fingers in home-key position as you use the shift keys.

1 Within Before Sales September Product Long Provide
2 District Include Doctor Student Purchase Financial
3 Enough Changes Center Morning Giving Title Serving

Keep hands and arms quiet; keep wrists low but not touching the machine.

4 On Tuesday, April 14, Mr. James will come to town.
5 Yes, Christmas Day is next Wednesday, December 25.
6 The winter sale is at Manhattan Sporting Goods Co.

| 1 | 2 | 3 | 4 | 5 | 6 | 7 | 8 | 9 | 10 |

40B

Speed Practice

Take a 15- or 12-second timing on each line. If you complete a line in the time allowed, go on to the next one.

Goal: To build keyboarding speed 6'

		15"	12"
1	A full sheet has 66 vertical lines.	28	35
2	Triple spacing provides two blank lines.	32	40
3	Enter/return moves a cursor to the next line.	36	45
4	Six vertical lines are equal to one vertical inch.	40	50
5	To leave an inch top margin, start on the seventh line.	44	55

| 1 | 2 | 3 | 4 | 5 | 6 | 7 | 8 | 9 | 10 | 11 |

40C

Technique Timing

Key as many of the letter closings as you can in 5 minutes.

Key your reference initials at the appropriate place in each closing.

TS after each set of closing lines.

If you finish before time is called, start again.

Goal: To build speed keying closing lines 6'

Resume keying without pausing after each enter/return.

1 Sincerely
  ↓ QS
  Cheryl J. Elkins
  Systems Analyst
  DS
  xxx

2 Sincerely
  ↓ QS
  Arthur M. Schmit
  Supervisor
  DS
  xxx

3 Sincerely
  ↓ QS
  Vivian D. Swanson
  District Director
  DS
  xxx

4 Sincerely
  ↓ QS
  Nelson G. Taylor
  Director of Education
  DS
  xxx

Checkpoint: Did you keep the cursor/carrier moving without pauses after enters/returns?

40D

Need to Know

Goal: To learn proofreader's marks 4'

Proofreader's marks are used to indicate corrections or changes in hard copy. Refer to the table that follows to learn what each mark means, how to use it, and what the corrected copy looks like.

Mark	Meaning	Example	Corrected Copy
∧	insert	Improve ^your keyboarding	Improve your keyboarding
ℛ	delete	using your software	using software
#	add a space	you#think	you think
◡	close up space	in denting	indenting

Technique Timing

Take a 1-minute timing on each line. Work on improving the technique shown.

DS after each timing.

Goal: To improve keyboarding techniques 12′

Return to home-key position after making reaches to new keys.

1 My construction project (Green Acres) is finished.
2 Kim (my foreman) and Earl (your foreman) are gone.
3 The store has Spring/Summer and Fall/Winter sales.

Keep your eyes on the textbook copy.

Repeat lines 1–3.

Keep the **j** finger in home-key position.

4 Two words (it's/its) were correct 95% of the time.
5 Which of the discounts (17% or 18%) do you prefer?
6 She could type the report and/or file the letters.

| 1 | 2 | 3 | 4 | 5 | 6 | 7 | 8 | 9 | 10 |

29E

Keyboard Composition

Key the question number and a short answer.

Do not correct errors.

Goal: To compose at the keyboard 5′

1. What is your street address?
2. How long have you lived there?
3. What school do you attend?
4. Why are you taking keyboarding?
5. Where do you usually study?
6. What are three of your favorite foods?
7. How long does it take you to get to school in the morning?
8. What courses are you taking this term?
9. What are three words that begin with **M**?
10. What foods can you name that are white?

29F

Technique Timing

Take two 2-minute timings.

If time allows, start again.

DS after each timing.

Goal: To improve keyboarding techniques 6′

Quickly return fingers to home-key position after using the shift keys.

1 Send me $25 (and not a penny more) on November 15.
2 The new rate ($10.50/hour) went into effect today.
3 Sales for three months (May–July) were 15% higher.
4 For $655, I can purchase most (about 75%) of them.
5 By 9:15 (or was it earlier?), about 75% were sold.

Checkpoint: Did you use the correct spacing with the symbols?

Use a comma to separate items as you key them across the page.

Check your answers in Appendix B.

Example:

```
commonwealth: com mon wealth, common—wealth, 5
```

1 commonwealth
2 grandfather
3 December 16, 1986

4 Ms. Lisa Thomas
5 $16,468,117.20
6 self-contained

7 superstar
8 well-mannered
9 Boston

39D

Need to Know

Goal: To learn about salutations in letters 5′

The salutation is a polite greeting to the individual receiving the letter.

1. Whenever possible, use the individual's name in the salutation. The correct form to use is the courtesy title (*Mr., Ms.,* etc.) and the last name. (If you know the person well, you can address him or her by first-name-only.)
2. The salutation generally used in personal and business letters is *Dear,* as in *Dear Dr. Feld.*

3. Sometimes the inside address does not contain the name of an individual. If the letter is addressed to a company or department, the accepted salutations to use are *Ladies and Gentlemen* or *Dear Sir or Madam.*
4. You may also use a business title in the salutation if you do not know the individual's name, as in *Dear Credit Manager.*
5. When open punctuation is used, no punctuation follows the salutation.

39E

Apply the Rule

Key all three parts using the spacing indicated.

In the *Application* section, key the first line of the inside address. On the next line, key the appropriate salutation.

Goal: To learn to format salutations 7′

<u>Rule</u> _{DS}

The salutation should contain a courtesy title and the individual's last name, as shown in the first line of the inside address. DO NOT use first names or initials with the courtesy title in the salutation. _{DS}

If the letter is addressed to a company (not an individual), the salutation is: Ladies and Gentlemen <u>or</u> Dear Sir or Madam. _{TS}

<u>Example</u> _{DS}

Dr. Jacquelyn Wood
Dear Dr. Wood _{DS}

West Bend Paints
Ladies and Gentlemen _{TS}

<u>Application</u> _{DS}

Mr. A J. Andersen
The Commonwealth Corporation
Mrs. Robert Valdez
Otis Life and Casualty Company
Dr. Juanita Carter
Mr. Merle Skare

Lesson 30

30A

Warmup

Key each line twice.
DS after each pair.

Identify misstrokes.

Goal: To strengthen keyboarding skills 5'

1 His new car will go very fast when it is tuned up.
2 "The greens complement the yellows," added Quimby.
3 The roof--costing $245,000--complements the house.
4 Complimentary donations are these: $67, $68, $40.

| 1 | 2 | 3 | 4 | 5 | 6 | 7 | 8 | 9 | 10 |

30B

Speed Practice

Take a 20- or 15-second timing on each line. If you complete a line in the time allowed, go on to the next one.

Goal: To build keyboarding speed 5'

GWAM

	20"	15"
1 Invoice No. 465 is for $46.50.	18	24
2 The fractions are both 1/3 and 3/4.	21	28
3 Your November 12 order has been shipped.	24	32
4 Well over 85% of the classes scored over 90%.	27	36

| 1 | 2 | 3 | 4 | 5 | 6 | 7 | 8 | 9 |

30C

Goal Writing

Default or DS

Take two 3-minute goal writings.

Key at a pace that is comfortable for you.

If you finish before time is called, start again.

Identify misstrokes.

Determine your GWAM.

Goal: To measure timed-writing progress 10'

	1'	3'
A robot is a computer-controlled mechanical	9	3
device. It is most often a large metal box with	19	6
long mechanical arms. A robot can be used effec-	29	10
tively in jobs that involve doing the same task	38	13
over and over so that it becomes boring.	46	15
A robot never tires, takes lunch breaks, or	55	18
goes on a vacation. It can handle dangerous sub-	65	22
stances, work in polluted air, and work in a very	75	25
uncomfortable position. It can even work in total	86	29
darkness.	87	29

1' | 1 | 2 | 3 | 4 | 5 | 6 | 7 | 8 | 9 | 10 | AWL
3' | 1 | 2 | 3 | 5.7

39A

Warmup

Goal: To strengthen keyboarding skills   5'

Key each line twice. DS after each pair of lines.

Speed   1 She thought she would earn a profit when she sold the homes.
Accuracy   2 Eva received Vincent's invoice covering convention services.
Number/Symbol   3 One square foot is equivalent to 929.030 square centimeters.
Data Entry   4 WAIT KEYBRD 60, NONE, '1',L1, '2',L2, '3',L3, '4',L4, '5',L5

| 1 | 2 | 3 | 4 | 5 | 6 | 7 | 8 | 9 | 10 | 11 | 12 |

39B

Goal Writing

Goal: To measure timed-writing progress   10'

Default or DS

Take two 3-minute goal writings.

If you finish before time is called, start again.

Record your speed and accuracy.

	1'	3'
Data-base management systems are special programs	10	3
designed to enable you to manage information on a computer	22	7
in a useful way. With such a system, you simply input the	34	11
contents of your index cards, notebooks, and file cabinets	46	15
onto disks. Then you can use the computer to retrieve,	57	19
update, or sort through the data to locate specific infor-	69	23
mation. All you have to do is to tell the computer what you	81	27
are looking for. In just seconds, it will retrieve it.	92	31

1' | 1 | 2 | 3 | 4 | 5 | 6 | 7 | 8 | 9 | 10 | 11 | 12 | AWL
3' | 1   2   3   4   5.7

39C

Language Arts

Goal: To learn rules for dividing words   8'

Read the rules in the box at the right.

For each word in the list on the next page, key the word and a colon (:).

Then, key in the following information:

1. Syllables in the word.
2. How the word is divided.
3. The number of the rule that applies.

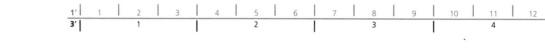

Rule 4. Avoid dividing figures, abbreviations, dates, or proper nouns.

Rule 5. Divide a compound word between the elements or after the hyphen.

Examples:

Word	Syllables	Divided Word	Rule Number
AFL-CIO	----	(avoid dividing)	4
basketball	bas ket ball	basket-ball	5
$46,668.17	----	(avoid dividing)	4
Dr. Howard Jones	----	(avoid dividing)	4
self-addressed	self ad dressed	self-addressed	5
June 16, 1985	----	(avoid dividing)	4

(Continued next page)

Take a 2-minute timing on each group of lines. Work on improving the technique shown.

Then take a 1-minute timing on the lines for the technique that needs the most improvement.

DS after each timing.

Goal: To improve keyboarding techniques 6′

Make the reaches with the fingers rather than the entire hand.

1 Write $40 and 50% and $60 and 70% and $80 and 90%.
2 (1/3), (2/3), (3/4), (4/5), (5/6), (1/10), (12/13)
3 She won in 1972, 1974, 1976, 1977, 1980, and 1982.

Try to key these easy words as words rather than letter by letter.

4 the can he of year to copy and letter order in all
5 you when we their for may such your these that new
6 our have me two on with most thank than them other

| 1 | 2 | 3 | 4 | 5 | 6 | 7 | 8 | 9 | 10 |

30E

Apply the Rule

Read the rule and the examples.

Then key the sentences in the *Application* section. As you key them, use the correct spacing with fractions.

Goal: To learn the spacing with "made" fractions 7′

Rule

1. When keying fractions, do not space before or after the diagonal.
2. Leave a space between a whole number and a "made" fraction.

Example

What is the sum of 14 1/2, 1/4, 2 1/3, and 2 1/12?

Application

1 He used 1 1/2 times the amount of salt called for.
2 She tried to add 1/2, 2/3, 3 1/2, 3/4, and 2 5/16.
3 The rate was 16 3/4 percent, but she wrote 16 1/2.
4 The recipe called for 3 1/2 pounds of wheat flour.
5 It cost her 2 1/2 times more to fly than to drive.

30F

Technique Timing

Take two 2-minute timings on each technique.

DS after each timing.

Goal: To improve keyboarding techniques 12′

Use word wrap or the margin signal to determine line endings.

In the United States, coins and paper money make up only about 20 percent of all the money in circulation. The other 80 percent consists of checking accounts, bank deposits, and various kinds of credit, such as credit cards.

Key handwritten copy without pauses.

Repeat the paragraph above.

38F

**Application:
Letters**

Default margins

T

Letterheads (2)
SM: 1¼"

Goal: To key business letters in block format 15'

JOB 1   File name: L38F1

Cue: Use your own initials as reference initials below the originator's name and title.

(Current date)

Ms. Jean Garvey
Manager
Baker Tools
15800 Pawnee Circle
Lincoln, NE 68506-6011

Dear Ms. Garvey

Business letters serve many important business functions, such as making sales, ordering products and services, informing customers, correcting problems, persuading buyers, making inquiries, and conveying goodwill.

Letters should make a favorable impression on those who receive them. Each letter should be arranged to be pleasing to the eye. It should be visually framed with approximately equal top and bottom margins.

Sincerely

Macie Hobkirk
Correspondence Specialist

xxx

JOB 2 File name: L38F2

Key the letter in 38E using the current date. Make these changes:

1. Change the inside address to:

   Mrs. Jeanne Manning
   Sales Manager
   Manning Office Supplies
   1110 Oakcrest
   Trenton, MI 48183

2. Change the salutation to:

   Dear Mrs. Manning

3. Key your own initials as reference initials.

Checkpoint: Did you key your own initials below the originator's name and title?

Keyboard Composition

Key each sentence and the phrase that best completes it.

Do not correct errors.

Goal: To compose at the keyboard 5'

1. I would like to spend my summer (at the beach, in the country, in the mountains).
2. This weekend, I might (read a book, go to a movie, go to a party).
3. I am better at (throwing a ball, playing the guitar, drawing).
4. I would like to (earn a lot of money, have a family, travel to new places).
5. Keyboarding will help me (write my school papers, input programs more quickly, get a job).
6. I would like to learn to (fix a flat tire, speak another language, keyboard more accurately).
7. For me, it is easy to (ride a bike, ride a horse, drive a car).

Lesson 31

M	Default Settings
T	SS SM 2" (12); 1½" (10) Tab ¶

31A

Warmup

Key each line twice. DS after each pair.

Identify misstrokes.

Goal: To strengthen keyboarding skills 5'

1 The book was thick and he did not want to read it.
2 Glendon accepted their offer; Lynette rejected it.
3 Use all the numbers except these: 34, 67, and 89.
4 "Why won't Quentin accept defeat?" asked Benjamin.

| 1 | 2 | 3 | 4 | 5 | 6 | 7 | 8 | 9 | 10 |

31B

Goal Writing

Default or DS

Take two 3-minute goal writings.

Key at a pace that is comfortable for you.

If you finish before time is called, start again.

Identify misstrokes.

Determine your GWAM.

Goal: To measure timed-writing progress 10'

	1'	3'
You have probably noticed that a major thing	9	3
you have done up to this point is to learn good	19	6
techniques of keyboarding. By now, you should be	29	10
able to employ those effective techniques without	39	13
consciously thinking of doing so.	46	15
You will now learn to format the typical	54	18
things you might produce from day to day for your	64	21
personal use. As you complete the lessons that	74	25
follow, remember to key by touch, to key without	83	28
pauses, to keystroke properly, and so forth.	92	31

	1	2	3	4	5	6	7	8	9	10	AWL
1'											5.7
3'	1			2			3				

Need to Know

Goal: To learn the block format for business letters 7'

The block format is a time-saving format for business letters.

1. Business letters are usually prepared on **letterhead** stationery. Letterhead

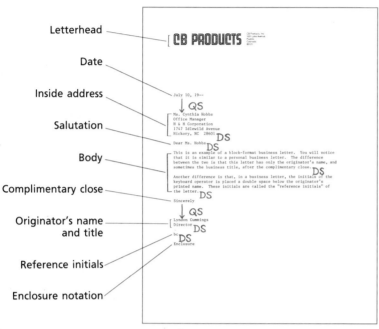

Letterhead
Date
Inside address
Salutation
Body
Complimentary close
Originator's name and title
Reference initials
Enclosure notation

BUSINESS LETTER IN BLOCK FORMAT

is printed with the name and address of the originator's company.

2. If letterhead is not available, regular bond paper is used and the company name and address are centered on line 7.

3. In **block format,** the margins, spacing between parts, and position of the date line are the same for personal and business letters.

4. Business letters may contain parts that do not appear in personal business letters: the originator's title, reference initials, and (if needed) an enclosure notation.

5. The **originator's title** is keyed as part of the signature lines immediately below the printed name.

6. The **reference initials** are the initials of the keyboard operator. They are keyed in lowercase letters a DS below the signature lines.

7. When additional items are being sent with the letter, an **enclosure notation** is used. It is keyed a DS below the reference initials.

Project Preview

 M

File name: L38E
Default margins

T

Full sheet
SM: 1¼"

Key as much of the letter as you can in 5 minutes.

Use the current year in the date.

Ignore misstrokes.

If you finish before time is called, start again.

Goal: To key a business letter in block format 8'

April 1, 19-- ↓ line 15

  ↓QS
Mr. Sheldon Keresey
Office Manager
Dunstan Corporation
3001 Ygnacio Valley Road
Walnut Creek, CA 94598 ˌDS

Dear Mr. Keresey ˌDS

This is an example of a block-format business letter. You will notice that it is similar to a personal business letter. The difference between the two is that this letter contains the originator's business title and the keyboard operator's reference initials below the originator's name. ˌDS

Sincerely

  ↓QS
Sally Waggoner
Director ˌDS

sbs

31C

Need to Know

Goal: To learn how to use other keyboard symbols 7′

Refer to the illustration to help you locate each new symbol key on your keyboard.

Determine which finger strikes each key.

Note: Some symbols may not appear on your keyboard.

Symbol	Spacing	Example
General Use:		
! (exclamation	2 spaces after	Ouch! That hurts.
@ (at)	space before and after	2 @ $1.69
# (number/pound)	no space between figure and symbol	#47 (number) 50# (pounds)
¢ (cent)	no space before	75¢ each
& (ampersand/and)	space before and after	Smidt & Sons
* (asterisk)	no space between symbol and word	*Note Total*
½ (one-half)	no space before	5½ oz.
¼ (one-quarter)	no space before	2¼ lbs.
Math Use:		
+ (plus)	space before and after	2 + 2
= (equals)	space before and after	2 + 2 = 4
Programming Use:		
@ (at)	no space after symbol	@4
+ (plus)	no space before or after	A+B
[(left bracket)	no space after	[UC
] (right bracket)	no space before	[UC]
> (greater than)	space before and after	AMT > than 10
< (less than)	space before and after	A < B
* (multiply)	no space before or after	5*8
= (equals)	no space before or after	C=C+1

31D

Keyboard Practice

Goal: To practice proper keystroking techniques 13′

Key each line twice.

Identify misstrokes.

1 Max cried, "Help!" Sue screamed, "I'm over here!"

2 Sharon bought 6 dozen @ $2 per dozen and paid $12.

3 Randy purchased 500 gallons of #2 grade oil today.

4 This order is for 350# of potatoes @ $1.98 per lb.

(Continued next page)

Lesson 38

Default Settings
T   SS   SM 1½" (12); 1" (10)   Tab ¶

38A

Warmup

Key each line twice.
DS after each pair.

Confusing words: it's and its

Goal: To strengthen keyboarding skills 5'

1 It's too soon to tell whether Anne passed the algebra class.
2 Northwest High chose its principal from the three finalists.
3 It's certain that Pamela's sense of duty was its own reward.

| 1 | 2 | 3 | 4 | 5 | 6 | 7 | 8 | 9 | 10 | 11 | 12 |

38B

Accuracy Practice

DS after each group of lines.

Goal: To build keyboarding accuracy 5'

Take a 3-minute accuracy timing on the lines in 38A. If you make an error, start again. Stay on a line until you have keyed it without error.

38C

Language Arts

Read the rules in the box at the right.

For each word in the list below the box, key the word and a colon (:).

Then, key in the following information:

1. Syllables in the word.
2. How the word is divided.
3. The number of the rule that applies.

Use a comma to separate items as you key them across the page.

Check your work with the key in Appendix B.

Goal: To learn rules for dividing words 10'

Divide words only when it is absolutely necessary to maintain proper line lengths. Refer to a dictionary or word book as needed for syllabication.

Rule 1. Never divide a one-syllable word or one with five or fewer letters.

Rule 2. Divide only between syllables.

Rule 3. Include two or more letters with the first part of the divided word and three or more with the last part.

Examples:

Word	Syllables	Divided Word	Rule Number
sought	sought	(do not divide)	1
undue	un due	(do not divide)	1
consume	con sume	con-sume	2
carefully	care ful ly	care-fully	3
abandoned	a ban doned	aban-doned	3

Example:

trimmed: trimmed, do not divide, 1

1 trimmed
2 gratefully
3 thought
4 abounding
5 compound
6 erasing
7 contained
8 overly
9 trapped

5 He bought at 60¢ apiece; she bought at 50¢ apiece.

6 The Martin & Watkins Company was closed yesterday.

7 *Note: Every score should be listed individually.

8 Suzanne very quickly added 30$\frac{1}{4}$ to 60$\frac{1}{4}$ and got 90$\frac{1}{2}$.

9 Please check this problem: 10 + 11 + 12 + 7 = 40.

10 180 PRINT "TYPE @12' "TO PRINT AN INCOME STATEMENT

11 A sample line in a program might read: PRINT A+B.

12 The program command to begin underscoring is [UC].

13 1050 IF AB IS > 18 THEN PRINT "MONTHLY DEDUCTIONS"

14 1060 IF AB IS < 18 THEN PRINT "PAYROLL DEDUCTIONS"

15 In a program 5*8 means 5 is to be multiplied by 8.

16 280 IF A=25 THEN PRINT "THESE PEOPLE MAY NOW VOTE"

31E

Technique Timing

Take two 3-minute timings on each group of lines.

Key each line once. Repeat if time allows.

DS after each timing.

Goal: To improve keyboarding techniques 15′

Key the numbers as quickly as you key the words.

1 sign 2856 work 2948 down 3926 then 5636 rich 4836

2 firm 4847 when 2636 form 4947 rush 4726 city 3856

3 wish 2826 owns 9262 both 5956 pals 0192 girl 5849

Quickly release the shift key and return to home-key position.

4 The decisions affected Sam, Rose, Mark, and Wilma.

5 Enterprise; Calendar; Maintenance; Mortgage; Brief

6 Has Fay Jacks passed the CPA or the CAM exams yet?

Lesson 32 / Measuring Mastery

32A

Warmup

Key each line twice. DS after each pair.

Goal: To strengthen keyboarding skills 5′

1 The new cook heated thick soup for the tired boys.

2 I am enclosing the four copies that you requested.

3 "Send him water-marked stationery," said Marjorie.

4 Invoice Nos. 2938, 4720, 3820, and 7564 were paid.

| 1 | 2 | 3 | 4 | 5 | 6 | 7 | 8 | 9 | 10 |

37D

Need to Know   **Goal: To learn the correct format for inside addresses** 6′

1. The first line of an inside address identifies the addressee, the person to whom the letter is written. The correct form consists of a courtesy title, the individual's first name, initial, and last name.
2. Courtesy titles include *Mr., Mrs., Miss, Ms.,* and *Dr.*

```
Addressee's name ──▶ Ms. Margaret A. Rice
Business title ──────▶ Office Supervisor
Company name ──────▶ Goldberg Office Supply
Street address ──────▶ 2437 Central Street
City, state, and ──────▶ Chattanooga, TN  37402
  ZIP Code
```

Use *Ms.* when you do not know the marital status of a woman or when she prefers this title.

3. The second line of the address usually contains the person's business title, if it is known.
4. If the letter is sent to a business address, the next line usually contains the company's name.
5. The most important address information is in the last two lines. The second line from the bottom usually contains a number and street name or a post office box to which mail is delivered.
6. The city, two-letter state abbreviation, and ZIP Code is on the last line. Separate the city and state abbreviation with a comma. Leave two spaces between the state and ZIP Code.

37E

Need to Know   **Goal: To learn to key unarranged copy** 5′

Some of the letters in this unit are set in unarranged format. When keying unarranged copy, you make decisions about the arrangement and spacing of the letter parts on the page.

Diagonal lines (/) are used to indicate the end of a line or a letter part. When you see a diagonal line, you need to decide how many times to press the enter/return key. For example, if the copy reads *Dear Mrs. Vlasuk/,* you press the enter/return key twice before keying the body of the letter.

Double space and begin a new paragraph when you see the paragraph symbol (¶).

37F

Application: Letters   **Goal: To key personal business letters in block format** 22′

JOB 1 **M** File name: L37F1   Default margins
     T Full sheet   SM: 1¼″

Mr. Larry Saindon / Director of Admissions / College of Southern Idaho / 8150 Lake Avenue / Twin Falls, ID 83301 / Dear Mr. Saindon / Please send me your catalog for the fall semester. I am interested in majoring in accounting or computer science. I would like to enter Southern Idaho in September. ¶ Also, please send me any information that is available on student housing and scholarships. / Sincerely / Catherine Morello / P.O. Box 310 / Grand Junction, CO 81501

> **Checkpoint:** Did you space correctly between the letter parts?

JOB 2 **M** File name: L37F2   Default margins
     T Full sheet   SM: 1¼″

Ms. Marianne Holmes / Information Director / Mission Viejo Construction Company / 15568 East Hampden Circle / Englewood, NJ 07632 / Dear Ms. Holmes / Because energy conservation is a top priority with our family this winter, I would like to know what types of insulation you recommend for a four-bedroom frame house with about 3,000 square feet of living space. We have two floors to the house, and the garage is attached. ¶ We have just had new storm windows and doors installed to reduce heat loss. Please list any other energy-saving measures we can take. / Sincerely / Alvin Rivera / 629 East Stanley Avenue / Minot, ND 58701

Goal Writing

Default or DS

Take two 3-minute goal writings.

Key at a pace that is comfortable for you.

If you finish before time is called, start again.

Identify misstrokes.

Determine your GWAM.

Goal: To measure timed-writing progress 10′

	1′	3′
The computer is being used today more and	9	3
more to help those in our midst who are disabled.	19	6
Electronic devices can help the severely disabled	29	10
use a computer to communicate, to feed themselves,	39	13
to operate entertainment devices, or even to per-	49	16
form tasks on the job. Computer-produced speech,	59	20
or voice synthesis, can help the blind to perform	69	23
tasks that may have been very hard or impossible	79	26
for them to do. Yes, the computer is doing a lot	89	30
to help the disabled.	93	31

1′ | 1 | 2 | 3 | 4 | 5 | 6 | 7 | 8 | 9 | 10 | AWL
3′ | 1 | 2 | 3 | 5.7

32C

Technique Review

Key the statement number (followed by a period and two spaces) and your answer.

Goal: To review keyboarding techniques and procedures 8′

True/False

1. Space once before and after a hyphen.
2. Always leave one space after a quotation mark.
3. Space twice after a semicolon.
4. Space twice after a period that ends a sentence.
5. Space once after a period used as a decimal point.
6. To figure the number of words in a line, divide the number of strokes in the line by 5.

Fill-in-the-Blank

M
7. Use the _____ to key all capital letters.
8. A command to the printer within text is called an _____ command.
9. Use the _____ keys to move through text.
10. The automatic return feature of a microcomputer is called _____.

T
7. The _____ sets a tab stop at any point on a line.
8. The _____ allows you to key beyond the left and right margins.
9. The _____ moves the carrier to the left one space at a time.
10. Use the _____ to key all capital letters.

32D

Punctuation Practice

Key each line twice, using correct spacing around the punctuation marks.

Goal: To review spacing with punctuation 9′

1 Wm. R. Jones Co. -- the state's leader -- can exhibit.

2 Ship the following: 8 red, 12 blue, and 12 green.

3 The correct numbers are 1 5/16, 15/32, and 19 3/32.

(Continued next page)

M Default Settings
T SS   SM 1½″ (12); 1″ (10)   Tab ¶

37A

Warmup

Key each line twice.
DS after each pair.

Two-letter ZIP Code abbreviations

Goal: To strengthen keyboarding skills 5′

```
1 States AL AK AZ AR CA CO CT DE DC FL GA HI ID IL IN IA KS KY
2 ZIP LA ME MD MA MI MN MS MO MT NE NV NH NJ NM NY NC ND OH OK
3 Code Abbreviations OR PA RI SC SD TN TX UT VT VA WA WV WI WY
```

| 1 | 2 | 3 | 4 | 5 | 6 | 7 | 8 | 9 | 10 | 11 | 12 |

37B

Comparison Copy

Default or DS

Take a 2-minute timing on each paragraph.

Try to keep your speed on the statistical copy as high as your straight-copy speed.

Goal: To build speed on a variety of copy 7′

	1′	2′
The mailing address on an envelope is single spaced and	11	6
contains the same information as the inside address of the	23	12
letter. Key the addressee's name on the first line and the	35	18
title on the second line of the inside address.	45	22
The No. 10 envelope used for most business correspon—	11	6
dence measures 9 1/2 x 4 1/8 inches. The mailing address is	23	12
keyed 2 1/2 inches (or 15 lines) from the top edge of the	35	17
envelope and 4 inches from the left edge.	43	22

1′ | 1 | 2 | 3 | 4 | 5 | 6 | 7 | 8 | 9 | 10 | 11 | 12 |
2′ | 1 | 2 | 3 | 4 | 5 | 6 |

37C

Keyboard Composition

Complete each sentence.

Do not correct errors.

Goal: To compose at the keyboard 5′

```
1. One place you can see lots of fish is ___.
2. When my keyboarding improves, I will be able to ___.
3. My keyboarding teacher, whose name is ___, uses a stopwatch.
4. I usually celebrate my birthday, which comes on ___, with ___.
5. My second period class, ___, begins at ___ a.m.
6. ___, my keyboarding teacher, is always telling us to ___.
7. In the ___, you are likely to find tigers and ___.
8. I like green vegetables, such as ___, when they are ___.
9. If I had ___ dollars, I would buy ___.
10. A coat will keep you ___, but an umbrella will keep you ___.
```

Checkpoint: Did you think of information for the blank spaces as you were keying the sentences?

Key each line twice.

4 "She can win it," said Jane. "Jack can win also."
5 Call Mary at 7:30 a.m.; I'll call you at 7:00 a.m.
6 He built 2,450 units; however, we sold only 1,830.
7 The figure is $65.39, but only $56.93 was written.
8 She told us <u>not</u> to go. Let's do what she says to.
9 Isn't Bob's car insurance just as good as Henry's?
10 Jo said, "Either one -- Kathy or Zoe -- is qualified."

32E

Technique Timing

Take two 2-minute timings on each group of lines. Work on improving the technique shown.

If time allows, start again.

DS after each timing.

Goal: To demonstrate keyboarding techniques 13'

Keep your eyes on the textbook copy when keying and entering/returning.

1 I inquired about proposed subordinated debentures.
2 Invoices 38209, 39576, 40730, and 41829 were paid.
3 Orion filed an action in the First District Court.

Key without pausing between words or lines.

4 Then--and only then--will I get the majority vote.
5 Her phone number (798-4005) is an unlisted number.
6 Nu-Ore has multi-million dollar lease obligations.

Keep hands and arms in correct position.

7 The Governor of Arkansas expressed his opposition.
8 Long-term debts exceed total shareholders' equity.
9 I enjoined further communications to shareholders.

> **Checkpoint:** Were you able to keep your hands and arms in correct position? If necessary, review 8D.

32F

Technique Timing

Take two 2-minute timings.

Use word wrap or the margin signal to determine line endings.

Goal: To demonstrate keyboarding techniques 5'

Use machine parts correctly and efficiently.

Dental insurance has become a <u>very</u> important employee benefit. About one of every three Americans is covered by some type of dental insurance plan. Dental plans have the support of employers and the American Dental Association (ADA) because, "they foster better dental care."

1. Store the document.
2. Select the print option from the main menu, or key in the print command for your program.
3. Select the appropriate format for the document. To print a document in a specific format, you may need to change the software program's default settings to match those of the document. The settings you change may include margin settings and line spacing.

   The procedure you use for making changes may vary, but it is usually done in one of two ways:
   a. Key in the desired format changes as they are requested by the print-program prompt.
   b. Move the cursor through a list of default settings, and key in the desired changes.
4. Check your printer to see that it is turned on and is ready to print the **hard copy.** Be sure the paper is aligned correctly.
5. Key in the command to start printing.

E *Electronic Typewriters*

Documents that have been stored in the memory of an electronic typewriter may be printed at a later date. The steps in the printing process vary but usually include the following procedures:

1. Insert paper. Use the same pitch printwheel/element and set the same margins, tabs, and line spacing you used when you keyed the document.
2. Position the carrier where you want the document to begin printing.
3. Depress the print key or command for your typewriter.
4. Key in the file name or the storage area.
5. Depress the key or command to start printing.

   Key the body of the letter in 35G. The file name is L36D. Print the document.

36E

Application: Letters

File name: L36E
Default margins

Full sheet
SM: 1¼"

Key the document. If your equipment has storage capabilities, store the document.

Retrieve and print the document.

Unless your teacher tells you differently, delete the document.

Goal: To prepare a personal business letter in block format 18'

Cue: Use today's date.

Mr. Harrison Tyler
Reynolds Computer Company
2767 Central Avenue
New Orleans, LA 70633

Dear Mr. Tyler

As a testimonial to the Rabbit 7000 computer you sold me recently, I should like to tell you how satisfied I have been. The Rabbit has helped me to keep accurate banking records for the first time in years. It has enabled me to keep up-to-date records of my appointments. It has helped me to improve my math skills through a program called "Math Teacher."

I am still finding many uses for my Rabbit, and I expect to use it for many years to come.

Sincerely

Marilyn Stokes
2373 Fairview Avenue
Bogalusa, LA 70427

Checkpoint: Proofread and correct all errors before you store and/or print this document. Check the format of your letter.

Part **2** // Developing Formatting Skills

M Default Settings
T SS SM 1½" (12); 1" (10) Tab ¶

36A

Warmup

Key each line twice.
DS after each pair.

Goal: To strengthen keyboarding skills 5'

1 Cassy has assured the astonished eastern Asian of the asset
2 Fong was fatigued with the frightening fight for five frogs.
3 Lanky Luke felt lucky to pluck the nickel from a clear lake.
4 This young man felt you were undoubtedly unduly in a stupor.

| 1 | 2 | 3 | 4 | 5 | 6 | 7 | 8 | 9 | 10 | 11 | 12 |

36B

Accuracy Practice

DS after each group of lines.

Goal: To build keyboarding accuracy 5' *36-1*

Take a 3-minute accuracy timing on the lines in 36A. If you make an error, start again. Stay on a line until you have keyed it without error.

> **Checkpoint:** How many error-free lines did you key?

36C

Language Arts

Read the rule in the box at the right.

Then key each numbered sentence, supplying the correct number style.

Check your work with the key in Appendix B.

Goal: To review rules for numbers 7'

> Use figures for the day of the month and the year in correspondence.
>
> **Example:**
>
> The U.S. Bicentennial was celebrated on July 4, 1976.

1. His order was received on January four and shipped on February 2.
2. John and Joe enlisted in the U.S. Air Force on April twelve, 1952.
3. Your letter of October 13 reported a shipment on May 15, 1983.
4. Her birthday was September fourteen, 1945.
5. The reservation is for November ten instead of November 12.

36D

Read and Do

Goal: To learn how to print a document 15' *36-2*

The final step in document preparation is the **printing** process. Before printing a document, proofread carefully and correct all errors.

M *Microcomputers*

The printing process varies depending on the software program you are using. Determine the procedures for your software program. Use the following steps as a guide to the printing process:

(Continued next page)

Unit 3 / Personal/Business Letters

One way of using your keyboarding skills is in the preparation of correspondence. In this unit, Lessons 33–45, you will learn to:

1. Increase your keyboarding speed and accuracy.
2. Prepare personal and business letters in block format.
3. Use open punctuation for salutations and complimentary closes.
4. Develop skill in keyboard composition.
5. Name, store, retrieve, print, and delete documents.
6. Key documents containing proofreader's marks.

Micro Dictionary

character	a letter, number, symbol, or blank space in a line of text
column	a term often used to refer to horizontal spaces across the screen of a microcomputer. An 80-column screen will hold 80 characters.
default settings	equipment settings that are preset into a software program or into the equipment's memory. These settings may include margins and tab stops.
document	a term often used to refer to letters, tables, reports, and other information prepared on electronic equipment
file	a stored document
file name	a name given to a document when it is stored
hard copy	a document that is printed on paper
print	the process of converting screen/disk copy to hard copy
retrieve	the transfer of stored documents from a floppy disk file to the computer's memory. On electronic typewriters with storage capabilities, documents are recalled from a storage area to the typewriter's memory.
store	the placement of documents on a floppy disk or into memory so that they may be recalled at a later time

Lesson 33

M Default Settings
T SS   SM 1½" (12); 1" (10)   Tab ¶

33A

Warmup

Key each line twice.
DS after each pair.

Goal: To strengthen keyboarding skills 5′

1 Teresa truly tried to treasure her trophy for a trapeze act.
2 Verbal brevity is a valuable trait a volleyball devotee has.
3 The dominant horseman rode a palomino through a wheat field.
4 Ora was open in her opposite opinion on population movement.

| 1 | 2 | 3 | 4 | 5 | 6 | 7 | 8 | 9 | 10 | 11 | 12 |

1. Select the files option from the main menu.
2. Select the delete option from the files menu.
3. Select the file that is to be deleted. File selection is usually done in one of two ways.
   a. The files are listed one after another. Move the cursor to the file you want to delete. Enter the command that deletes the file.
   b. When a prompt asks for the file name, key in the appropriate file name. Be sure to key in the file name correctly.

Most software programs give you an opportunity to change your mind about deleting a file. After you indicate the file you want to delete, a prompt usually appears on the screen to ask you if you want to delete the file. Proceed to delete the file by giving the appropriate response (usually a Y for yes). You may cancel the delete by entering the appropriate cancel command for your program.

E *Electronic Typewriters*

Some electronic typewriters use a delete key while others use one or more commands to delete a document or file from memory. Depending on your typewriter, you may use the following steps:

1. Press and hold down the delete key, or key in the command for your particular typewriter.
2. Key in the file name or the storage area.
3. Key in the other commands as necessary.

Delete L35D.

35G

Application: Letters

File name: L35G
Default margins

Full sheet
SM: 1¼"

Key the document. If your equipment has storage capabilities, store the document.

Unless your teacher tells you differently, retrieve and delete the document.

Goal: To key a personal business letter in block format 16'

(Current date)

Mr. Alvin Pittaro
Director of Admissions
Allegheny Technical Institute
4455 Mountain Way
Harrisburg, PA 17105

Dear Mr. Pittaro

Thank you for the very helpful talk you gave to my computer class. Most of us did not realize that so many careers in computer technology are open to us.
That is why I am writing to you. I would like to enter ATI in September. Please send me the name of a career counselor that I can contact for aptitude testing.

Thank you for taking time to visit our class. I look forward to seeing you in the fall.

Sincerely

Jeffrey Clarkson
148 Maple Avenue
Mount Airy, PA 19119

Technique Timing

Take two 3-minute timings.

If you finish before time is called, start again.

Goal: To improve keying techniques on blocked paragraphs 7'

Cue: SS lines of paragraphs. DS between paragraphs.

Single—spaced paragraphs are used mainly in personal and business letters. When paragraphs are single spaced, the operator must touch the enter/return key twice to begin a new paragraph. This procedure will leave a blank line between paragraphs. DS

Paragraphs that are not indented are called blocked paragraphs. All lines in a blocked paragraph, including the first line, begin at the left margin. The letter format that will be used in this unit is called a block format. Block format means that all letter parts begin at the left margin.

| 1 | 2 | 3 | 4 | 5 | 6 | 7 | 8 | 9 | 10 | 11 | 12 |

Need to Know

Goal: To learn the block format for personal business letters 10' 33-1

The block format is a time-saving format for preparing personal business letters.

1. In **block format,** all lines begin at the left margin.

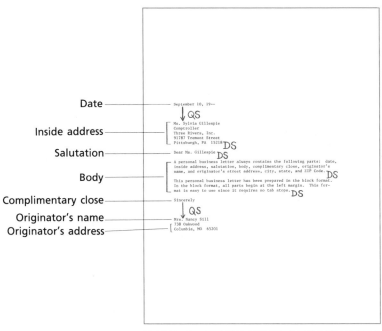

Date

Inside address

Salutation

Body

Complimentary close

Originator's name
Originator's address

PERSONAL BUSINESS LETTER IN BLOCK FORMAT

2. The letter should be approximately centered on the page. Use the following guidelines for formatting letters.

M Use default margins. Press enter/return for cursor returns in the opening and closing lines of the letter. Allow word wrap to determine line endings in the body of the letter.

T Set 1¼-inch margins, or use a 6-inch line length. Each of these settings contain space for 60 pica (10-pitch) **characters** or 72 elite (12-pitch) characters. Press the return key for carrier returns in the opening and closing lines. Use auto return or the margin signal to determine line endings in the body of the letter.

3. The **date** line always contains the month (spelled out in full), the day, and the year. The position of the date line varies according to the length of the letter. Key the date on line 15 for the average-length letters in this unit.

(Continued next page)

E Electronic Typewriters

The procedure for storing text varies depending on the kind of typewriter you are using. However, the basic process includes these steps:

1. Insert paper; determine whether your print-wheel/element is 10-pitch or 12-pitch; set margins, tabs, and line space.
2. Depress the store key or store command for your equipment. Some typewriters have numbered storage areas; others require a file name. Depending on your equipment, you may need to specify a storage area or give a file name.
3. Key the document as you usually would.
4. Depress the store key or store command to close storage.

Key and store the sentences in 35B. Use L35D for the file name.

> ## 35E

Read and Do Goal: To learn how to retrieve documents 6'

After a document has been stored on a disk or in the memory of an electronic typewriter, you must have some method to recall or **retrieve** the document to use it at a later time.

M Microcomputers

Before you retrieve a file, you may need to clear your computer's memory. Also, remember to store or save a document before starting a new document.

The procedure for retrieving stored files may include the following steps. Select and follow the steps that apply to your software program.

1. Select the retrieve or recall option, or key in the command to retrieve a file.
2. Key in the name of the file that is being retrieved. If you have a dual disk drive, you may need to tell the computer which drive contains the file.

   If you can't remember the name of a file, you may be able to display a list of the names of files that are stored on a particular disk by keying in a directory command.

When you retrieve a document, the computer puts a duplicate of the document into the computer's memory as a working copy. The original document remains in storage. You may change or print the working copy. If you make changes, the changes occur only in the working copy until you store it. When you store the working copy, it usually replaces the original document stored in the file.

E Electronic Typewriters

Some electronic typewriters play or print a stored document. Others send the document through the typewriter's display one line at a time. The process usually involves these steps:

1. Insert paper; set margins and tabs if your typewriter prints the document. Position the carrier and paper where you want the document to begin printing.
2. Depress the retrieve key or the retrieve command.
3. Key in the file name or the storage area.
4. Depress the key to start the process.

The typewriter either plays back the entire document or displays the first line of the document. Typewriters that display stored text usually have a command or key to allow you to scroll the text forward. Use this feature to continue your review of the stored document.

Using the key or command for your particular equipment, recall file L35D.

> ## 35F

Read and Do Goal: To learn how to delete a stored document 5'

When a document or file is no longer needed, it can be deleted or removed from a disk or from the memory of an electronic typewriter.

M Microcomputers

The deleting process on microcomputers varies according to the software package you are using. Determine the procedure for your program. The basic procedure usually involves these steps:

(Continued next page)

M Use the enter/return key to space down to line 15. Some software programs have a default setting for the top margin. That is, a certain number of lines are set aside for a top margin. Include these lines in your count to line 15. For example, if the top margin default is 6 lines, count down 9 more lines (6 + 9 = 15).

4. The **inside address** is keyed a quadruple space (QS) below the date. (When you see QS, strike the enter/return key four times.) The inside address usually contains the name, title, company name, and address of the addressee (the person to whom the letter is written).

5. The **salutation** is keyed a double space (DS) below the inside address. It usually begins with *Dear* and contains a courtesy title and the addressee's last name. When open punctuation is used, no colon is keyed after the salutation.

6. The **body** is single spaced with no paragraph indentions. Use a double space between paragraphs.

7. The **complimentary close** is keyed a double space below the body. When open punctuation is used, no comma is keyed after the complimentary close.

8. The **originator's name** (the name of the person who wrote the letter) is keyed a QS below the complimentary close to leave room for the handwritten signature.

9. The **originator's address** is keyed below the name to make it easier for the addressee to respond to the letter.

10. Two spaces are left between the two-letter state abbreviation and the ZIP Code. (When ZIP-Plus is used, a hyphen and four figures follow the ZIP Code.)

33D

Project Preview

Default margins
Word wrap: body

Full sheet
SM: 1¼"
Margin signal: body

Key as much of the letter as you can in 5 minutes.

Use the current year in the date.

Ignore misstrokes.

If you finish before time is called, start again.

Goal: To key a personal business letter in block format 7'   *33-2*

July 23, 19-- ↓ line 15
    ↓ QS
Mr. Charles Gibbs E/R
General Manager E/R
Windsor Corporation E/R
1180 Sherwood Drive E/R
Farmington, NM 87401–2310 DS

Dear Mr. Gibbs DS

A personal business letter always contains the following parts:
date, inside address, salutation, body, complimentary close,
originator's name, and originator's street address, city, state,
and ZIP Code. DS

This personal business letter has been keyed in the block format.
In the block format, all parts begin at the left margin. This
format is easy to use since it requires no tab stops. DS

Sincerely
    ↓ QS
Mrs. Jodell Cash E/R
921 East Second Street E/R
Apple Creek, OH 44606–7794 E/R

35B

Speed Practice

Goal: To build keyboarding speed 5′

Take a 20- or 15-second timing on each sentence. If you complete a sentence before time is called, go on to the next one.

1 Hyphenate words only at a syllable.   21 | 28

2 Often businesses do not hyphenate words.   24 | 32

3 Line-ending decisions take time and practice.   27 | 36

4 Not dividing words at the right margin saves time.   30 | 40

5 When you hyphenate a word, hyphenate between syllables. 33 | 44

| 1 | 2 | 3 | 4 | 5 | 6 | 7 | 8 | 9 | 10 | 11 |

35C

Language Arts

Goal: To review rules for capitalization 7′

Read the rule in the box at the right.

Then key the paragraph, supplying correct capitalization where needed.

Check your work with the key in Appendix B.

> Capitalize days of the week, months of the year, and holidays.
>
> **Examples:**
>
> The reports will be presented on Monday, Wednesday, and Friday.
> All state offices will be closed for Memorial Day on Monday, May 27.

His report of august 8 requires several adjustments. In the first place, all committees meet on tuesday, september 3, not on monday, september 2. As monday, september 2, is a holiday, labor day, our offices will be closed so every employee can enjoy a long weekend. Other holidays to be observed the rest of the year are in november and december. On november 28, the corporate office will close for thanksgiving. Most offices will also close on wednesday, december 25, for christmas. Customer service operations resume on tuesday.

35D

Read and Do

Goal: To learn how to store documents 6′

A feature of most software programs and of some electronic typewriters is the ability to store documents for later recall or retrieval.

M *Microcomputers*

On many software programs, storing is referred to as saving a file. To store or save a document, select an option or use a command to move the document from the microcomputer's memory to a floppy disk. Until you store a document, it exists only in the microcomputer's memory. If you turn the microcomputer off, you may lose the copy you have keyed.

While each program has its own menu or its own commands for storing documents, the procedure usually includes the following steps. Key the document as you usually would; then select and use the steps that apply to your software program.

1. Select the store or save option, or key in the store command for your program.
2. Key in the name of the document, if prompted to do so.
3. Respond to any other prompts that may appear on your screen. If you have a dual disk drive, you may need to tell the computer which disk drive contains the file.

(Continued next page)

Key as many of the opening lines as you can in 5 minutes.

Use the current year in the date.

Leave two spaces between the two-letter state abbreviation and the ZIP Code.

TS after each set of opening lines.

If you finish before time is called, start again.

Goal: To build speed in keying opening lines   6'

Resume keying without pausing after each enter/return.

1 November 15, 19--
   ↓ QS
   Mr. Stephen Karampalas
   50 Ashland Street
   Farmington, NM 87401 ₁ₛ
   DS
   Dear Mr. Karampalas

3 December 12, 19--
   ↓ QS
   Dr. Norman Dodge
   2307 Cherry Lane
   Palo Alto, CA 94303 ₁ₛ
   DS
   Dear Dr. Dodge

2 January 27, 19--
   ↓ QS
   Mrs. Elaine C. Williams
   Admissions Officer
   Bedford Business College
   Bedford, MA 01730-0381 ₁ₛ
   DS
   Dear Mrs. Williams

4 April 2, 19--
   ↓ QS
   Ms. Olive Troy
   Office Manager
   Strobel Oil Company
   Camas, WA 98607 ₁ₛ
   DS
   Dear Ms. Troy

Default margins
Word wrap: body

T

Full sheets (2)
SM: 1¼"
Margin signal: body

Use the current year in the date.

Goal: To key a personal business letter in block format   15'   33-3

JOB 1

November 7, 19-- ↓ line 13
   ↓ QS
Ms. Mary Zolar
Office Manager
Technical Systems, Inc.
9023 West Parmalee Circle
South Bend, IN 46601 ₁ₛ
DS
Dear Ms. Zolar
   DS

I understand you have just purchased a new EASYUSE personal computer. I am thinking of purchasing the same model and would like to have some information about it. ₁ₛ
DS

How much memory capacity does your computer have? Does it use floppy disks from other manufacturers? Do you find the word processing software does everything that the advertisements say it will do? Do you have a maintenance contract? ₁ₛ
DS

I appreciate your taking the time to answer these questions for me. If the EASYUSE can do all that I think it can, it will be a great help to me in my home office. ₁ₛ
DS

Cordially
   ↓ QS
Don Lewis
285 Courtland Avenue
Indianapolis, IN 46259

(Continued next page)

Check your answers in Appendix C.

3. The inside address is keyed a double space below the date.
4. The salutation is keyed a double space below the inside address.
5. In block format, the first line of a paragraph indents five spaces.

34H

Application: Letters

File name: L34F
Default margins

Full sheet
SM: 1¼″

Note: Beginning in this lesson and continuing through the book, file names are given.

Unless your teacher tells you differently, use the suggested file names for the documents you prepare.

Goal: To key a personal business letter in block format 10′   34-3

Cue: Use today's date in the date line.

(Current date)

Ms. Eileen Ricchio
Office Director
Communications, Inc.
P. O. Box 310
Conifer, CO 80233–7278

Dear Ms. Ricchio

In answer to your letter of October 20, I agree that most of us have many opportunities to send block-format personal business letters. This method of communication can help us accomplish a variety of personal tasks.

At times we all need to order goods, request or give information, and confirm or make plans. These are all situations in which sending a personal business letter is the most effective means of getting the job done.

Sincerely

Kaye Roll
2411 East Madison Avenue
Los Angeles, CA 90067–1231

Checkpoint: Did you use a QS after the date and the complimentary close?

Lesson 35

M Default Settings
T SS   SM 1½″ (12); 1″ (10)   Tab ¶

35A

Warmup

Key each line twice.
DS after each pair.

"ing" combinations

Goal: To strengthen keyboarding skills 5′

1 skating dancing talking wishing skiing singing eating buying
2 I feel like singing while I am dancing or skating or skiing.
3 Stopping those running around the swimming pool is her duty.

| 1 | 2 | 3 | 4 | 5 | 6 | 7 | 8 | 9 | 10 | 11 | 12 |

JOB 2

Key the letter in 33D using your own name and address as the originator.

Lesson 34

	Default Settings
M	
T	SS SM 1½″ (12); 1″ (10) Tab ¶

34A

Warmup

Goal: To strengthen keyboarding skills 5′   *34-1*

Key each line twice. DS after each pair of lines.

Speed   1 Their theory is that the woman got the quantity right today.
Accuracy   2 Different friends of Fred offered to forward funds for food.
Number/Symbol 3 Four quarts, 1 gallon, and 3.785 liters are identical terms.
Data Entry   4 Their fourth quarter tax installment is $14,056.12 + 749.15.

  | 1 | 2 | 3 | 4 | 5 | 6 | 7 | 8 | 9 | 10 | 11 | 12 |

34B

Goal Writing

Goal: To measure timed-writing progress 10′   1′ | 3′

Default or DS

Take two 3-minute
goal writings.

If you finish before
time is called, start
again.

Record your speed
and accuracy.

	1′	3′
One type of nondisplay word processor is the electronic	11	4
typewriter. Since it has the capability to edit text, it	23	8
may be called a word processor. It is easy to operate, and	35	12
no time is lost for training. It does not take up any more	47	16
space than an electric typewriter. The initial purchase	58	19
price is much lower than that of a higher-level word pro-	70	23
cessor. No additional money need be spent for software, and	82	27
it can be upgraded.	86	29

1′ | 1 | 2 | 3 | 4 | 5 | 6 | 7 | 8 | 9 | 10 | 11 | 12 | 5.7
3′ | 1 | 2 | 3 | 4 | AWL

34C

**Keyboard
Composition**

Goal: To compose at the keyboard 5′

Complete each sen-
tence.

Do not correct errors.

```
 1. The title of this course is ____.
 2. The teacher's name is ____.
 3. In this course, I am learning ____.
 4. To improve my keyboarding, I need to ____.
 5. I like to be with people who are ____.
 6. My favorite way to spend a rainy day is ____.
 7. Something that always makes me laugh is ____.
 8. When it is warm and sunny, I like to ____.
 9. My favorite ways to spend time are ____.
10. One job I don't think I would like to do is ____.
```

Technique Timing

Take a 2-minute timing on each set of closing lines.

TS between sets.

If you finish before time is called, start again.

Goal: To build speed in keying closing lines 5'

Resume keying without pausing after each enter/return.

1 Sincerely

   ↓ QS
Ms. Karen Carter
Halekulani Apartments
2199 Kalia Road
Honolulu, HI   96815–3315

2 Sincerely

   ↓ QS
Mrs. Sue Smialek
85 Barnham Street
Seattle, WA   98178–0823

34E

Need to Know

Goal: To learn how to name a file 6'

34-2

Documents that are prepared on some electronic equipment can be saved for future use. When the document is saved or stored, the computer creates a file for the document. The file is stored with other files on a floppy disk.

To enable the equipment to locate a file at a later date, give the file a name. Because stored documents are usually referred to by their file names, choose names that will help you remember the contents of the files. For example, if you wrote a report on tourism in New York, you might name the file—Tourism in New York.

To name a file, you need to know the requirements of your software program. Some programs may require the file name to begin with a letter instead of a number or a symbol. Other programs may not accept marks of punctuation or blank spaces within the name. Still other programs may limit the number of characters in the file name.

If your program limits the number of characters in a file name, you may need to abbreviate words. For example, let's assume you are using a program that allows a maximum of eight characters in a file name, and you want to give the report on tourism in New York a file name. You might abbreviate the words Tourism in New York and use a name such as *TourNY*.

34F

Application: File Names

Create appropriate file names for the document summaries shown at the right.

Use the naming requirements for your software program.

Goal: To create file names 5'

Document Summaries

1 Letter to Micro Magazine
2 Science class project
3 Term paper on Cable TV
4 A video game named "1995 Space Flight"
5 A list of expenses for December

34G

Self-Check

Key the statement number and your answer: True or False.

Goal: To review the block format 4'

1. In block format, all lines begin at the left margin.
2. The date of a letter in block format is always keyed on line 14.

(Continued next page)

Appendix **A:** Ten-Key Numeric Keyboard

The ability to key numbers by touch is an important skill. You have already learned to key the top row of numbers on the alpha-numeric keyboard by touch. In the following activities, you will learn to key the ten-key numeric keyboard (keypad) by touch.

Ten-key numeric keyboards are usually found on microcomputers or electronic calculators. When you are keying quantities of numerical data, your ability to input numbers by touch will make the task easier and faster.

The ten-key numeric keyboard is especially useful when large quantities of numbers are to be keyboarded. The arrangement of the ten-key keyboard into three columns down by four rows across allows for more rapid keying of numbers than the top-row of the alpha-numeric keyboard.

The location of the ten-key numeric keyboard varies on microcomputers. Some microcomputers have the ten-key numeric keyboard located to the right of the alpha-numeric keyboard. Other microcomputers have a separate ten-key keyboard that is attached to the microcomputer when a large quantity of numerical data is to be keyed. Regardless of its location on the microcomputer, the ten-key keyboard has the same basic key positions to be learned by touch.

Key Locations

The locations of the numbers from 0 to 9 are usually the same on all equipment. The locations of the enter and decimal keys, and of other function keys, vary from one model of microcomputer to another. Locate the number keys, the enter key, and the decimal key on your keyboard. The following illustrations show some typical ten-key numeric keyboard arrangements.

Home Position

On the ten-key numeric keyboard, ④, ⑤, and ⑥ are the **home keys.** When the hand is in home-key position, the **j** finger is over ④, the **k** finger is over ⑤, and the **l** finger is over ⑥. The **j** finger is also used for ① and ⑦. The **k** finger is used for ② and ⑧, and the **l** finger is used for ③ and ⑨.

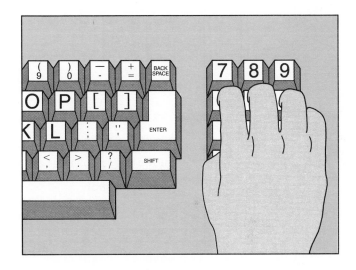

Fingers used for the keys ⒺⓃⓉⒺⓇ, ⓪, and ⨀ depend on the arrangement of the keyboard. On some numeric keyboards, the thumb is used for ⓪ and the **l** finger is used for ⒺⓃⓉⒺⓇ. Study your machine's keyboard to see which finger should be used for ⒺⓃⓉⒺⓇ, ⓪, and ⨀.

Entering Numbers by Touch

Your primary objective while using these materials is to learn to locate the ten-key numeric keys by touch. Your practice materials consist of columns of numbers. After you key a number in a column, strike the enter key to force a line break. That is, each time you strike the enter key, the cursor will move to the next line. At the end of each column, press the enter key twice to leave extra space between the columns.

You are not to total these columns of numbers. You are learning a new key position—not how to add numbers. Also, most microcomputers require a special software program that enables the microcomputer to add columns of numbers.

PROOFREADING/ERROR CORRECTION

Proofreader's Marks

Symbol	Meaning
℘	delete, take out
CAPS or ≡	use capital letter
lc or /	use lowercase letter
∧	insert here
⌃	insert comma
⌄	insert apostrophe
⌄⌄	use quotation marks
⊙	use period
⊙	use colon
⊙	use semicolon
◡	close up
#	insert space
⁋	indent for paragraph
no ⁋	no paragraph
∼	change the order
⊏	move to left
⊐	move to right
(sp)	spell out in full
stet	let stand as is

Proofreading

Follow these steps to help ensure the accuracy of all keyed documents.

1. Review any special instructions for preparing the document. Be sure they have been carried out.

2. Decide whether the document is properly formatted on the page.

3. Look over the document for obvious omissions or errors.

4. Read the document for understanding.

5. If the document contains unfamiliar content or technical matter, ask a coworker to help. The keyboard operator should read from the original, the coworker should follow the screen/printed copy.

6. Double-check names, figures, addresses, amounts, spellings, and dates to be sure they are accurate.

7. Proofread again line by line, checking the screen/printed copy against the original.

New-Key Orientation

Goal: To learn the location of ④, ⑤, ⑥, and ⏎ENTER

1. Locate ④, ⑤, ⑥ (the home keys), and ⏎ENTER on the keyboard chart.
2. Next, locate the keys on your keyboard.
3. Position your **j, k,** and **l** fingers over ④, ⑤, and ⑥. Reach to ⏎ENTER with your **l** finger.
4. Input the columns, keeping your hand in home-key position.

Technique Timing

Take two 2-minute timings on these columns.

If you finish before time is called, start again.

Press the enter key twice after each column.

Goal: To key the home-row and enter keys by touch

Keep your eyes on the textbook copy, not on your fingers, as you input numbers.

1	2	3	4	5	6
444	555	666	456	554	664
555	666	454	654	445	446
666	444	545	465	564	566
456	654	446	556	664	645
564	546	646	656	565	465
646	465	546	465	655	654

Checkpoint: How often did you look at your hands: not at all; once; twice; more?

Keyboard Practice

Key each column twice.

Press the enter key twice after each column.

Goal: To practice proper keystroking techniques

1	2	3	4	5	6
456	564	646	555	666	444
654	546	465	666	454	545
446	646	546	456	654	465
556	656	465	554	445	564
664	565	655	664	466	566
645	465	654	444	555	666

7	8	9	10	11	12
654	666	464	666	456	555
546	456	565	655	455	554
456	546	656	654	454	545
465	646	546	555	446	454
444	654	654	556	445	456
555	564	546	554	444	654

Ten-Key Numeric Keyboard

Special Report Pages

Examples are shown in format for an unbound report. Use the same format for these special report pages as was used for the report.

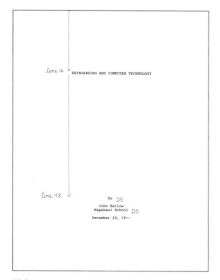

Title page

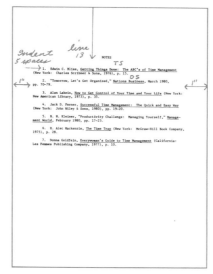

Endnotes

Bibliography

Footnotes. Footnotes can be used (instead of endnotes) to give credit for quoted material and provide additional information or details. Indicate a footnote at the point of reference by keying a superior number. The footnote itself is placed at the bottom of the page on which the reference occurs. All footnotes are numbered consecutively throughout the report.

Begin formatting the footnote by keying a 1½-inch separating line a single space below the last text line. Double space after the line. Indent the first line of the footnote 5 spaces and key the following information: author's name, title, publication information, and page reference. If the footnote contains two or more lines, single space the lines. Double space between footnotes. Be sure to plan ahead so you can provide enough space for the footnotes and still leave a 1-inch bottom margin on the report page.

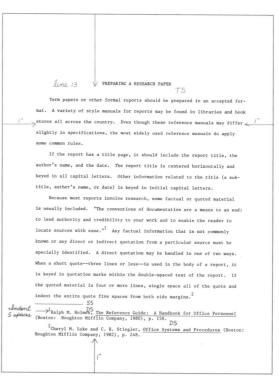

Footnotes

New-Key Orientation

Goal: To learn the location of 1, 7, and 0

1. Locate the 1, 7, and 0 on the keyboard chart.
2. Next, locate the keys on your keyboard.
3. Position your hand over the home keys. Practice the reach from the home keys to each new key. Reach down to 1 and up to 7 with the **4** finger. Strike 0 with your thumb.
4. Input the columns, keeping your hand in home-key position.
5. Practice at a comfortable pace until you feel confident about each key's location.

Technique Timing

Take two 2-minute timings on these columns.

If you finish before time is called, start again.

Press the enter key twice after each column.

Goal: To key the left-column and 0 keys by touch

Keep your eyes on the textbook copy, not on your fingers, as you input numbers.

1	2	3	4	5	6
444	014	140	107	011	141
471	107	701	074	170	117
174	740	701	104	710	417
741	101	704	007	004	047
710	114	471	411	471	104
407	441	117	047	174	114

> **Checkpoint:** How often did you look at your hands: not at all; once; twice; more?

Keyboard Practice

Key each column twice.

Press the enter key twice after each column.

Goal: To practice proper keystroking techniques

1	2	3	4	5	6
741	710	407	014	147	740
101	114	441	140	701	701
704	471	117	107	074	104
007	411	047	011	170	710
004	471	174	141	117	417
047	104	114	444	471	174

7	8	9	10	11	12
170	140	104	111	777	410
701	147	107	147	111	140
107	014	401	174	444	014
741	041	701	741	714	741
147	074	101	710	741	471
410	047	010	410	704	147

Ten-Key Numeric Keyboard

MEMOS

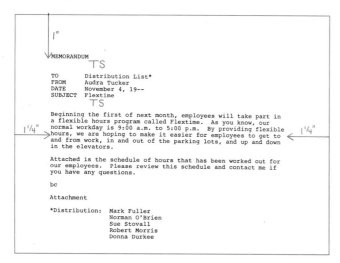

Memos can be keyed on printed forms or on plain paper. Printed forms vary in size and format, but usually have the guide words *To, From, Date,* and *Subject* printed on them. Set tabs and side margins to align with the guide words.

When keying memos on plain paper, use a 1-inch top margin and 1¼-inch side margins. Key the heading lines single spaced, then triple space to key the body. Single space the lines of the body, leaving a double space between paragraphs. Place your reference initials a DS below the last paragraph.

REPORTS

Formats

Unbound Report

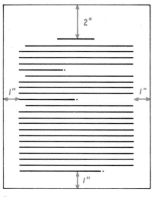

Page one

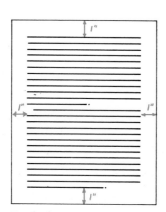

Continuing pages

Top-bound Report

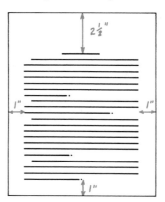

Page one

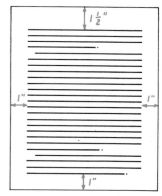

Continuing pages

Left-bound Report

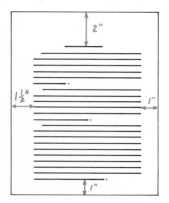

Page one

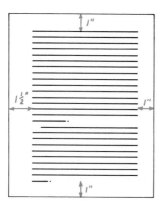

Continuing pages

New-Key Orientation

Goal: To learn the location of ③ and ⑨

1. Locate ③ and ⑨ on the keyboard chart.
2. Next, locate the keys on your keyboard.
3. Position your hand over the home keys. Practice the reach from the home-row key to each new key. Reach down to ③ and up to ⑨ with your **6** finger.
4. Input the columns, keeping your hand in home-key position.
5. Practice at a comfortable pace until you feel confident about each key's location.

Technique Timing

Take two 2-minute timings on these columns.

If you finish before time is called, start again.

Press the enter key twice after each column.

Goal: To key the right-column keys by touch

Keep your eyes on the textbook copy, not on your fingers, as you input numbers.

1	2	3	4	5	6
666	669	339	966	939	699
999	663	363	393	363	936
333	936	336	966	393	939
963	396	936	633	639	336
639	936	636	393	369	696
399	363	996	993	369	939

Checkpoint: How often did you look at your hands: not at all; once; twice; more?

Keyboard Practice

Key each column twice.

Press the enter key twice after each column.

Goal: To practice proper keystroking techniques

1	2	3	4	5	6
963	639	399	669	663	936
396	936	363	339	363	336
936	636	993	966	393	966
633	393	993	939	363	393
639	369	369	699	936	939
336	696	939	666	999	333

7	8	9	10	11	12
369	333	963	639	669	339
396	666	369	963	663	336
393	999	639	936	636	933
696	369	396	966	363	699
693	963	393	939	939	633
639	639	693	333	393	399

Ten-Key Numeric Keyboard

LETTERS

Formats

Block format

Modified-block format
Indented paragraphs

Special Letter Parts

Attention line. An **attention line** directs a letter to a person or a department not named in the address. When used, it is keyed as the second line of the mailing address in the letter or on the envelope. Use all caps, no colon, and leave one space between the word *Attention* and the name or department that follows.

Subject line. A **subject line** calls attention to the topic of the letter. It is keyed a double space below the salutation at the left margin. Key the word *Subject* in all caps, followed by a colon, two spaces, and the topic of the letter, with the main words keyed in initial caps.

Copy notation. When a copy of a letter is sent to a person other than the addressee, a **copy notation** is added a double space below the reference initials. Key a lowercase *c*, followed by one space and the person's name (courtesy title, first name, and last name).

Postscript. A **postscript** is a brief addition to a letter. It is positioned a double space below the last line of the letter at the left margin. Key *P.S.* in all caps with no space before the *S*. Leave one space after the *S*. before keying the message.

Second-page heading. When a letter is too long for one page, the letter is carried over to a second page of the same quality as the letterhead. A **second-page heading** is keyed 1 inch from the top edge starting at the left margin in block format, as shown.

```
Mr. Norman Baker
Page 2
February 14, 19--
```

Letter Placement

The date on line 15 is generally acceptable for average-length letters. However, you may need to prepare letters of varying lengths. Use the letter placement table to center these letters horizontally and vertically on the page. Position the date line higher when the letter contains special letter parts (such as a subject line) or a table. Use side margins of 1¼" regardless of the length of the letter.

Length	*No. of Words*	*Date Line* *10-Pitch*	*12-Pitch*
Short	Under 100	20	20
Medium	100–200	16–14	18–16
Long	201–300	12–10	14–12

Postal Abbreviations

U.S. States, Districts, Possessions, Territories

Alabama	AL	Montana	MT
Alaska	AK	Nebraska	NE
Arizona	AZ	Nevada	NV
Arkansas	AR	New Hampshire	NH
California	CA	New Jersey	NJ
Colorado	CO	New Mexico	NM
Connecticut	CT	New York	NY
Delaware	DE	North Carolina	NC
District of Columbia	DC	North Dakota	ND
Florida	FL	Ohio	OH
Georgia	GA	Oklahoma	OK
Guam	GU	Oregon	OR
Hawaii	HI	Pennsylvania	PA
Idaho	ID	Puerto Rico	PR
Illinois	IL	Rhode Island	RI
Indiana	IN	South Carolina	SC
Iowa	IA	South Dakota	SD
Kansas	KS	Tennessee	TN
Kentucky	KY	Texas	TX
Louisiana	LA	Utah	UT
Maine	ME	Vermont	VT
Maryland	MD	Virgin Islands	VI
Massachusetts	MA	Virginia	VA
Michigan	MI	Washington	WA
Minnesota	MN	West Virginia	WV
Mississippi	MS	Wisconsin	WI
Missouri	MO	Wyoming	WY

Canadian Provinces

Alberta	AB	Nova Scotia	NS
British Columbia	BC	Ontario	ON
Labrador	LB	Prince Edward Island	PE
Manitoba	MB	Quebec	PQ
New Brunswick	NB	Saskatchewan	SK
Newfoundland	NF	Yukon Territory	YT
Northwest Territories	NT		

New-Key Orientation

Goal: To learn the location of ② and ⑧

1. Locate ② and ⑧ on the keyboard chart.
2. Next, locate the keys on your keyboard.
3. Position your hand over the home keys. Practice the reach from the home-row key to each new key. Reach down to ② and up to ⑧ with your **5** finger.
4. Input the columns, keeping your hand in the home-key position.
5. Practice at a comfortable pace until you feel confident about each key's location.

Technique Timing

Take two 2-minute timings on these columns.

If you finish before time is called, start again.

Press the enter key twice after each column.

Goal: To key the middle column keys by touch

Keep your eyes on the textbook copy, not on your fingers, as you input numbers.

1	2	3	4	5	6
555	228	885	285	582	828
888	852	285	258	558	825
222	522	825	525	582	852
582	252	588	858	825	258
822	528	258	582	525	885
522	855	852	825	582	282

> **Checkpoint:** How often did you look at your hands: not at all; once; twice; more?

Keyboard Practice

Key each column twice.

Press the enter key twice after each column.

Goal: To practice proper keystroking techniques

1	2	3	4	5	6
582	822	522	228	852	522
252	528	855	885	285	825
588	258	258	285	825	525
858	582	825	582	558	582
825	525	582	828	528	852
852	885	282	555	888	222

7	8	9	10	11	12
888	585	222	828	522	228
222	522	555	825	852	822
852	555	888	852	285	825
258	582	258	258	852	828
582	258	852	885	825	258
528	282	528	282	558	522

Ten-Key Numeric Keyboard

Lesson 5F

(1) False (2) True (3) True (4) False (5) True
(6) False (7) False (8) True

Lesson 11F

(1) 8 (2) 32 (3) 14 (4) 26

Lesson 22F

(a) True (b) False (c) False (d) False (e) True
(f) False (g) False

Lesson 34G

(1) True (2) False (3) False (4) True (5) False

Lesson 39F

(1) True (2) False (3) False (4) False (5) False
(6) False (7) False (8) False

Lesson 44E

(1) salutation (2) date (3) writes (4) single spaced
(5) double space (6) courtesy title (7) open (8) Ladies and Gentlemen (9) reference initials

Lesson 47C

(1) True (2) True (3) False (4) False (5) True
(6) True (7) True

Lesson 49E

(1) 1 (2) 3 (3) 0 (4) 2

Lesson 50F

(1) True (2) False (3) True (4) False (5) False
(6) True

Lesson 53D

(1) True (2) True (3) False (4) True (5) True
(6) False

Lesson 57D

(1) False (2) True (3) True (4) False (5) False
(6) True

Lesson 63E

(1) 4 (2) 7 (3) 2 (4) double (5) 6

Lesson 65E

(1) True (2) False (3) False (4) True (5) True
(6) True

Lesson 69D

(1) 13 (2) triple (3) double (4) 7 (5) 1 inch (6) 6
(7) double (8) endnote (9) bibliography (10) alphabetical

New-Key Orientation

Goal: To learn the location of ·

1. Locate the · on the keyboard chart.
2. Next, locate the decimal key on your keyboard.
3. Position your hand over the home keys. Practice reaching to · with your thumb. (Depending on the arrangement of keys on your numeric keyboard, you may need to use a finger other than your thumb for the decimal key.)

Keyboard Practice

Key each column twice.

Press the enter key twice after each column.

Remember to keep your hand in home-key position as you enter the numbers.

Goal: To practice proper keystroking techniques

1	2	3	4	5	6
777	978	998	878	788	879
888	987	879	889	787	798
999	878	787	887	897	989
789	987	878	788	977	987
897	789	797	987	797	789

7	8	9	10	11	12
111	132	231	221	331	223
222	213	211	322	232	321
333	123	223	312	133	122
123	213	233	322	312	113
321	231	321	212	123	312

13	14	15	16	17	18
468	48.2	.8	284.0	41.87	154.88
0.489	02537	5827	100	4058.4	888
214.2	852	.024	8.45	08945	.0082
712	.3978	18.73	560	2.25	20008
63944	257.0	85.00	23.00	20.0	632.48
.58	.2684	1045	0.89	36.248	64.1

Speed Practice

Take two 2-minute timings on these columns.

Try to increase your speed on the second timing.

Goal: To build speed on the ten-key numeric keyboard

1	2	3	4	5	6
61.96	446	2.067	78.3	519.2	3372
96	53.94	595.9	3425	60.5	547.4
452.6	9.520	799	53.59	3.678	48.8
2396	101.8	11.5	94.6	4557	2.9
2.8	78.97	543	6.224	431.9	5.973
42.48	11	97.34	40.08	72.6	8.68

Ten-Key Numeric Keyboard

Lesson 65C

(1) Send copies to Roth, Dallas; Solti, Toronto; and Wise, Akron.

(2) We ordered these: A35, 10 sets; A61, 3 sets; and K37, 2 sets.

(3) Invite Casey, Operations; Alves, Personnel; and Ricks, Sales.

(4) On Monday, we sold 130; on Thursday, 175; and on Friday, 220.

(5) She travels to Boise, Idaho; Peru, Indiana; and Dallas, Texas.

(6) Trophy winners were Dick, 1984; Jeanne, 1983; and Tommy, 1982.

Lesson 66D

(1) Linda is reading my copy of the book <u>Stories of the Wild West</u>.

(2) She wrote six automotive columns for <u>Lake Charles Weekly News</u>.

(3) His book <u>Byways</u> was reviewed in this issue of <u>Literary Digest</u>.

(4) They will use this textbook: <u>Our Business and Economic World</u>.

(5) The magazines I like best are <u>Sports World</u>, <u>Flying</u>, and <u>Forum</u>.

Lesson 67C

(1) "Pioneers of the Old West" was the title of the first chapter.

(2) He wrote an article entitled "A Computer for You" last August.

(3) They made "Rhythmic Raindrops" a song remembered by everybody.

(4) James read Longfellow's "The Village Blacksmith" to the class.

(5) "Sign of the Times" was the first movie filmed by Mitch Alder.

(6) Bonatello's "Circle of Gold" was the best speech he ever gave.

Lesson 68C

(1) Can Sue study Greek in Athens while she and Fay are in Greece?

(2) My friend, Dean, is in the U.S. Navy in San Diego, California.

(3) Will Raylen be attending Franklin Roosevelt College this year?

(4) His teacher at Faulkner Junior High School was Ms. Rutherford.

(5) The soccer team at Lexall University played in the Pearl Bowl.

(6) She saw a Shakespearean play in Dallas at the Westone Theatre.

(7) Did Ms. Wilkes work for the Knox Company in Saginaw, Michigan?

(8) Ask Mr. Leu to compare Marxist doctrine with Russian policies.

Lesson 8E

(1) Let Ned sign the letter. He will do it.
(2) Katie will do it faster than Ned or Ken.
(3) Just write Helen; he will write her too.
(4) It takes too long. Use a different one.
(5) Look in here first. Look there in June.
(6) Now I write songs. Let Jewell sing one.

Lesson 35C

His report of August 8 requires several adjustments. In the first place, all committees meet on Tuesday, September 3, not on Monday, September 2. As Monday, September 2, is a holiday, Labor Day, our offices will be closed so every employee can enjoy a long weekend. Other holidays to be observed the rest of the year are in November and December. On November 28, the corporate office will close for Thanksgiving. Most offices will also close on Wednesday, December 25, for Christmas. Customer service operations resume on Tuesday.

Lesson 36C

(1) His order was received on January 4 and shipped on February 2.
(2) John and Joe enlisted in the U.S. Air Force on April 12, 1952.
(3) Your letter of October 13 reported a shipment on May 15, 1983.
(4) Her birthday was September 14, 1945.
(5) The reservation is for November 10 instead of November 12.

Lesson 38C

Syllables	Divided Word	Rule Number
(1) trimmed	trimmed	1
(2) grate ful ly	grate-fully	3
(3) thought	thought	1
(4) a bound ing	abound-ing	3
(5) com pound	com-pound	2
(6) e ras ing	eras-ing	3
(7) con tained	con-tained	2
(8) o ver ly	overly	3
(9) trapped	trapped	1

Lesson 39C

Syllables	Divided Word	Rule Number
(1) com mon wealth	common-wealth	5
(2) grand fa ther	grand-father	5
(3) —	December 16, 1986	4
(4) —	Ms. Lisa Thomas	4

Syllables	Divided Word	Rule Number
(5) —	$16,468,117.20	4
(6) self con tained	self-contained	5
(7) su per star	super-star	5
(8) well man nered	well-mannered	5
(9) Boston	Boston	4

Lesson 41C

(1) Mandy's three favorite colors are yellow, brown, and burgundy.
(2) Now I know how to key columns, business letters, and reports.
(3) The theatre will show the new movie at 7:30, 10:00, and 11:30.
(4) Did you strongly agree, moderately agree, or totally disagree?
(5) Her pets included a dog, a cat, and a three-foot garter snake.

Lesson 42D

(1) My tennis team plays every day at Racquets and Nets Unlimited.
(2) Harvey went to work for Aschetino, Williams, and Turnage, Inc.
(3) While on vacation, he stayed at a place called Inn on the Sea.
(4) At an antique shop, The Yankee Traveler, we found an old desk.
(5) She interviewed at Whitcomb and Sons as well as at McKinley's.
(6) We'd prefer to eat at either The Big Apple or at Pete's Patio.

Lesson 44C

(1) You may write to that company at their Seventh Street address.
(2) Stephanie's parents will live in Newburgh at East 40th Street.
(3) The fires on Sixth Avenue spread to the houses on 22nd Street.
(4) Many cities have a Second Avenue, but few have a Hound Street.
(5) The company's offices are located at One Hanover Place.
(6) Marita joined a health club on East 36th Street.

Lesson 48C

(1) We were told that the interest rate for savings was 6 percent.
(2) Mary Lou was told to use 3.1416 in order to solve the problem.
(3) The stock moved from 9⅜ to 16⅜ before dropping to 4⅞.
(4) Mrs. Ray said that over 16 percent of the workers were absent.
(5) We were quoted rates of 6%, 7%, 8%, and 9% by different banks.
(6) To add ½ and ³⁄₁₃, you must first find a common denominator.
(7) Mr. Pang said the average time spent on the job was 2.3 years.
(8) Nearly 70% of the students in my class failed the test.

Lesson 51C

(1) Billy charged 10 cents a glass for his lemonade; Ava, 9 cents.
(2) The architect charged $10,000 for the drawings of the mansion.
(3) Of the $300.00 collected, $275.28 will be used for publishing.
(4) My utility bill was $131.75 this month and $300.00 last month.
(5) A strip of stamps that costs $22.00 today used to cost $16.50.
(6) If you collect 15 cents from each person, we will have $23.10.
(7) Mary said the bill was for $10.00; I wrote a check for $10.75.
(8) Fees for jogging are $4; for racquetball, $8; for tennis, $10.

Lesson 55C

(1) It was about nine o'clock when Jack and Sarah finally arrived.
(2) Madeline's work started at 8:15 a.m.; she arrived at 8:00 a.m.
(3) The party was supposed to begin around two and end around six.
(4) My class began at 10:15 a.m. and ended much later at 3:15 p.m.
(5) The factory's last shift begins work at exactly 4:30 each day.
(6) I will have to hurry to catch the nine o'clock commuter train.
(7) It was almost twelve o'clock before they finished the project.
(8) Complete that letter by 3 p.m. to get it in the mail at 4 p.m.

Lesson 57C

"What new software do you have to show to this group today?" asked Mr. Jones. "Well," said Miss Conway, "we have a spelling verifier that will certainly improve the spelling on all your letters and reports." As Mr. Jones and the team watched, Miss Conway showed them how a spelling verifier checked the spelling of every word in several letters and reports. "It will show you which words are misspelled so you will be able to correct them," said Miss Conway. "Isn't that amazing?" asked Mr. Jones. As heads nodded, he tossed his dictionary aside.

Lesson 59D

(1) Mr. Williamson assigned the problems from Chapter 43, page 16.
(2) In Volume 2, Chapter 4, page 116, he found the secret formula.
(3) Yesterday, Mrs. Henrique asked us to complete Lessons 1 and 2.
(4) Did Mrs. Ridley say the answer to the question was on page 16?
(5) Judy said that the outline for Chapter 19 required 5 pages.
(6) Franklin read 4 passages from Volume 6, Chapter 9, page 43.

Lesson 60C

(1) The words affect and effect are very frequently used wrongly.
(2) Recently, the term information processing has been used more.
(3) Practice reaches to numbers 6 and 7 using only your j finger.
(4) Lee still isn't sure whether to write take or to write bring.
(5) Sandy will be asked to define the term scrolling.

Lesson 62C

(1) The suffix osis also means "a diseased or abnormal condition."
(2) In phonetics, the phrase glottal stop refers to "speech sounds."
(3) The phrase touch and go means "a precarious state of affairs."
(4) The word justify means "make all lines end at the same point."
(5) The term buffer refers to "a temporary storage area for data."
(6) The word scroll refers to "moving text displayed on a monitor."

Lesson 64C

(1) Ms. Donner said, "Be very judicious in the use of the copier."
(2) Jenny asked, "How many copies of the report will you require?"
(3) "Do you suppose," Mr. Canady asked, "that you could help him?"
(4) Ms. Leu told Timothy that he would have to reprint the letter.
(5) "Incidentally," Janet said, "the copier needs to be repaired."
(6) "The order from Boston must be processed today," said Mr. Lee.